The Old Jarhead's Seabag
Short Stories, Essays and Irish Pennants

Robert A. Hall

(An "Irish Pennant" is--or was--a loose thread or loose end in Marine slang. Doubtless not politically correct today, but the Irish folks I know are passionate about Ireland, music and whiskey, intent on having a good time, rich in humor and serious about serious issues, not gotcha trivia, so I think they'll not be too upset.)

I0423435

All author's proceeds from this book are donated to
The Injured Marine Semper Fi Fund
to help wounded troops and their families

Dedication

For Bonnie, who has enriched my life since we were married in 1992. I can't imagine what my life would have been like without her.

Cover Photos

Front: The author catching a nap on his seabag.

Rear: The author at the Marine Corps Ball, November 10, 1982, his last year in the Reserves, and today.

Royalties

The author has directed that all his royalties from this book be directed to the **Injured Marine Semper Fi Fund** (www.semperfifund.org), which is a nonprofit set up to provide immediate financial support for injured members of U.S. Armed Forces and their families. They direct urgently needed resources to Marines and Sailors, as well as members of the Army, Air Force or Coast Guard who serve in support of Marine forces. Checks may be sent to the Injured Marine Semper Fi Fund, 825 College Blvd, Suite 102, PMB 609, Oceanside, CA 92057. This book is, however, not endorsed or supported by the Semper Fi Fund, and in fact they had no advance knowledge the author was going to write it or to direct the royalties to their cause. The author is solely responsible for it, including all opinions, typos, and errors.

About the Author

Robert A. Hall was born in Philadelphia, PA April 15, 1946. He graduated from Collingswood High School in NJ and enlisted in the US Marine Corps on his 18th birthday, serving from August of 1964 to August of 1968. He volunteered for Vietnam where he was a Radio Relay Team Chief at Khe Sanh in 1967.

In 1968, Hall decided to leave the Corps for college and go into politics. He holds an Associate Degree in liberal arts from Mount Wachusett Community College (1970), a Bachelor's Degree in government from the University of Massachusetts (1972), and a Master's of Education degree in history from Fitchburg State University (1980).

Hall next served five terms in the Massachusetts State Senate. He was first elected in November, 1972, the year he graduated from U-Mass, defeating an incumbent Democrat by nine votes, the first Republican elected in that district since 1938. He was reelected four times by large margins, including being nominated by both parties in 1976. He was Republican Whip when he retired undefeated in 1982. While in the Senate, Hall earned his master's degree at night and served another six years in the Marine Reserves, finishing with the rank of Staff Sergeant. He had to leave the Reserves in 1983, as his new responsibilities as an association executive required too many weekends, creating a conflict.

Hall was a successful association executive from 1982 until pulmonary fibrosis forced his retirement on October 1, 2013. During that period, he managed six different associations, each of which was stronger fiscally and had more members when he left than when he accepted the position. He had a right lung transplant through the Madison, WI VA hospital on December 23, 2013, and has been struggling to recover since that time.

A frequently-published freelance writer, Hall's columns, articles, short stories, and poetry have appeared in over 75 local and national publications. In all, he has 12 books in print, with the royalties going to charity. His Old Jarhead blog gets 3,000-11,000 page views a week. www.tartanmarine.blogspot.com.

He has been married to his first wife, Bonnie, since 1992. They met when she came to a Scottish Country Dance class he was teaching, an activity his health has forced him to give up. They currently live in Madison, WI, to be close to the VA and their grandkids.

Other Books by Robert A. Hall (Royalties to charity)
http://tartanmarine.blogspot.com/2010/07/new-book-published.html
All books may be locared on Amazon by searching for the title or going to the
Author's page.

The Good Bits: The Marines, the Massachusetts Senate and Managing Associations
Author House, 2005.
A collection of life stories and anecdotes the author gathered for his granddaughter.

Chaos for Breakfast: Practical Help and Humor for the Non-profit Executive
American Society of Association Executives, 2008
http://www.asaecenter.org/Shop/BookstoreDetail.cfm?ItemNumber=36447
All author royalties from this book on association management go to the Orthopaedic
Research and Education Foundation and The Center for Association Leadership. It
may only be available in electronic form now.

The Coming Collapse of the American Republic: And what you can do to prevent it
CreateSpace, 2011
A discussion of the state of our nation and trends that are working against us. Since
the publication of this book in 2011, the situation has grown worse in all areas.All
author royalties go to The Injured Marine Semper Fi Fund to help wounded veterans.

Old Jarhead Poems: The Heart of a Marine
Create Space, 2011
All author royalties go to The Injured Marine Semper Fi Fund to help wounded
veterans. This collection of Marine and patriotic poetry was awarded the Marine
Corps Heritage Foundation's 2012 Robert A. Gannon writing award for poetry.

Advice for my Granddaughter: For When I'm Gone
CreateSpace, 2012
A book to provide practical guidance on life decisions for 'tween and teen girls. All
author royalties are donated to the Pulmonary Fibrosis Foundation.

Share the Cup: Poetry of Love and Life
CreateSpace, 2012
A collection of traditional, structured poetry, including many in the sonnet form,
written over a period of almost 50 years. All author royalties are donated to the
Pulmonary Fibrosis Foundation.

The Hand of the Prophet: A Novel of Islamic America, 2053
CreateSpace, 2012
By the year 2053, large parts of the United States have fallen under the rule of fanatical, home-grown Sunni Muslims, who have established the Islamic Republic of America, an Islamic theocracy under Shari'a religious law. Now, the Christians are the terrorists. All author's royalties from this book are donated to a charity to help those who have suffered in the War on Terror.

C.Y.A. Protecting Yourself in the Modern Jungle
CreateSpace (Revised Edition) 2013
First published in 2010, this book has been reissued through CreateSpace/Amazon at a lower price, with all royalties going to the Pulmonary Fibrosis Foundation. A humor/ self-help book, this is advice with an attitude.

Eddie Grabowski's Gift: A Marine Christmas Story
CreateSpace, 2013
Eddie Grabowski's Gift is a short novella, with an old Marine's lessons on life, love and giving. All author royalties are donated to the Marine Corps Heritage Foundation to support the National Museum of the Marine Corps.

Advice for Boys: From an Old Marine
CreateSpace, 2013
A refocus of *Advice for my Granddaughter* for boys, with all royalties going to the Pulmonary Fibrosis Foundation.

The Old Jarhead's Journal: Random Thoughts on Life, Liberty, and Leadership.
CreateSpace, 2013
The Old Jarhead's Journal is a collection of Random Thoughts on politics and life and Conservative Political Essays, mostly published on the author's blog, including the essay "I'm Tired" which went viral on the Internet in 2009, "The Hall Platform," "This I Believe," and "Why I'm a Republican." All royalties are donated to the Injured Marine Semper Fi Fund.

Contents

Note that these short stories and essays were written between 1985 and 2016. Therefore, please excuse any elements that time has passed by.

Trigger Warning: Short Stories to Offend Every Variety of Genteel Political Correctness

Essays to Make Pajama Boy Seek His Safe Space

188-196.....Irish Pennants - Poetry

Most of my poetry is in my two books, *Old Jarhead Poems* and *Share the Cup*. These were written post publication of those volumes.

Casualty Call
Mother Corps
I loved Heroin more than you
LCpl John Payne
Marine Air
Molon Labe
Sonnet for AJ
There's Nothing Dignified in Death
We will come for you
Who is "Iron Mike"?
You'll never be alone

Short Stories

The Price

"The Price of Freedom is the willingness to do sudden battle; Anywhere, Anytime, and with utter Recklessness." --Robert A. Heinlein

Top was scanning the tree line ahead when from the corner of his eye, he saw Kat rein in her sorrel. He pulled his mount up, raised a hand to stop the twelve other troopers behind them--one of whom was dead and slung over his horse--and turned to see why she had stopped. Kat was staring intently into the trees to the left, about thirty yards from the road. He nodded approvingly; she was covering her sector. Kat had the best eyes in Zeblon. Looking back, he saw the other riders were scanning their sectors as he had trained them. He took a quick look to the front and saw nothing. But situational awareness was key to survival. History was littered with the bodies of good troops who'd been distracted by a diversion, before being annihilated by a larger force coming from another direction.

"What do you see?"

Kat had nocked an arrow. They all had guns, hers a revolver which she preferred, but ammo was almost as scarce as gasoline. "I'm sure I saw someone, probably a young girl, watching us from the trees."

Top nodded. If Kat said she saw something, she did. "Trap?" he asked.

"Doubtful. From this distance they'd just open up. Unless they had no firearms at all and are trying to lure us into knife range." She slid from her horse, dropped the reins so it would stay and stepped towards the side of the road.

Top pulled his carbine from the homemade scabbard--a Henry 357/38 lever action--and scanned the woods. He called to Anson to cover her as well; the others automatically widened their areas of scan. Surprises were only fun on Christmas.

"Hello," Kat called. "Don't be afraid. We're friends, we won't hurt you." There was no movement. Well, evil folks could claim to be peaceful friends too. She laid her bow down and took a step towards the woods, hands raised and extended.

Top was nervous, tempted to order her back and everyone to ride on. But if there were people this close to Zeblon's Mill, they needed to know who they were. As far as he knew, other than a few straggler families trying to hold out on their own or drifters, everyone in the area was either part of the Zeblon Freehold, al-Rashid's mini-Caliphate on the other side of the river, or the barbarians in the city thirty-seven miles away. Or slaves of either al-Rashid or the barbarians. Besides, Kat would insist. A wise commander doesn't give orders if they are likely to be challenged in the field, unless necessity requires it.

Kat took another step towards the woods, holding up her empty hands. "You don't have to be afraid," she called. "We will help you."

To Top's surprise, a small figure stepped around a tree and took a step forward. He had figured whoever Kat had seen would be slipping away through the trees as silently as possible. Kat took two more steps towards the girl and beckoned her to come forward.

She was wearing a Muslim dress, but no head covering. A fugitive from al-Rashid, Top thought. It was a complication they didn't need, but he gave no thought to leaving her. Since the start of the Chaos three years ago, everyone had daily complications they didn't need. They would just have to deal with it. Besides, she could be a source of intel about Rashid's plans and strength. They had an uneasy truce with the Muslim leader, but were constantly aware that he thought all living persons should be under Muslim rule and should live by the unchanging strictures of Shari'a Law--however he interpreted Shari'a in his domain.

The girl--she couldn't be more than fifteen--took two steps toward Kat and said in a barely audible voice, "I'm hungry."

"We have food," Kat replied. "I'll get some." She went back to her horse, pulled a packet from her kit and started back to the girl, smiling reassuringly. The girl waited for her, while Top and Anson scanned the woods behind her. The other riders had cast quick glances toward her, but were focused on their areas of responsibility, aware that one mistake could cost their lives.

Kat reached the girl, her eyes flickering between the child and the woods behind her. "Are you alone?"

"Yes," the girl replied. Opening the packet, Kat tore off a small chunk of bread and handed it to her. The child stuffed it in her mouth, hardly chewing before she swallowed. Then she retched, but kept it down. Kat decided to hold back on the meat.

"Let's get you some water," Kat said, taking the girl's hand and leading her toward the horses. "You can't eat too much at once, it will make you sick. You can have more in town, a bath, and a rest."

"Al-Rashid will come for me," the girl said as Kat helped her onto her horse. "He will try to kill you." They had less than five miles to go and could ride double.

Kat's face tightened. "He won't find you. His writ doesn't run in Zeblon Freehold."

Top turned his attention back to the front. "Let's ride in," he called. "And let's stay alert so we get there."

On the ride the girl told Kat that her name was Aisha. "That's a Muslim name, after Mohammad's favorite wife; are you a Muslim?" Kat asked.

"I am--was--al-Rashid's slave, so they made me swear the *Shahadah* which they said made me a Muslim. My real name is Maddy Mahan; we had a farm about ten miles west of al-Rashid's stronghold. We are--were--Catholic."

"Ah, I thought those freckles and hint of red in your hair might be Irish, certainly not Middle Eastern. How old are you, Maddy?"

"I'm fourteen--I think. I'm pretty sure I was twelve when I was taken, about two years ago. And my mother, father and brother were killed."

"I'm sorry, Maddy. There's been a lot of death and terror since the Chaos started. You were older than your namesake when, according to the Muslim texts, Mohammad took her to wife, then to his bed."

"We were so happy before the Collapse; I just didn't realize it. But afterwards, we were always hungry and afraid. When al-Rashid and his raiders came, my father and brother were killed fighting them, but they killed three of Rashid's men and wounded two. They made me pay for that, though I was considered lucky that Rashid wanted me for himself. I hid, or mother would have killed me like she did herself. I have often wished in the time since that she had killed me first."

"You're with us now, Maddy, free people--and we intend to stay that way. Life is hard for us, as for everyone since the Chaos started, but you will be free and not harmed," Kat said, holding the frail child close. "And if you remember anything of farming, you will be more than welcome." As she talked, she continued to scan her sector of fields to her left, though they were drawing close to home. But almost safe and safe were two different things. And safe was dear purchased and very relative.

"Al-Rashid used me to work the gardens. At least during the day," Maddy said. Kat had no need to ask about the nights.

They relaxed a little when they rode past the ZDF--Zeblon Defense Force-- checkpoint and cantered past houses and into the small downtown of what was once a struggling Midwest farm community. The local joke was that the founder had meant "Zebulon," but couldn't spell. The adjective "struggling" was now moot--every person still alive was struggling. And tens of millions, perhaps billions, had died; no one would ever know the total death toll. That the human race would continue seemed assured. That civilization and freedom would go on, well, that was a lot more chancy. The Zeblon Freehold was one attempt, and they knew of others farther south, and assumed there were more.

There was a crowd downtown--crowded being relative post-Collapse in a very small town--but it was market day. Stores went out of business soon after the Collapse, as they couldn't get merchandise and everyone realized that paper money, credit cards and checks were worthless. But people fell into the habit of setting up tables midweek to barter goods, food and crafts. Everyone ate in groups they called messes, with those who had chipping in food and cooking skills. The top currency was ammunition, medicine, canned goods and gasoline, but supplies were small and dwindling. They had a local retired chemist and a gun enthusiast who did his own reloading working on gunpowder. Gas was hopeless, hence the horses, though they had an SUV and a four-wheel-drive pickup fueled and ready for emergencies in a garage. No one went hungry, but the meals were plain and meager.

Jackson, the ZDF second-in-command, came out of the storefront they were using as headquarters. He raised a hand to Top, then his glance took in the body slung over a horse. "Who'd we lose," he asked tersely.

"Wolf," Top replied.

Jackson looked down, his black features hard, and spat on the ground. "Shit," he said. Wolfgang McDonald was not only well liked, he had been Army infantry, though unlike Jackson had not seen combat. "I hope it was worth it."

"Nothing's worth losing troops," Top replied, "But we stung them pretty good, which is why we went. There were over twenty of the barbarian raiders, and we killed at least six, wounded others. The rest fled. They were all on foot, as usual. Thank God they have no discipline; there are so many of them. But they had three women with them they must have taken as slaves from stragglers while they came south, and they killed them first thing. Wolf went berserk, killed two raiders, exposed himself and was hit. Nothing we could do for him. We buried the women, left the dead raiders for the scavengers. We also collected five guns from the dead, and more ammo than we expended, plus some pills they had scavenged." Drugs were far more valuable than gold in the cities.

"Yeah, sounds like Wolf." Jackson shifted around, planting his prosthetic leg firmly in the street.

Top had argued that while he had retired from the Marines as a Master Sergeant, he was admin, so Jackson with combat infantry experience should have been the commander of the ZDF. He'd kept up his rifle skills and physical fitness, but basic infantry training was a long time ago--and he was fifty-seven. Unfortunately, Jackson's leg made riding hard for him, though he was fourteen years younger and in good shape.

"I keep going over in my mind what I could have done differently," Top said.

"Andy, it wasn't your fault," Jackson said. Top's name was Andy Turner, but everyone called him Top because Jackson usually did. "Shit happens in combat. Actually, shit happens anywhere, but especially in a firefight. You know that. Wolf knew we had to burn them to make them choose another direction--we all knew it after that traveler brought word raiding parties were out from the city. And we know the survivors in the cities are getting more desperate."

"I wish you could lead patrols," Top said. "Your experience is better than mine."

"Yeah, and after thirty minutes I can't concentrate on anything but the pain in my leg. Who's the girl?" He nodded towards Kat and Maddy.

"Her name's Maddy," Kat said. "She escaped from Rashid. Now if you soldier boys are done talking military stuff I want to get her inside for food and rest." She slid from her horse, then helped Maddy dismount.

Jackson cast a meaningful glance at Top. He knew what that had meant for the girl. And what it could mean to the fragile peace between the Freehold and Rashid's Caliphate. They were about evenly matched in fighters; so far neither side was willing to pay the cost of trying to destroy the other. That didn't mean they were friends.

He stepped toward Maddy, holding out his hand, his famous sunny smile splitting his face. "Welcome to Zeblon's Freehold," he said. "I may look black, but I'm really white--Jackson White at your service." It was a favorite joke of his. Kat rolled her eyes, but Maddy took his hand and smiled tentatively. It appeared the girl was better than she had a right to be--farm folk were strong.

Top went to see Wolf's wife; the burden of command. She had already heard from the other women and was bearing up stoically. Anyone still alive this long after the Collapse was inured to bad news; it was as common as fleas. He promised that the body would be cared for and they would hold the funeral in the morning. No rifles would fire, though. Ammo was too precious.

Two hours later, after they had eaten, he called a council of war. Present were Hal Anderson, President of the Zeblon Board of Freeholders, Jackson as second in command of the ZDF, Anson Pittenger, who was a lieutenant, Katrina "Kat" Tennent, who was a fine scout, but refused any leadership role, and Top. They had rescued Kat from barbarian raiders about two years ago, though she had been held by them for over a week. The raiders hadn't killed her because she'd taken the opportunity of the ZDF attack to grab a gun and kill two of them, then terminated four more of their wounded with her knife to save ammo. She turned out to be an accomplished equestrian and good with both a gun and a bow, having lettered in archery in college; she was putting the archery component of the local sporting good store to good use. Since she was utterly ruthless and her only interest was in killing slavers, she was full time with the ZDF, but preferred to operate without the responsibility of directing others. Still, Top and Jackson found her counsel valuable.

"How's Maddy?" Top asked Kat. "And do you think she knows anything of value about Rashid and his Holy Warriors?" The sarcasm in his voice was plain.

"What's the phrase they used to use in TV medical shows before the stations went off the air? Doing as well as can be expected--for a child that has suffered sexual abuse for two years. But she is strong. She had a 38 revolver tucked inside her clothes, and there was blood on them. Not hers--it came from one of Rashid's wives who she apparently killed to escape."

"That will bring Rashid down on us," Hal said. He had been elected President of the Board because no one else wanted it. Neither did he, but he had served on the pre-Collapse town board and had a sense of duty. And his dental practice had become rudimentary.

"Maddy has the protection of the Freehold," Top said flatly. They were a community trying to maintain human rights, the rule of law, and as much freedom as the times would allow. Though the law was harsher now; a man caught stealing food the year before was simply expelled from the Freehold. Most things including food belonged to the community now. Top joked that after hating them all his life he'd become a kind of communist. Jackson said really a community-ist.

"I questioned her very gently," Kat said. "She said Rashid bragged about having two hundred Holy Warriors ready to die for Allah, though that may be inflated, likely is. She thinks they have four to five hundred people in the Caliphate. But that includes slaves, many of them young girls like her. They can hardly trust slaves and have to detail guards."

"*Those whom thy right hand possesseth of those whom Allah hath given thee as spoils of war,*" Top said bitterly, quoting the Qur'an's justification of sex slavery.

Jackson said, "I wish we could do something about that."

"We can put about a hundred-thirteen troopers in the field, if need be, and have total a hundred sixty-seven effectives--minus Wolf--in the ZDF to stave off an attack here," Top said. "Putting that many in an attack against two hundred hardly seems wise, not to mention that Zeblon would be held by only fifty-four fighters who can't take the field, good as some of them are." He nodded at Jackson, who tossed him a mock salute.

"Rashid is in the same situation," Jackson said. "He has to leave, say, a third of his soldiers to guard their base, keep out raiders and prevent the slaves from escaping. That's why neither Zeblon nor the Caliphate has attacked before. We'd both have to attack outnumbered; the results of victory wouldn't be worth the loses. If victory was to be had."

"And the surviving entity would be more vulnerable to the barbarians, who have to get more aggressive or starve. I doubt any of them has grown anything other than pot in their lives," Top replied. "But Rashid will come round to see what we know. We need to keep Maddy out of view for a while, and increase perimeter security. If he doesn't know she's here, he's unlikely to attack on speculation alone."

"We had some news from the south while you were out," Jackson said. "Two men from a freehold about twenty miles down, well-armed of course. They weren't travelers, nothing to sell, though they did ask if we had anything useful as surplus they could send a traveler to trade for. Unfortunately, we all need the same things, though I told them we had a bumper corn crop. For these times."

"Be hard to move bulk corn twenty miles nowadays, and the things we want they probably wouldn't trade," Hal said. "But they could probably take a wagon load."

"If they had a sporting goods store there, and they haven't gotten into bows themselves, any archery supplies would be welcome," Kat said.

"They mentioned gold," Jackson grinned. "I said you can't eat it, but that the old paper money made nice fire starters."

"You said they had news?" Top replied.

"Yeah," Jackson said, "But it's old and been passed through a succession of travelers."

"So, as reliable as the Internet before the Collapse," Hal smiled. "Jackson, you tell everyone what they said; you may have noted security details that passed me by."

"They had a group of five travelers come through with a wagon, looking to trade. Apparently so well armed that they even had a little ammo they would let go of." Jackson grinned. "And they were willing to take a little gold, but the price was high. Apparently folks out East will still take it on spec, if the price is right. They were also scavenging abandoned homes and towns, of course."

"Any news of the Government in DC? We've heard nothing since about three weeks after the nuke destroyed New York City," Top asked. "Once the Internet, satellites, TV and radio packed it in, just silence." They still turned on a radio and computer once a week to check, briefly, as generating electricity was costly.

"Well, we know that Washington retaliated, destroying Tehran and the rest of Iran's cities, military bases and nuke facilities, despite supposition that the terrorists' nuke could have come from North Korea or Pakistan," Jackson said. "What we didn't know was that the President and the Veep were in NY, as well as the two former Presidents living there, and are presumed killed. The nuke strike on Iran was ordered by the Chairman of the Joint Chiefs, who apparently headed the government after the hit."

"A coup? Or was 'greatness thrust upon him'?" Top asked.

"The travelers thought the latter," Hal said. "But remember their news was passed from ear to ear."

"Anyway, after the stock market vanished, the economy seized, and the government stopped paying entitlements as it had no money and couldn't borrow any, the riots swept the cities from coast to coast. Probably worldwide, as they said the economy of the rest of the world followed us off the cliff."

"Even without the nuke, it would have happened eventually. Almost all levels of government in the world were mortgaged to their hairline with debt and unfunded promises of wealth transfer." Top said. "Though I know Hal disagrees with me. That's why we elected him; we needed one sunny optimist to keep us from all going bat-shit crazy."

"Too late for some," Kat said, smiling at Top to show she was kidding.

"That may not be a joke," Top replied. "Like everyone else I wake up sometimes and think it's just a nightmare."

"Anyway," Jackson jumped back in, "There has been no known contact with the rest of the world since. The U.S. of A. appears to have shrunk to about 100 miles around DC, as there were troops to enforce martial law and protect the food depots. They believed that all the big and most medium cities are under the control of some kind of barbarians and local warlords--though many are still fighting for supremacy. And they were not surprised to hear about Rashid's personal Caliphate--apparently they were set up or tried wherever there was a sufficient Muslim population."

"The Muslims have the discipline of their religion, US military and vets have the discipline of their training, but the barbarians have none at all," Top said. "And they produce nothing, probably grow nothing. Their canned goods and stored food have to be running out. That means they have to spread out from the cities to try to take what they need from folks like us. I expect bands of them may cut loose from the cities entirely, perhaps forced out by bigger gangs."

"Well," Jackson replied, "They have to have used up a lot of ammo in their internal debates as to who's in charge. That helps."

"Yeah, but we're getting low as well," Top replied. "I don't fancy fighting off a thousand crazed barbarians with clubs! Or with the lances and swords Sam is making." Sam Kenton had been a blacksmith by hobby; now it was his full-time trade.

"Just shoot the first one," Kat smiled. "When they stop to eat him, you can get the rest--or run for it."

Everyone chuckled, but not heartily. "Let's call it a night," Top said, "If that's okay with you, Mr. President. We have Wolf's funeral at nine.

"Of course. Wolf's widow, Ellen, wants to stay in their house with the boys," Hal said. "I agreed, but told her if she changed her mind, two families had already told me they'd love to have them move in."

They held the funeral for Wolfgang McDonald at 0900 the next morning. Or at what their mechanical watches told them was about 9:00 am. Anson had taken charge. He'd served one hitch in the Marines, infantry, but served mostly as an embassy security guard, so he was good at ceremony. Combat experience would have been better, but ceremony helped to keep up morale and remind them of what they were trying to preserve. And he could drill in small unit infantry tactics.

The service was held at the small white church on the edge of Zeblon, Pastor Jackson White presiding. Jackson had heard the call while in the hospital recovering from his wounds and had built up quite a following after being medically retired from the Army. Almost everyone not on security guard or vital work was there, over four hundred folks, including Zeblon's well-known atheist, Mike Schmidt, several Jews, the Amish Yoders and their one Muslim family, Ali, his wife Maryam and their kids. Their parents, Shi'a Muslims, had come to the US long ago. Ali and Maryam had been born here and were westernized. They had as much reason to fear al-Rashid and his fundamentalist Sunni "Caliphate" as anyone in the Freehold. Ali had served in the Navy and was a member of the ZDF. Maryam was an RN, skills more valuable in the post-Collapse world than brain surgery.

Wolf was interred in the churchyard behind Zeblon Baptist, next to his German mother. His Scots-Irish father had taken his car the week after the Collapse and driven into the city to find out, "When the government expected to get things straightened out." He had not been heard from since.

Trees had been cleared to make more room for graves; there were more dead now than living. Headstones were no longer made, but a cross with his name was put up next to a large rock someone had hauled from the stream in the small woods to the west of town. Mario Blanco, a former member of the high school band played taps. Only Ellen wept, and not much. Since the start of the Chaos, folk were as used to death as people in the dark ages.

As the service was finishing up in the graveyard, a rider came in from the outpost on the road to the west. Top heard the hoof beats and went to meet him, recognizing 17-year-old, George Edwards. "Rashid coming with riders, maybe ten, and a flag of truce," he said without preliminaries.

Kat and Anson had arrived on Top's heels. Jackson wasn't far behind. "Anson, take ten troopers and go with George to reinforce the western picket. I'll be right behind you. Kat, you get Maddy inside and well out of sight."

Jackson had quickly come up and Top briefed him. "I'll get every man armed, in case," Jackson said.

"And every woman who carries arms as well," Kat said, smiling, "I do hope they start trouble." When she was in a flip mood she called herself the, "Last living feminist." She turned and waved reassuringly at Maddy who was watching them fretfully from a small group of women offering support to Ellen.

Top caught up to the troop he'd sent out before they reached the picket. Kat was with him, having left Maddy with Ellen McDonald. Might do some good for both of them.

Rashid was drawn up by the picket of two men. Top knew that two others had faded out of sight, but were covering them. The Muslim party carried a white flag next to their black and green banner with Arabic writing. He'd been told it was a Qur'an quote from the Sura of the Sword, "Slay the idolaters wherever you find them." For all he knew it said, "Coexist with all creatures."

Rashid held up his hand as they trotted up. "Peace be upon you." His warriors were bunched around him, Top noted, while his own troop had spread out a little in a semi-circle. "And also on you," Top replied. Both were wryly aware of the irony. "What brings the holy warriors to Zeblon Freehold"

"First, to thank you for sending a rider to warn us that barbarians were out. We met a party and, by Allah's will, inflicted a rebuke upon them."

"It's in both our interests to keep the raiders at bay, so we can live our lives at peace," Top said. Privately he though that Rashid's people and the barbarians fighting was a grand thing.

"We also come because we have lost something that belongs to us," Rashid said. "A girl."

"We have nothing here that belongs to you," Top replied.

"Under the civilized laws of the Freehold, people are not possessions," Kat said. She was smiling, but it was the smile of a predator about to strike. Top agreed with the sentiments, but wished she had not drawn attention to herself. She was an attractive woman, little romantic interest as she'd had in men since her ordeal.

"The Holy Qur'an teaches us that 'Men are in charge of women, because Allah hath made the one of them to excel the other' and has made lawful to us that which our right hand possesses," Rashid replied, eyeing Kat thoughtfully. Top noticed others staring at her and two other armed women in his troop; knew that they thought her a wanton for riding with men and behaving immodestly. He didn't like the idea of including women in a combat formation, it degraded efficiency. But with the shortage of effective fighters, needs must.

"Why would you think your missing person is here?" Top asked. "There's nobody here who doesn't belong to the Freehold, though we had some messengers from the south a few days ago."

"News of interest?" Rashid asked.

"Only that they had travelers from the east and the country is still having trouble reestablishing itself," Top replied, aware that was an understatement.

"America is finished," the Muslim said. "In it's place, Allah will raise a new Caliphate!"

And we know who you think should be Caliph, the Marine thought, but didn't say. "God defend the right," he said ambiguously. "But back to your business today."

"We searched to the west," Rashid said, "Where the girl, Aisha, came from. There was no trace."

"Perhaps she went to another freehold; I hear there is one further west of you--and larger than us." Top said, emphasizing "larger," to stress Rashid's tactical position. "Aisha is a Muslim name--why would a Muslim leave you?"

"She saw the light through Allah the Merciful after she came to us, but a jinn possessed her and she murdered my wife out of jealousy. The infidels to the west are over thirty-five miles," Rashid said. "We have little contact and do not think she could have gotten that far. May we view your village from inside to be sure she isn't hiding there?"

"Sure," Top said. "Right after we search the Caliphate for Christian slaves being held against their will. But I am sorry for your loss. Which wife was killed?" He tried to keep any touch of sarcasm out of his voice.

"My first wife, peace be upon her," Rashid replied, seeming unaware of any undercurrent in the question. "So we seek not just a fugitive, but a murderer. And will not rest until she is brought to Allah's justice. Both murder and apostasy--leaving Islam--are punished with death under Shari'a Law." He waved at his men, and they turned to ride off.

"Go in peace," Top called after them. He waved a hand downward to calm Kat and the others. He knew they would have liked to set upon Rashid and his men, killing all of them. But he also knew that whoever took Rashid's place would declare a holy

17

war on them, and though he thought they would win, there would be too many dead, and the survivors less likely to hold off barbarian raids. Freedom and civilization hung by a thread in these parts as it was. He waved Anson up.

"Follow them?" his lieutenant asked. Pittenger was no fool.

"Yes," Top said. "Take two troopers." He saw Kat edge her mount forward and resigned himself to what he didn't have to like. She was arguably the best scout they had. "Stay well back, try not to be seen, and avoid contact. But I want to know if they all go home. Oh, and try not to get yourself killed--we cannot spare anyone."

Anson laughed. "Well, getting killed wasn't on my agenda today; I have some chores to do." He pointed at Kat and another trooper, Jefferson White, Jackson' thirty-year-old brother. They waited until the Islamists were out of sight before riding slowly after them, following the crumbling road that led to the bridge to the "Caliphate," alert from the start, scanning the fields and occasional abandoned farm, buildings gutted. Almost anything worth scavenging in them was long gone.

"Better to lose them than ride into an ambush," Top called to Anson. Then leaving two men to reinforce the picket, he led the rest back into the village.

Anson kept his patrol at a walk, spread out, studying the sides of the road for signs that riders had left it. It was Kat that spotted it, about three miles out. She let them go on about a hundred yards, then spurred up to Anson, pointing ahead to throw off an observer.

"Brush marks on the left side, a bit back. Beyond them what looked like tracks, or broken grass stalks. Couldn't be sure without riding over to look, but I suspect Rashid circled back a rider to watch for us."

"Nice work," Anson said. "We'll ride on to the top of the next rise, maybe a half mile, scan the countryside, then turn back. Give a watcher something to chew on." He trusted Kat's report.

Atop the slight hill, Anson used his binoculars to scan a 360 degree arc, particularly studying buildings and groups of trees that might hide people. There was no sign of Rashid or anyone else. He noted how fast the fields were going wild, but thought they needed to get a party out this way. Might be some food they could harvest, growing wild now. Or feral farm animals.

He turned and led them back toward Zeblon, as alert as if they'd been on the trail of a barbarian raiding party. Once they were far enough to be out of sight of Rashid's observer, assuming he's set up to watch where they had been, they circled off the road across old corn fields in the direction of the tracks.

Coming up to the military crest of a slight hill, more of a rise, they dismounted. Jefferson held the horses while Anson and Kat crept to the summit. They found themselves looking down on the old Yoder farm. The Yoder family had fled to Zeblon about two weeks after the Collapse, after getting warnings from others of the Plain People. They were pacifists, but not fools. They still would not fight, though Samuel, the oldest boy at fifteen, was showing interest in defiance of his father. Regardless, the Amish had the kind of primitive skills that made them valuable in the post-Collapse world, and were looked to for advice. Anson wished they had more Amish, but the others in the small community had fled further south. Or died.

Nothing was stirring around the deserted farm. Anson wondered if he'd guessed wrong, though it was the best vantage point. "Scan the country side. He may not be there. Or there might be two, at different points."

"Got it," Kat said. The sun was behind them, so both were comfortable using binoculars. And that was what gave Rashid's man away. He was inside a barn, where he could watch the road from windows, but apparently came to the door to check his rear, scanning the hill. A glint of sunlight reflected off his binoculars. "And got him," she said.

They concentrated on the barn, but didn't neglect to scan the countryside at intervals. After a forty-minute wait, it was Anson who picked up the two riders coming down the road from the direction that the Muslims had taken. They cut off before the place where Kat had seen the tracks of the watcher, riding directly to the Yoder farm, apparently secure that they were the only players on the board.

As they rode up, the watcher, who had seen them coming of course, rode his horse out of the barn. They conferred on horseback, the watcher pointing first down the road that led to Zeblon, which was north of them, then to the grassy fields to the south of their hill. Apparently satisfied, the watcher rode back the way the men had come, while they headed cross country to the south, where their watcher had pointed.

"They don't ride well," Kat said.

"Compared to you, who does?" Anson replied. "Apparently they don't know the advantage of being on the high ground." Then he slid back to where Jefferson waited with their horses and had him shift them to the north slope, still on the military crest so they'd be below the top and out of sight of the riders.

As it transpired, it hardly mattered. The two riders turned west towards the woods that were west of Zeblon, but were in sight of the village on their far side across the fields. They rode without looking back.

"It looks like we have two spies," Jefferson said.

"Yeah, and dumb ones," Anson replied. "Mount up. We'll give them ten minutes to work their way into the woods then head north so we can swing around to the Freehold out of their sight."

Top was on the east side of the village watching three men and two women, including Maddy, being taught knife fighting by Ed Rajewski. He heard hooves and turned to see Pittenger, Kat, and Jefferson ride in from the north. He was unsurprised at the direction; wise patrols seldom came back the way they went out. He raised a hand in greeting.

"Well, Zeblon has picked up a couple of lice," Anson said. "They are apparently watching us from the woods on our west."

"Tell only those who need to know," Top said. "And make sure no one shows inordinate interest in the woods. Our knowing they are there may give us some advantage we haven't thought of yet."

Kat slid from her horse, smoothly pulled the flat knife sheathed on her back below her neck, and flipped it end over end to quiver in a target board about fifteen feet away. "I can do that two out of three times," she told the students. "The problem is the third time--now your opponent has your weapon. Never throw your knife unless it's a last resort." Ed smiled; he had just told them much the same thing.

Top called Maddy over and gave her strict instructions to stay away from the west side of the town. Cautioning her to keep it confidential, he told her they thought Rashid had a spy there; people followed orders better when they knew the reason. Then he took some troopers to the east of town to practice with the new lances. The troopers weren't yet bad with them, but were working up to that level. Mediocre would come later. Maybe even proficiency with enough practice.

Just after the noon meal the following day, a rider from the western picket came to tell Top that two Muslims were again riding in under a flag of truce. He took Pittenger and two other troopers out to meet them. One of them identified himself as Mohammad, "Son of Mohammad, the Caliph."

"How may we be of service?" Top inquired. It never helped to give offense to enemies. Unless you wanted them angry.

"It is we who can be of service. The Caliph returns your favor by warning you we have had word that a very large party of kuffer barbarians are headed south, coming right at you, maybe a little to our side to the west. He rides to meet them with the Holy Warriors, and suggests you do the same." Turning abruptly, the two Muslims spurred off.

Top turned to Pittenger. "I wonder what this means for the two spies in the woods?"

Anson laughed. "Those *are* the two spies in the woods. I recognize them and their horses."

Looking after the riders, Top said thoughtfully, "So they weren't spies, but set there to give us this warning after Rashid and his men were on the road to the north of us."

Anson laughed again. "Surely you don't think our brethren from the Religion of Peace might be planning a nasty surprise?"

"I think they have decided we have Maddy, and that we are an intolerable threat to their dreams of a Caliphate. I think they are planning a trap to try to cripple us, so that Zeblon comes under their sway. And I think we may have a surprise for them, Insha'Allah!"

Top called the usual suspects for a council of war. "I believe Rashid means war against the Freehold. If we don't take his bait in this, he will find another ploy, or just assault us. If we move now, we have the advantage of knowing he's setting a trap."

"Are we sure of that?" Hal asked. "I hate the thought of more war, more deaths."

"Unfortunately, Hal, it take two sides to make peace, only one to make war," Anson replied. "One of the reasons the country was in decline before the Collapse was that there was too much wishful thinking about that, especially among so-called leaders."

"Gentlemen may cry, 'Peace, peace, but there is no peace,'" Top replied. "If it's not a trap, but there really are many barbarians, we need to put everyone we can in the field anyway. We will go cautiously, scouts out, and let the situation develop."

"I'll alert the ZDF," Jackson said. "Every possible fighter under arms, to ride with you or to protect the Freehold while you're gone. Damn, I wish I was going."

"Me too, though we need someone to command here as well." Top replied. "My whole time in the Corps I got zero cavalry tactics! Tell them we will ride before dawn, just like some damn movie."

Jackson laughed. "I can't help you. The only cavalrymen I met in the Army rode around in choppers." He went out the door.

Top, Anson, and the others were up before dawn. They had mounted slightly over a hundred troopers, almost their full field strength, leaving behind only the sick or those with urgent tasks in town, who would augment Jackson's defense force.

Top selected two scout teams to ride forward about fifty yards and to the left and right of the main column, Kat and Jefferson to the left, two others to the right. The scouts had orders to proceed with caution, expecting an ambush.

The column would move by twos cautiously along a secondary road, parallel to the main road where Rashid would expect them. They didn't like using the road, but they knew it was the only way to get to the area with a large force reasonably fast. So did Rashid, of course.

About 30 troopers carried lances in addition to their firearms, Kat and at least ten others had augmented their weapons with bows.

Every trooper carried ammo and food for two days. They assumed there would be forage for the horses on the route. Top and Anson had been training the troops as cavalry, as best they could, and to respond to simple bugle calls from Mario, who rode just behind him. If they were in open area they could be ordered to swing right and left to form a battle line, Top leading the left, Anson the right. Generally, they expected to fight on foot, using every fourth trooper as a horse handler. Dragoons, really. Not, Top thought, quite up to riding with Wade Hampton or Phil Sheridan.

About three miles out of town, he saw the scouts on the left, Ali and Edward Rajewski, known as Ski of course, pull up. Ski was a another Marine vet, a communicator, but one now without a radio. He'd served with artillery, which they also lacked.

Ski signaled them to hold, which they already had, then he and Ali rode cautiously around a bend in the road. The scouts had to pull in close to the road when there were woods. Getting tangled in forest wasn't going to help, but such areas required extra caution.

Top's anxiety level increased when Ski disappeared from sight, but Ali halted so he could observe both Ski and the column.

Anson asked if Top wanted him to take some troopers forward to provide backup. He nodded yes, and Pittenger had just started forward with ten men when Ski appeared, walking his horse. Behind him crept a decrepit wagon, pulled by an old horse, from his gait, driven by a man who looked ancient.

Anson came up to them and stopped to confer. Then he ordered his men to spread out as a picket, where Kat and Jefferson, seeing the commotion, joined them. He waved Top forward, and rode back towards the column, the wagon creeping along behind him.

When Top came up to them, he saw the man was not nearly as old as he thought, but seemed old, defeated, slumped over. "What's your name, friend, and what brings you this way?" Top asked.

"Name's Walter," the man said softly. "Walter Penneat, the damn fool."

Top chuckled. "Well, we're all fools from time to time. What brings you to our area?"

"I'm running from the barbarians what took my wife and daughter," the man whispered. "All my fault. I thought our hidey hole was safe, we'd wait it out. Save the property when things was restored. Wife begged me to come south for safety. But I said we were safe. I was out scavenging, came back to hear a commotion. Barbarians had caught my daughter out getting water, wife ran out to try to save her. It was useless. All I had was this." He held up a small 32 auto, the kind of gun women used to carry in their purses. Then he began to weep.

"How many barbarians were there, and where were you located?

Walter lifted his head. "We were about ten miles south of the outskirts of the city," he said. "Thought it was safe enough. But there were hundreds of them. Nothing I could do, except die. Didn't have the guts even for that."

"Can't see what good your dying would have done, and your warning us like this did a powerful lot of good," Top said. "How'd you get away."

"I stayed hidden until they moved away west," Walter replied. "And then after dark I went to the shed where I kept the horse. Either they missed it, or thought he wasn't worth taking. I hitched up the wagon, loaded what supplies I could, and headed south like Betsy wanted me to. Too late for her and poor Maggie, damn fool that I am."

"I'm sending you into town with two men, you'll be safe there. Meanwhile we will ride towards where the barbarians went. Long shot, of course, but you might see your women again."

He detailed two troopers. One rode in the wagon with Walter, who had broken down completely. The other followed behind, leading the extra horse.

Top called a quick council of war with Anson and the scouts. "Maybe Rashid was telling the truth," he said.

"More likely Taqiyya," Anson replied. "Lying to advance the cause of Islam."

"It's just possible that Rashid is setting a trap for us and is unaware that a horde of barbarians are headed south and west from the city," Kat said.

"Yes," Top said. "I don't think he would knowingly put himself between two hostile forces. I think the only thing to do is continue with extreme caution, and to head west at the next crossroad. I doubt the Caliph is ahead of us. I think he would have stopped Walter, just for the news, if he had seen him."

"And Walter doesn't look like one of Rashid's Holy warriors," Ski laughed. "Nor does he have the nerve to carry off such a deception."

"Agreed. Forward. Very slowly," Top ordered.

They advanced another three miles, turning west at a crossroad at about mile two, then back north at the main road. Top alternatively fretting they were moving too slow or that they were riding into a trap. He wanted to find Rashid, but not in a killing zone.

They passed another east-west crossroad, then came to a place with few houses, where the road bent left and the woods closed in on both sides to about twenty yards from the crumbling road. It seemed a likely place for an ambush, and his anxiety level went up, though he trusted his scouts. Or maybe in a location like this, scouts were a trip wire for an ambush.

Both teams of scouts drew closer to the road, to avoid going in the trees, but stayed at the wood's edge. They spread out, Kat maybe thirty yards ahead of Jefferson, and Ed the same distance in front of Ali. About thirty yards on, Kat must have seen something and wheeled her horse, waving to Jefferson, Ali and Ski to retreat. Horrified they saw a line of riders come from the woods on either side. These began firing. Kat's horse went down, badly wounded. Ski turned and rode toward her, as did Jefferson and Ali. She frantically waved them back to warn the column.

Ali and Jefferson reluctantly turned and spurred their horses. Ski realized the riders were too close and would be on him immediately. He pulled his horse to the ground and had killed or wounded three of Rashid's men before a shot took him in the head, killing him instantly.

Kat had pulled her revolver, they were too close for the bow. She realized they were not shooting at her, obviously trying to capture her alive. Five shots for them, she thought, and one for me.

Ali and Jefferson reached the bend in the road, and looked back to see Ski go down and a swarm of Muslims close in on Kat. Ahead the column had spread out in ranks ten across, a difficult maneuver they had practiced, not with perfect success, and was coming at the gallop. They met the main body about fifty yards from the bend. "Ski's dead," Jefferson shouted. "Kat spotted the trap, but her horse went down. She waved us off to warn you. I think she's dead too."

They fell in beside Top, who had not slowed at all. "She was right, no use getting all four of you killed," he shouted. "And we needed to know what was happening."

They thundered up to the bend, reining in to see Rashid's men, about thirty in all, riding away from them. One of the horses was carrying double. Ali and Jefferson kicked their winded horses back into motion. "Hold," Top commanded. His voice left no room for response, and they pulled up. Jefferson swore, the first time Top had ever heard him do so. "I think the real ambush, the main force, is ahead," he said, his voice sharp, but calm. "These troopers were too close behind us after the main group hit us from the front. But Kat made them, and blew their plan."

"We can't let then get away with her!" Ali said.

"If we ride straight into them now, they will hurt us badly, even if we win, which isn't likely as they are in fixed positions," Top said.

"And if we got close to rescuing Kat, they'd kill her anyway," Anson chipped in, a bitter tone in his voice. He was very fond of Kat, little interest as she'd shown in him.

"We have to do something," Jefferson said. There were grunts of agreement from those near enough to overhear the conversation.

"And so we shall, but where they don't expect it. We will watch for a few minutes, then turn and ride slowly back as if we were going home," Top said.

"They won't believe that," Jefferson said.

"They may," Ali replied. "The fanatics think that all infidels are cowards."

"Let's hope so," Top said. "We'll swing west at that crossroad, and try to get around to their flank, maybe hit them after dark. It's our best chance. And Kat's too, if she is alive. I think they probably set up a camp to the west; Rashid seldom moves without his comforts." He was thinking, 'Not without a sex slave or two' but said nothing. Their thoughts were on Kat, but his had to be on winning the fight.

"Having run us off, as they think, they may sit there a day or so to see if we creep back, hoping we will still hit their entrenched position," Anson said. "Might even put those riders back in the woods, a little deeper though, thinking we won't expect them to stay in the same place."

They turned right at the crossroad, heading west, walking the horses to preserve their strength. Top rode up and down the line, passing the word on what they were trying to do, encouraging and calming the troopers. "Stay focused. We are all angry, but don't let it cloud your mind. Anger is a good servant, but a bad master. It won't help Kat and might get you killed. No one wants that, least of all her."

As evening came on, they stopped at a creek to water and feed the horses and do the same for themselves. Top overheard a trooper offering to trade his dinner with his horse, bringing a chuckle from those around him, and smiled. Troops were the same throughout the centuries. They were settling down now, their spirit returning. If things worked out as he hoped, they would need spirit.

About an hour after dark, they came to yet another crossroad, which headed north and south. Top had brought forward a trooper who had lived in this area, could confirm what he was pretty sure of, that the road would take them about three miles to the west of Rashid's position. They spotted some droppings on the road and figured this was the route the Muslims had taken north.

Abandoned farms were a particular worry. Barns could hide a number of riders, too few to take them on, but enough to follow behind, snipe at them, or maybe scouts to ride cross country to warn Rashid. They saw nothing suspicious, but Top had four scout teams out now, and they proceeded slowly, ever alert. No one felt sleepy, though tomorrow when the adrenalin wore off there would be a crash.

They passed several side roads, but the scouts confirmed that the droppings, which had to be from the Muslim force, continued. Finally they came to another crossroad, and the droppings turned right, back east. Top figured they were pretty close to Rashid. He sent Anson and a party of twenty forward to try and locate the Muslim camp and position. Very carefully and very quietly. The main body let them get a half mile ahead, and still with scout teams out, went forward.

Kat was pulled roughly from her horse. Her head throbbed and she was woozy; apparently someone had clubbed her from behind in the melee. She cursed herself for not using her last bullet to end her life before they got that close; she had been caught up in the heat of the fight. Her hands were tied behind her, but not tightly. She inwardly thanked Allah that Muslims were careless, or thought so little of women they didn't fear them. She was thrust into a tent. Rashid's camp was about fifty yards to the rear of the Muslims fighting positions. Apparently Rashid liked to travel in some comfort, though there were only a few tents, she assumed for the leaders.

Seeing how dug in they were as the party rode through made Kat grateful that the ZDF had not hit them head on. They might have won, but the losses would have been disastrous.

The tent she was pushed into looked big enough to hold four comfortably, but there was bedding for only one spread on the ground. She assumed this was the Caliph's tent.

A guard was posted over her. He told her to lie on the bedding and keep quiet. She lay on her side, due to her tied hands, and tried to work gently at the knots without calling attention to what she was doing. The guard squatted down and studied her with some interest. "Kaffir women are always immodest, in violation of the laws of Allah," he said. "The Caliph will teach you a woman's place." Kat didn't respond.

They were there for a couple of hours. She could tell from the growing darkness that night was falling. The tent was in deep gloom when a young man entered. Kat saw it was the one who led the ambush party that had taken her.

"I am Mohammad bin Mohammad, son of the Caliph," He said. "What are you called?" He looked about seventeen and was very cocky.

"My name is Katrina Tennent," she said, "A free woman of Zeblon freehold," staring defiantly into his eyes. Kat realized he was one of the Muslims who had come to "warn" them into coming here. He must have ridden hard to get here first, but he knew where to go and wasn't worried about an ambush.

"My father intends to add you to his household as a concubine."

We will see if I will be Rashid's sex slave, Kat thought. She said nothing, keeping her face blank.

"But since I took you in battle, he said it is Allah's will that I have you first. Untie her hands," he snapped to the guard.

That one hesitated. "Do it," Mohammad said. "I have had many Kaffir women. I do not need them tied. Unless I feel like making them scream with a hot iron." *His smile would chill a lava flow*, Kat thought.

The guard handed his rifle to Mohammad and motioned her to sit up. Kneeling behind her, he loosened the rope, then removed it. *Well, that saves time*, Kat thought. Her efforts had loosed the knot hardly at all.

The guard rose and Muhammad handed him back his rifle. "Take off your trousers," the boy ordered, grinning hungrily. Kat just stared at him. Stepping forward, he hit her with the butt of the AR-15, not enough to knock her out, but she went black for a few seconds. Pain flashed through her already aching head, and a trickle of blood slid down her left cheek.

Realizing she was facing overwhelming force, Kat moved to comply, kicking her shoes off and pushing her jeans down, followed by her panties as he gestured at them. She hoped a better moment would come. Mohammad's smile widened. "Truely Allah is generous and merciful, to bring you to my bed," he leered.

He handed his rifle to the guard, then his revolver, so she couldn't grab it while he raped her. "You can watch," he told the guard, "If I say the word, hit her again." Then freeing himself from his pants, he climbed on top of her.

Pittenger's party proceeded cautiously towards where they though Rashid's positions were, a scout on foot about thirty yards in front of them. There was enough ambient light that they could just make him out. Suddenly the scout's hand went up. Slowly he edged back towards them.

"Sentry," he said. "The idiot was smoking; I saw the glow through his cupped hands, but smelled it first."

"No surprise," Anson replied. "Except that they have tobacco. Maybe scavenged it from an abandoned house."

"What's the plan?"

"Since you know where he is, do you think you might slip behind him and arrange a date with some Houris, Insha'Allah?"

The scout grinned. "Tom's dating service for careless Muslims," he said.

"Take another man in case there are two."

The two scouts, now sentry assassins, slid into the night. Pittenger and the other men waited nervously, keeping their horses quiet. Top threw out another scout to their front and rear. It never hurt to be careful.

There was no sound from their front, but the two scouts slipped back to them in about fifteen minutes. They were smiling. "There was just one. Apparently he thought guard duty was a bore. If we had waited until he finished his smoke, he'd have been asleep."

They got close enough to see dim outlines of the tents, and the glow of a banked fire. "Still in position, expecting us from the south," Tom said.

"Yes, some people hate to change their plans, because they have such faith in them," Anson replied. "We'd better go back. No use alerting them."

Suddenly there was a shot from their left, north of the camp, then several more. Men began running around. A horn blew, and fighters, suddenly awake, trotted back from their fighting positions set for the ambush to the south. They could see more figures running towards the camp from the north.

"What the Christ is that?" the scout asked.

"The barbarians the old man warned us about. They aren't an invention of Rashid's fevered mind," Anson replied. He raised his voice, "Back to the column at a gallop," He ordered. The need for silence was gone.

Shots and screams echoing behind them, they raced for the ZDF expedition.

In the tent, Kat, trying desperately to keep her mind from what was happening to her, heard the sounds of fighting first. Hoping it was the ZDF attacking, she looked at the guard, who noticed it about that time. He had been enjoying watching Mohammad rape her, hoping he might be given a turn. "Mohammad?" he said tentatively.

The teenager heard it then, but was too close to climax to stop. "Find out what's happening," he ordered.

The guard ran from the tent, leaving Mohammad's weapons on the floor, his master thrusting rapidly at the Kaffir woman. Kat pulled the knife from behind her neck and had it deep in Mohammad's throat before the guard had been gone five seconds. Suddenly a bright plume of arterial blood covered them both. She rolled the boy's gurgling body off her, used the bedding to wipe at the blood on her face, and quickly pulled on her jeans and shoes.

Picking up the boy's weapons, she checked to be sure they were loaded. Both were. Peeking from the tent, she determined the attack was coming from the north. She turned to look at Mohammad's body, the blood had slowed to a trickle, convulsions stopped. "*So it was learned among the heathen host,*" she quoted in a whisper, "*How much a freeborn woman's favor costs.*"

The guard burst back into the tent yelling, "Barbarians!" He had no time to comprehend the changed circumstances as Kat shot him twice in the chest with Mohammad's revolver. It kicked like a bastard and she realized it was a 44 magnum.

Looking out the flap of the tent, she saw that there was no one in sight; the Muslims had passed her, running towards the melee a few yards to the north of the camp. She scurried to a supply wagon and climbed in, crouching behind some boxes.

Knowing it wasn't the ZDF, she had a free fire zone of Muslims and barbarians struggling about thirty yards north of her position, and that she could happily shoot anyone she could see. It was doubtful that either side would realize where her fire was coming from; the din was awful. Her plan was to do some damage, then slip away to the southeast, avoiding Rashid's fighting positions. She was sure there was no one there, but that would be their fallback position if the barbarians were winning. Right now it looked as though that was not the case, so she drew bead on a Holy warrior who was calmly shooting barbarians down. He fell. "One" she said, counting her rounds. She couldn't stay too long.

Top had the column moving forward at the first shot. Anson and his riders thundered to them, shouting, "Zeblon!" Pulling up, Anson panted, "Barbarians. Attacking Rashid from the north."

"Any sign of Kat?" Anson shook his head.

"Normally, I'd be delighted to sit back and watch them kill each other," Top said. "But there is a possibility Kat's alive. More important, we have the opportunity to take both in a flank attack, destroy Rashid's power and hurt the barbarians so badly they won't come this way anytime soon. I'm going to attack."

"Good," Anson said. "The land opens up before the camp, so we can form a battle-line." He pulled his horse to the right wing, where he would command.

Top raised his voice, "We are going to hit them hard. Shoot anything male that moves. If it looks female it could be Kat or other slaves. Other than women, no prisoners. Pass it on." Turning to the bugler, he said, "Sound forward at the trot." Beside him the flag bearer unfurled the stars and stripes. Their country might be defunct, but they were used to serving under it.

They came in sight of the fighting, but no one seemed to notice them. He signaled them to spread out in a battle line. There was room for them to form double ranks to his left and right, though they were pretty ragged by the standards of 19th century armies.

"Forward at the trot." They picked up a little speed. Those with lances lowered them. "Charge!" Top commanded. He was surprised that it felt thrilling, rather than foolish. Where is *John Wayne* when we need him? He thought.

The ZDF charge was on top of the fighting before either the Muslims or the barbarians noticed that there was a third player on the field. Struggling for their lives, they were slow to turn from the danger in front of them towards the new threat. But as the ZDF troopers started killing them, they swung to face them, firing blindly as panic set in. The ZDF riders with lances discovered that once you speared someone, you had to let your lance go. Still, they accounted for several enemies put out of the fight. And a screaming Muslim running through the field with a lance bobbing from a welter of blood in his side terrorized all.

Within minutes, panic set in and both the Muslims and the barbarians turned to run. They had already lost a great many of their fighters on both sides and the new attack was too much to bear. Many even threw down their weapons, to facilitate a rapid retreat.

"Nine" Kat counted, bringing down a barbarian. "Two more and it's time to go." Then she heard the new fighting to the west. Seeing horse mounted fighters in the melee, killing both barbarians and the holy warriors, she realized it was the ZDF. *Maybe I'll stay a bit and help out*, she thought. She looked around for discarded weapons or ammo that she could retrieve with relative safety, saw none. But she did spot Rashid surrounded by several Muslim warriors, his bodyguard she assumed. They were not fleeing like most on both sides, but were fighting their way with difficulty toward the ZDF line, which was breaking up in the melee. She tried to get a clear sight picture.

Rashid had spotted Top at the head of the ZDF riders, and was trying to get close enough for a clear shot. *If, Insha'Allah I can kill the infidel leader, we may save this*, he thought. He wondered where Mohammad was, hoped his son was safe.

Suddenly, a huge barbarian lunged at Top, and the Marine turned sideways. He killed his assailant with a pistol, but was exposed for just the time Rashid need to aim and put a round in Top's chest, slamming him off his mount.

At the same moment he fired, Anson saw him and snapped off a shot, which took Rashid in the head, his brains exploding onto the bodyguard behind him. The man screamed, and every Muslim thought then only of safety, running from the fight, throwing down their weapons. The barbarians took the hint, and they streamed off north together, heedless of the fact they were running with men they had been trying to kill moments before.

The ZDF, maddened by battle and seeing Top go down, pursued the panicked fighters, killing them as fast as they could.

Anson rode by a wagon, heard his name called. He looked around, heard "Anson!" again, and saw a hand waving at him over the side of the wagon. Riding carefully over, he saw Kat smiling at him from behind the fort of boxes she had made.

"Thank God," he said. "Are you okay?"

"I'm some the worse for wear," she said. "But I'm alive and those who abused me are not, so I think I'm ahead. I saw Top go down; do you know if he's okay?"

"The medic went to tend him, but I don't know. Suddenly I was in command. Which reminds me." He signaled to the closest riders, sent them to call off the pursuit. Looking around, he saw Mario, beckoned him over.

"A grand night, Boss," Mario said. "I still have my horn!"

"Grand except for our dead and wounded. Sound assembly."

Anson pulled them off to the other side of the Muslim entrenchments. He put out double pickets and told the rest to get some food and sleep if they could. Few could sleep. The medic and two others came in bearing Top's body slung over a horse. "Nothing I could do," he said, tears on his cheeks. "He was hit close to the heart, bled out in minutes."

"Not your fault," Pittenger replied. "And there's no better death for a Marine."

Men straggled in all night. Some were wounded, some lost and some so taken by battle fury they wouldn't stop killing while there was a live target or they had ammo.

They counted eighteen dead ZDF troops, including Top and Ski and twenty-four wounded, three seriously. Ali was among the slightly wounded. They also tallied seventy-eight Muslim dead and a hundred and twenty three barbarians. There were no prisoners. They went through the battle area and killed any wounded with the lances. They didn't have the facilities to care for their own.

In addition to rescuing Kat, there was another bright spot. Maggie Pennant, the old Wagoner's daughter, had managed to hide when the fight went against the barbarians. They had killed three other women they had taken as slaves, including Maggie's mother, Betsy. They put Maggie under the care of one of the women troopers.

The other positive was the number of weapons, ammo and supplies they recovered from both Rashid's men and the barbarians, which equaled about what was presently available back in Zeblon. Since they needed wagons for the wounded, they had to find a place to cache about half of it. Anson sent fast riders back to the Freehold with news of the fight and for the motor vehicles. A haul like this justified the use of gasoline.

A day later, back in Zeblon, Jackson gathered the ZDF leadership and Freehold Board, though they mostly overlapped, for a council of war. "This is a half-finished victory," he said. "But now is our chance to permanently destroy the Caliphate. If we hit them now, we can free their slaves, bring in any folks who are not fanatics, gather in all their materials and remaining weapons and rid ourselves of this danger. Plus any holdouts within twenty miles should rally to us."

"Who will lead?" Kat asked.

Anson was relieved when Jackson answered, "I will. I'll take the pickup. I propose we leave in the morning. We'll bury our dead when we get back." That there would likely be more, he left unsaid.

"Is it wise to risk our victory?" Hal asked. Kat gave him a look, but he didn't see.

"We risk our victory if we don't follow up now. They have lost the majority of their warriors, a lot of weapons and ammo, and their leader and his heir," Jackson replied. "And the pickup will bring in the last of their guns, ammo and supplies shortly."

"So, easy pickings?" asked Sam Kenton, who when not blacksmithing, served on the Board.

"There's no such thing in battle, Sam," Jackson said. "But the odds are heavily on our side for the first time. In a year, they may recover, if we don't finish this now. Every day we wait, they will grow stronger."

"I say we ride," Kat said. "Every day we wait is also a day in hell for their sex slaves."

"Are you sure you are up to it?" Anson asked.

"Try and stop me," she snapped. "I live--I survived--only to kill slavers!"

Only Jackson caught the pained expression fleetingly on Anson's face. "We all hate slavery," he said. "Part of the country's problems were that many people thought that only black folks like me were ever enslaved. But every society held slaves. The word comes from the word Slav, so many were enslaved in Europe in the middle ages. And slavery is justified in the Holy Qur'an. But our first duty is the safety and freedom of Zeblon Freehold."

"True," Anson said. "But I agree with you. We can secure that freedom and safety if we can eliminate permanently the threat of the Caliphate, and strengthen ourselves in the bargain. I move we ride, the sooner the better."

Hal called the question. Every hand but his went up. He looked from face to face, signed and raised his hand to make it unanimous. "I hate violence," he said to himself more than the group. "But needs must."

"Anson, issue the orders. We will leave twenty-five fighters here, including walking wounded, and arm every citizen. With what the pickup already brought in, we could arm a third world army. I hope to leave at first light, destroy them by noon, and send half our troopers back here immediately."

"Worried about the barbarians?" Sam asked.

"Not really," Jackson replied. "I expect after yesterday's bloodletting, we won't have any problems with them for a year or more. But eternal vigilance and all that. By the way, Anson, you did a fine job after you had to take command yesterday. Top would be proud of you."

Anson looked down. "Well, he and you and my DIs all trained me hard. I guess there was a reason."

"May I go with you, as a regular trooper?" Hal asked plaintively. "If I can vote for it, I can damn well do it."

"Certainly, Hal," Jackson answered. "I know this is very hard for you. It's actually hard for everyone, even those who talk and act tough." He glanced at Kat; she was staring at the window. "Most folk in our country were not raised to live in a constant state of fear and war. But if we want to keep freedom alive, well, freedom has always had a price. My great, great grandfather was in Union service at the Crater. It's just that since the Collapse, the resulting Chaos has demanded the price be paid almost on a daily basis. Top, Ski, and sixteen other Freeholders paid it yesterday. More of us will pay tomorrow, and in time to come."

He turned and limped toward the door, setting his prosthetic leg down harder than usual, perhaps to emphasize his words.

Anson glanced at Kat. There were tears on her cheeks. She glared at him, daring him to say something. He looked about the group. "It's a price we have to pay," he said. Then he turned and followed Jackson outside to begin preparations.

The Hunt

Tramdill knew a Seeker was hunting him. So was an enraged mob from the village a mile back, but that worried him not at all. The ignorant peasants on this feudal world were no more capable of destroying one of his kind than they were of appreciating advanced sentient beings like himself—or like a Seeker either, for that matter.

Shouting erupted behind him. He turned to see a group of angry folk emerge from the grove of oaks where he'd left the cooper's apprentice, when he mind-jumped to the elderly peddler whose body he occupied now. They were carrying the struggling boy, trussed like a wild boar.

Tramdill stood by the side of the road, secure in his new persona, and watched as they bore the terrified apprentice to his place of execution. Doubtless they would drive a wooden stake through the youth's heart, as was their barbaric custom when confronted with a Feeder. The fools didn't realize that only his brain was vulnerable—a new heart came with each new host he seized.

Shaking a knurled fist, Tramdill cursed at the boy whose body he had inhabited when he coupled with the miller's daughter, then drew her life force into himself. It was the discovery of her nude and drained body that had set the mob on the hunt.

Tramdill was enjoying himself, despite the threat posed by the Seeker. Primitive as it was, this world offered good sport. He liked the aftermath—the chase, the inevitable murder of his temporary host—almost as much as he enjoyed the coupling. Often he would allow himself to be captured in his host body, taken with a woman's corpse lying at his feet, and dragged out to be killed. Then he would brain-jump to a man in the mob before his former host was put to death.

But that was nothing to the sheer pleasure of drawing a female's life force into his soul, sucking her dry, feeding his energy reserves with her very essence.

It was this female life-essence that let Tramdill live, and provided the energy for his brain-jumps, as he moved from host male to host male. That his unwilling hosts had their minds destroyed, and were then killed by their own kind, or that the females who provided the vital essence did so at the cost of their lives, bothered Tramdill no more than a lion was bothered by feeding on a slaughtered wildebeest. Humanoids were Tramdill's natural prey. And this world was a virtual larder. He'd sent for his mate, Trindara—there were plenty of males here for her to feed on, no reason to keep the wealth to himself.

He'd been lucky to find a humanoid planet so technologically backward they had almost no defenses against Feeders, making life easy and sweet. Especially as it had apparently been well over fifty of the local years since one of his kind had fed here.

Or at least he was lucky until the Seeker arrived. And maybe lucky still, because she'd been careless, allowing some of the local folk to see her in her natural form. He'd heard the tales of a great monster ten days ago, and had moved rapidly away, hoping to draw her on, following his feeding trail, until he could trap her.

Tramdill had been hunted by a Seeker before, long ago, and had killed her, mostly by accident. He assumed there must be male Seekers on their home world, but the hunters were, as far as he knew, always female. They were mortal enemies of his kind; he knew not why but assumed it was some old feud. Or perhaps they wanted the humans for themselves, though he had not heard of a Seeker feeding. Once on the hunt, a Seeker never wavered. Tramdill would have to kill this one as well, or perish. Before he could take in enough essence to mind-jump to another world, she would be on him, drawn by the mass feedings necessary to fuel long jumps.

A Seeker in her natural form was invulnerable to him. But she would move too slowly that way, be too conspicuous, draw down attacks from the humans. She would have to assume human form to hunt him. Seekers did so without occupying a human the way he did, but they always became females, preserving their gender in the transition, just as he occupied males and fed on females. What was easier for him than killing a woman?

His problem was identifying her, the one woman hunting him among the multitudes he hunted. Her situation was similar, of course, since he could be any of the men on the planet—and could move from host to host as long as he had reserves of life essence. She could only track him by his kills.

Still, the Seeker on Andertin Four had known him. He was only saved because she struck too soon, before he coupled, rather then waiting until he was vulnerable at the climax of the coupling, almost catatonic for the moments before he drew the essence. Perhaps she was trying to save the girl's life, but why? Certainly there was no shortage of humanoids on Andertin Four. It made no sense to Tramdill—like losing your life to rescue an ant.

He'd killed her rather easily, stabbing the old woman, then finished his coupling with a now-terrified young girl. Tramdill had been startled to glance at the body of the dead crone when he was done feeding and discover it transforming into the repugnant natural shape of a Seeker. He'd immediately gone on a feeding frenzy and mind-jumped from Andertin, fearful another Seeker would come hunting him.

And now one was here, on Sol Three.

Tramdill fed on a goatherd in her hut, but she was old and ugly, her essence thin. And the peddler's body was too decrepit to provide much pleasure from the coupling. He decided to mind-jump as soon as a suitable candidate came into short range, where he would expend less of his reserves. Taking over a human's body gave him human tastes, talents and pleasures, but also the afflictions of that particular male.

Fortune smiled before he'd gone two miles. A young itinerant troubadour came up behind him, singly gaily, harp slung over his back. He asked the old peddler if he had any gut for harp strings, as he was headed to the nearby castle to entertain, the local Earl giving a great wedding feast. Moments later the peddler lay gurgling in a ditch beside the road, and Tramdill enjoyed the feel of young muscles stretching out as he swung down the track, harp slapping his side.

He liked the wedding, taking special delight in the attentions of several young women who made eyes at him as he sang romantic ballads in the great hall. Tramdill wondered if the Seeker could be here ahead of him, but thought it unlikely. Besides, he felt safe with the large number of men present—how could she pick him out?

Testing, he composed a sad song about a young girl who was murdered by a lover from far away. None of the women seemed overly interested. He thought the Seeker would be testing men also, and watched to see which women flirted with the most men, thinking to avoid them to be safe when feeding.

A serving wench caught his eye. Blond, sassy, she managed to exchange taunts and greetings, occasionally a slap or tickle, with almost every male there. If the Seeker were here, she would be the one. But she would have to catch him feeding to be sure, and that was his chance to trap her as well.

Carefully he selected his target, a young woman with flame-red hair piled in a bun on top of her head, who disdained the men, conversing only with two of the older women. Her flawless skin, blue-gray eyes and the expanse of freckled bosom exposed by her gown were much to his taste—or, to be precise, to the taste of his young host body.

Artfully he pursued her; singing praises to her beauty, concentrating his mental powers and the troubadour's charm on winning his way to her bed for the evening. She ignored him at first, than gradually let him engage her in conversation.

She was from a land to the north, a distant relative of the bride through an aunt's marriage to a mountain chieftain. Her name, she said, was Mairi MacKenzie. Her father had left her here for the celebration, and gone south to the capital on business.

Soon they were laughing together between his songs, and she was taking more wine. Eventually he knew all he needed to about Mistress MacKenzie.

She flushed hotly when he asked her to leave her door unbarred, so he could come and "sing her a love lullaby to sweeten her dreams."

"Och, ye are bold, Sir Minstrel, and me but a lass far frae hame," she said. But she told him which tower room was hers—and confided that, knowing none of the other women, she had no bedmates.

Tramdill continued to sing and play long after Mairi had departed—and most of the guests were well taken in drink. But he made certain the blond wench saw him when he took the stairs to the tower where the MacKenzie girl was bedded.

Then he waited, pressed against an arch at the top of the stairs, dagger in hand, for a full thirty minutes. Had the blonde or any other woman appeared, she would have died, whether she was Seeker or serving girl.

None did, and, satisfied he was safe for the moment, Tramdill made his way to Mairi's chamber. He smiled when a slight pressure swung the door open. Stepping inside, and taking no chances of being surprised, he barred it quietly behind him. Without waking her, he made a quick inventory of the room, looking for weapons that might be used against him when he was vulnerable. Finding none, he knelt by the sleeping woman and began to croon a sweet ballad of love. Her eyes fluttered open, and she smiled.

The coupling was glorious, the lass from the north country proving passionate, energetic and more than a little vocal, making Tramdill grateful for the thick stone walls of her chamber. Afterward he buried his face against the base of her throat, mouth kissing the tender spot where he would sink his teeth to draw her life essence, and slept for a moment, needing as always to regain his strength.

When his breathing grew shallow, Mairi carefully withdrew the long, titanium spike hidden in her hair, and centered it in Tramdill's left ear. With a powerful thrust, she drove it into his brain, killing him and his troubadour host almost instantly. He jerked once and went limp. She rolled the singer's body off hers, and stood, shaking herself as if to get mud off her person.

Looking at the corpse, she thought that except for a trickle of blood from his ear, he could be sleeping. She had known him immediately. This was the fourteenth Feeder she had killed, easily identifying them from their odor. By the Mother—didn't they know they stank of death?

Dressing quickly, she let herself out the postern gate, thankful that everyone was sleeping off the effects of the feast. She desperately wanted to shed the fleshy human body she had adopted for the hunt, so grotesquely soft and vulnerable. But she waited until she was out of sight of the castle, deep in the nearby forest, before transforming to her own shape, and summoning the lifter beam from her ship. This planet must be watched more closely, she thought, it was too vulnerable to Feeders. She would return soon, perhaps in two years.

"It were a dragon, my Lord, all blue and yellow scales," the frightened woodcutter said, fidgeting before his betters. "It were taller than ony tree, and it rose right into the sky and flew away."

"And I suppose it breathed fire!" the Earl said sourly, bringing a bark of laughter from the assembled knights. His head was pounding, his mouth tasted like a stable and there had been the murder of a troubadour, apparently by a Scotswoman no one recalled inviting to the wedding. And now this woodcutter had stirred up the village with tales of dragons, and must be dealt with. What could go wrong next, the Earl wondered?

At that moment, from fifty parsecs away, Trindara brain-jumped into a new host body on the world Tramdill had summoned her to. It had taken her long to gather strength for the jump. She was eager to see her mate and famished from the effort. Picking up a tray of ale flagons, she shook out her new blond hair and made her way into the great hall, where the local Lord and his knights were making sport of a poorly dressed old man. Her whole being warmed—such a lovely feast of men was laid before her, glowing with their essence.

She must find Tramdill and thank him. Funny she wasn't picking up his brain waves.

"The Hunt" was published in *Calliope*, Jan-Feb, 2006. It was the First Place Winner in the 2005 Mensa Writers SIG Fiction Contest.

Billy's Birthday

Walter took a last look around the campsite. Satisfied they had followed the Boy Scout dictum of "leave it better than you found it," he climbed into the truck cab and pulled around to the office. Margaret had just finished paying the young woman in the ranger hat and blue jeans. She tore herself away from a one-sided conversation to join him in their camper.

"I wish Billy had married a girl like that ranger," she said.

Walt decided there was no cause to mention the "ranger," while too old to be called a girl, was still young enough to be Billy's daughter--and their granddaughter. He turned east on the road running by the campground and changed the subject.

"Think it might warm up again today." Weather made a good topic, though after serving on both Iwo Jima and at the Chosin Reservoir, hot or cold, it hardly bothered him.

Margaret was studying the map. "Next week is Billy's birthday, Walter. I'd like to be there."

"Been working towards home for the past week, Maggie." He kept his voice free from inflection. "We'll be there."

They settled into the comfortable silence of forty-plus years of marriage, enjoying the ride, occasionally commenting on houses or scenery. Avoiding the interstates, preferring country roads, liking the familiarity of small towns, Walter and Margaret McClintock were no longer in a hurry. A few years ago they set out to explore America's backroads, first through the Midwest, but lately further afield. Every year they spent more time on the road, seeing the country.

"Next big town, lets stop at an outlet center so I can pick up a gift for Billy," she said.

Walter smiled at her request. Always an outlet center, discount store or flea market. Thank God, though they still owned the McClintock farm, after Korea he'd taken a job with a decent pension. Like most country women, Margaret was careful with the pennies. He didn't begrudge her the little she spent on discounted gifts.

"You got it," he said. The easy-listening station was fading, so Walt unzipped the cassette holder she'd bought him last Christmas--no doubt at a discount. Driving with one hand, he fumbled open the case and slid the Jean Redpath tape into the player. He'd been looking through the Scottish section for a bagpipe tape to annoy teenagers with boom boxes, and had found the Redpath tape with a song called "Maggie" on it.

Even turned low, Redpath's clear, sweet voice filled the cab. When "Maggie" came on, he reached out and took Margaret's hand.

"...when I first said I loved only you, Maggie,
and you said you loved only me..."

Margaret turned from studying the countryside. "I love you, Walt," she mouthed at him. He squeezed her hand and concentrated on the road, stretching out in front of them, long and empty.

35

Margaret was only ten minutes late for their appointed meeting in the mall, something of a record. He's spent the two hours in Terry's Table & Tavern, drinking non-alcoholic beer. Walt liked the real stuff, but at 74, he figured his driving didn't need any added risks. The barkeep was a retired Marine, so time had gone quickly, trading sea stories. Maggie was laden with three bags.

In the cab, she showed him her treasures: six pair of heavy socks for him, a Shetland sweater for her, and a Black Watch tartan shirt for Billy. All were seconds, purchased at half of retail.

"You can't even notice it," she said, pointing out the flaw on Billy's shirt, a double row of stitching on the left cuff. "Besides, none of you McClintocks is all that picky about what you wear."

"If we was picky, I'd never married a woman with a smart mouth," he kidded back.

Maggie was grinning broadly now. "I got an extra large shirt for Billy--don't you think that'll be right?" She reached over and patted his paunch. "You McClintocks run to lard when you get older, too."

"I don't know, Mag--I think that blond ranger kind of had an eye for me."

"If she did, it was cause she thought you were Santa Claus."

"And I could of been, given the right incentive."

Maggie poked him in the side. "Now, what's the right incentive at your age?" she laughed.

The last night, they stopped at a favorite campground 200 miles from home. Taking their evening walk around the camp, they held hands in the cool September twilight. Six teenagers were grouped around a fire, singing Sixties' folk songs with more volume than talent. They paused to listen and were invited to sit. Walter grumped it was horrible to reach an age when kids thought you were cute. Maggie cried at "Where Have all the Flowers Gone." She invited the kids for pancakes in the morning, so they made a late start.

Two hours out they stopped at a roadside farm stand. Maggie bought a half bushel of apples.

"You figure we'll eat all those?" he asked.

"I'll take half up to Billy and make a pie with the rest. You know how he pestered us for canned fruit when he was away."

It was past two when they pulled into the farm. Maggie turned to him, eyes glistening. "It's a beautiful day for Billy's birthday," she said.

Walt nodded. There was a soft breeze from the west, moving the clouds slowly across the pale sky. Soon it would be time for their fall leaf-tour.

They unpacked the food and dirty laundry. Maggie started a load of wash while Walt pulled the truck on a homemade ramp in the yard. He walked back to the barn for five cans of oil and a filter. The Marines taught him survival meant taking care of your gear first, and he saw no reason to break a good habit. He set the oil down by the truck and was preparing to crawl under when Maggie came out with the shirt and a bag.

"I'll go give Billy his present while you work on that old truck" she said, "but he'll expect you to come by later."

"I'll do so."

He stood and watched her climb the hill, her figure strong and slender for 69 years. In the soft light, Maggie looked like the same girl he proposed to the day he'd come home from the Pacific war. She wore her new sweater over a "Sunday" dress, not fancy, but clean and bright, and the breeze flipped her skirt from time to time. When she reached the wall at the top, he went back to his chore.

Maggie came in as he was getting out of the shower. "You better go see Billy while it's still light," she said, "I'll start dinner."

He pulled on a plaid short-sleeve shirt and clean denims. "I'll go now."

Walt climbed the hill in stages, stopping frequently to breath deep and admire the rolling hills of eastern Ohio. At each rest he vowed to take off twenty pounds. It was coming on evening when he entered the grove of trees at the top and pushed open the iron gate. The wall was cemented here, some fancier than the loose collection of stones with which previous McClintocks had bordered the rest of their land, clearing it for the plow.

He stopped and looked at his father's grave, brushing some lichen off the stone. His dad was a World War I Marine who died while Walter was in Korea fighting his second war. "Hi, Dad," he said, "Semper Fi."

Then he looked over to where the tartan shirt was hung over the arms of a Celtic cross standing at the left of the McClintock family plot. The bag of apples rested uncomfortably against the stone that formed the base.

Moving slowly to the cross, he pulled the flannel shirt off and hung it over his shoulders. It felt good against the evening chill. He would add it to the other gifts locked in the shed. In all the years, Maggie never missed a birthday or Christmas. Despite the fading light, he could clearly read the inscription cut neatly into the stone:

In loving memory of
Lance Corporal William Jefferson McClintock
United States Marine Corps
Born September 19th, 1947
Missing in Action
August 15th, 1967
Quang Tri Province
Vietnam
"Proud to Claim the Title"

He bent and picked up the apples. "Happy Birthday, Billy." Turning, he began to toss them slowly into the woods for the raccoons. Anger overwhelmed him, and he rocketed the apples into the grove, startling some crows, splattering them against the trees. He ran out of apples before his anger cooled, and looked around for a rock. Not finding one, he kicked the granite base of the cross. The sudden pain calmed him.

Walter glanced around the orderly graveyard. Six McClintocks had worn the uniform of the United States in war. Three of them were here, five if you included Billy and himself. He wondered who would care for McClintock graves when he was gone. Great-Grandpa was down at Gettysburg, so he'd be taken care of, at least.

For several minutes Walt stared over the farm, McClintock land for generations, looking toward the rising hills. He wondered idly if it would all be vacation condos someday. Turning, he looked down at the neat house where Margaret sometimes scolded an imaginary grandchild, a child who never grew up, a child lost in Vietnam as surely as Billy. "God curse all politicians," he whispered.

Putting his hands in his pockets, the last McClintock went down to dinner. It was easier going down.

Published in *Capper's Magazine*, November 4, 1997.

Get A Cat

Harold was bent forward on the couch, his left foot doubled onto his lap, alternating his attention between cleaning his toenails with a pen top and watching the Mets lose a double header. "You'd think" he said, "that in a burg this size a guy with average looks would have a date for Saturday night. I keep reading in Ann Landers about all the women looking for nice guys, but where are they?"

"Actually, Hal, I think the guys with average looks are scoring at least twice a week, the nice guys are making out on alternate Saturdays regular, and those of us blessed with superior features have to carry a stun gun to protect ourselves!" Ron replied, giving his friend a smile to show it was just their usual banter.

Harold shot him a sour look and got up to fetch two more beers from the fridge. "It's not funny, ya know. Last year you were dating Tracy and Jennifer at the same time. I was lucky to get two dates in a row with the same girl."

"Woman!" Ron injected.

"What?"

"Woman, Hal. This is not 1960. You're twenty-nine years old. Anyone old enough to date you is a woman and will resent being called a girl. Where did you spend the last decade--doing research on seal snot in Greenland?"

Harold bristled. He felt that any reference to his job at the lab implied he was a nerd. He'd stopped wearing the white coat except at work and gotten rid of the pocket protector he'd carried his pens in, though the price had been heavy in ink stains on the pockets of his K-Mart shirts.

"Look Ron, cut the crap. I'm really starting to think I've got a problem. The longest relationship I've had in ten months is three dates with that, ah, woman my mother introduced me to at Christmas--the one who flunked out of astrology school! You do okay, you've had a great thing going with Mildred..."

"Bunni!"

"Bunny?"

"Yes, Bunni, with an I" Ron smiled, "I've changed Mildred's name to Bunni."

"Why--and how--could you change Mildred's name" Harold asked. This turn of events fascinated him. If Ron could go around exercising such power over women that he could even change their names, there might be some secret to be learned here.

"Sit here at my feet and absorb wisdom from the master" Ron said. "And stop picking your toes while you're at it." He took a long swallow of beer to lubricate the coming discourse. "You see, Mildred--now Bunni--as cute as she is, as sexy as she is..."

Harold nodded, rapt. Mildred-Bunni had not escaped unappreciated from his fantasies.

"...As bright as she is, has always had an inferiority complex because of her name. Her mother named her for her great-grandmother. Bunni always wanted a modern, cute name, and her self-esteem has suffered. Ever sensitive to the plight of my fellow humans," Ron smiled his superior, master of pop-psychology smile, "I discerned this flaw and moved to correct it. She liked it when I told her she was 'cute as a bunny,' so I started calling her Bunni. I then enlisted her two best friends in the

cause. Now I'm getting all my friends--you included--to call her Bunni. In another
month, I'll have her mother calling her Bunni. Her happiness has soared and, in the
pantheon of her existence, I am the god who has given her the one thing she has
always wanted--a cute name!"

Harold was impressed. "Bunni wouldn't have a friend in need of a cute name,
would she? Bubbles? Cuddles? Kitti with an I?"

Ron gave him an appraising glance. "You don't need introductions, Hal, you need
a complete remake."

"Gee, thanks, remind me to say something nice about you."

"I'm serious, Hal. You want to improve your chances with women, you need to
refurbish your image. You've got to change your life style. Look, you're basically a
nice guy, college educated, a good job, and, not to put too fine a point on it, not all that
bad looking--you're just not very smooth."

Harold switched off the TV, abandoning the Mets to their fate in the sixth. "Okay"
he said, "I'm appointing you my PR man and campaign manager. Solitary sex may be
safe sex, but it sure is lonely. What do I do?"

"First, get two more brews and something to take notes on" Ron replied. He
waited while Harold complied, sublimely confident of his suitability for the role of a
Yuppie Professor Higgins.

"You've gotta put yourself in the woman's place" Ron said. "Learn to think like
them. What's a woman want in a guy? A sense of humor and brains, which you've got.
But she also wants class, neatness, warmth, sensitivity, and a touch of romance. Even
if you're Clint Eastwood on the outside, she wants some Alan Alda underneath."

Two hours, three beers, and much argument later, Harold had four pages of
notes on his laptop computer. The list was pretty much an indictment of the way he
presented himself to potential partners. It contained things like: clean apartment and
keep it neat; throw out nerdy clothes; learn at least three obscure love poems by heart;
dress neatly, but cool and casual; remove the pictures of nude women thumb tacked in
the bedroom and replace with framed art prints; find a better barber; don't pick toes,
ears or nose around women; eliminate sexist language; learn where to buy inexpensive
flowers; stock a few bottles of decent wine; tape some soft background music; and
talk about something besides the lab and the Mets.

Lastly, get a cat.

"A cat!" Harold choked. "Why would I want a cat? I don't want a cat, the last
thing I want is a cat."

Ron patiently tried to overcome Harold's objections, as he had for other items
on the "New, Improved Harold Holcroft" list. "Look, Hal, you're going to become a
sensitive, caring, post-modern kind of guy. You'll be a bright, well-employed, regular
guy, but, without being sappy about it, you'll also be romantic. You'll like a little
poetry, long walks on rain-swept beaches, fireplaces, flowers, soft music--and animals.
Why do you think I got Marmalade at the pound?"

Marmalade was Ron's lazy, yellow tabby. Harold had nothing against her, but
could see no real use for her, either.

"Women like guys who like animals" Ron went on. "To show you like animals,

40

you gotta have one. It has to be something cuddly they can pet, a cat or a dog. Dogs are hell in the city, so that leaves cats."

"Animals have to be taken care of," Harold objected, "and they cost money."

"All you do with a cat is put down food and fresh water in the morning, and change the kitty litter once a week or before you have a date over, whichever comes first. Best of all, they're free. People are always giving cats and kittens away. Just make sure the cat is affectionate, like Marmalade. Believe your old buddy, she's improved my sex life two hundred percent."

Harold remained dubious, but agreed to think it over.

On Sunday, while Ron supervised and drank Harold's beer, Harold cleaned and redecorated his apartment and reduced his wardrobe. On Monday, Ron joined Harold after work for a shopping safari that threatened to max Harold's VISA card. His purchases included eleven trendy items of apparel, five inexpensive art prints, six CDs (Ron vetoed "Bolero" as too obvious), four bottles of chardonnay and white zinfandel, a book of "Best Loved Poems," several candles and a vase for flowers. Harold balked when Ron tried to steer him into the mall's pet store "just to look."

On Thursday, Harold met Helen.

"She was in the cafeteria and all the other tables were filled, so I was able to join her without being obvious" he told Ron, who doubted that Harold was ever anything but obvious. "I started reading that poetry book over my chicken sandwich, and she asked me about it. I told her I was just getting interested in poetry, so she wouldn't expect me to know too much. We're having lunch again tomorrow!"

Harold met Helen twice for lunch the following week, and was ecstatic when she accepted his invitation for dinner Saturday night.

"You're a genius," he told Ron, who naturally agreed. "This is really working."

Saturday morning Harold recleaned the apartment, chilled the wine, put the music in the CD player, changed the sheets, got a haircut and sprang for $4.99 for flowers at the supermarket. He also made reservations at Angelo's, a nearby, inexpensive and Ron-recommended Italian restaurant, complete with red checkered tablecloths and candles in Chianti bottles. Then the doubts set in.

Ron answered his emergency call on the second ring. "Can I borrow Marmalade?" Harold asked.

"What?"

"Look, you've been right about everything else. You're probably right about the cat. I don't want to blow this with Helen, I think it could be the real thing. I think she'll probably come back to my place tonight--at least I hope so. Can't I borrow Marmalade for the night?" Harold pleaded.

"What happens when she finds out it isn't your cat?"

Harold could see his chance at happiness and romance slipping away. He quickly improvised. "She won't find out. If it works out, next time she comes I'll tell her Marmalade had to go to the vet. Then I'll tell her Marmalade died. She'll feel sorry for me and I'll get her to help me pick out a new cat" Harold said, desperately falling in with Ron's original plan.

"Well, it might work" Ron agreed. "Since you're my best buddy--come get her.

But I wouldn't do this for everyone."

"This is my roommate, Marmalade," Harold introduced the cat to Helen. Marmalade had been keeping her distance from him, but played like a trouper and came to greet them as he was hanging up Helen's jacket, rubbing against her legs. So far, it had been a perfect evening. Helen had laughed at his jokes and loved Angelo's. She'd responded to his kiss outside the restaurant and agreed to come over for a glass of wine "if you promise to behave." At that point, Harold would have promised to teach her to fly.

Harold installed Helen on the couch, lit two candles, clicked on a CD of harp music Ron had chosen, and poured two glasses of Ron's favorite chardonnay. Marmalade played her part to the hilt, jumping on the couch and curling up in Helen's lap, purring like a miniature chain saw. Ron left them to get acquainted and slipped into the bedroom to dispose of his tie and shoes, only to discover that Marmalade had thrown up in the middle of his bed. Well, he reasoned, that fitted well with her planned demise.

"I'll just be a minute" he called to Helen. "Marmalade's been sick. I'll have to take her to the vet tomorrow." He quickly stripped grandmother's quilt from the bed, rinsed the offended area under the bathroom tap and stuffed it in the hamper in his closet.

When he returned to the living room, Marmalade was contentedly enjoying the music by herself on the couch. Helen was in the hall, putting on her jacket. Harold was startled to see she had tears in her eyes.

"I'm sorry Hal, but this isn't a good idea. I shouldn't have agreed to come over. Thanks for dinner." She was out the door, closing it softly behind her, before Harold could recover from his disappointment and shock enough to ask what was wrong--or even say goodby.

From the living room came the unmistakable sounds of Marmalade being sick on the couch.

Helen's roommate was reading the Sunday paper in the kitchen when Helen wandered in and poured herself a mug of coffee. "How went last night's big date?" she asked. "Grim, I'll bet. You look like hell."

"It was fine 'til we got to his place," Helen replied. "I really liked the guy. Unfortunately, it turns out he has a cat. I tried to pet it because I like animals too, but my allergies took hold and I had to blow out of there. There's just no way I can date a guy who owns a cat. You'd think in a city this size, I could find one nice guy who doesn't have one of those furry sneezeballs living with him."

A Bit of Colored Ribbon

They killed Alex Johnson in the first block. He was checking the upper windows of burned-out tenements, just as they'd been taught, when a girl stepped out of an alley, swung a chain around his neck and dragged him down. Her partner thrust a long knife under Johnson's chin, grabbed his taser-rifle, and tried to duck back into the alley. Haskel, one of the newies, burned them both. Not that it did Johnson any good. His life bubbled out on the dirty concrete before they could get a lifepatch on his neck. Eddie thought it probably wouldn't have taken there anyway. Cutting throats was a Raider trademark.

Bronski stripped Johnson of anything usable and pushed his body behind a trash heap with the dead Raiders. The girl looked about fourteen, but she had a crude spider tattooed on her upper arm, totem of a raiding tribe. The Government killer team rallied in an abandoned store, and Eddie posted Haskel and Bronski at the doors. There wasn't a sound in the building. He hoped it wasn't home to a nest of Raiders, or all three of them would be the subject of dignified ceremonies.

Eddie reported the action and location on his comm-pad, and was ordered to continue the mission. Another team would retrieve Lance-Sergeant Johnson's remains, if the rats left enough. There would be a suitable rite and a Valor Cross for his grieving family, who would doubtless appreciate the bit of colored ribbon.

If he wasn't so terrified, Eddie thought he might laugh. Probably a touch of hysteria. Johnson was an arrogant berk, but he was the team leader. Always bragging about his "intuition," developed on thirty-plus killer missions in the deadly streets of a dozen old cities, hunting Raiders. Bugger-all good his experience had done him this time. He dare not let Bronski and Haskel see his fear. Corporal Edward McFee, 20, veteran of all of three missions, was now team leader. He couldn't abort the mission. Intel had identified the nest of a Raider leader, what the scum called a tribal chieftain, and they had been the only available killer team. It was too important a target to pass up. Burn a tribe leader and decent folk who lived on the city's periphery would be safer. For awhile.

Bronski motioned him over. In the rear alley, a dirty child of five or six was picking through another trash heap, hunting scraps of food. Eddie shook his head. Nits in a Raider nest were one thing, but there were lots of desperate people still living in the old cities who didn't belong to Raider tribes. This kid might grow up to be a tribesman, raiding for a living, murdering without remorse, but Eddie didn't kill children on spec.

He whispered an order to Bronski, then moved over and repeated it to Haskel. Both men were "newies"--troopers on their first mission--and would look to him to keep them alive. Eddie grimaced as they moved back onto the dark street. Without Johnson, they would be very lucky to survive hitting a chieftain's nest.

Concentrating on moving the team through the dead streets, Eddie's fear left him. Troopers were finely trained. Dressed like well-armed Raiders, they mostly blended in. With care and luck, they could carry out the mission and survive. With real luck, the nest would be abandoned.

Three or four people scurried out of their way, like small animals avoiding a hawk. Eddie burned one, a scrawny man armed with an old hunting rifle. The others appeared unarmed, and they let them go, hoping they were being taken for Raider tribesmen. Anyone in the city would shop Government troopers for a can of peas.

At 2:15 a.m., only 30 minutes behind schedule, they reached their target. The building was silent, but the team didn't show as much as a finger. If it was a nest, there would be watchers. Eddie prepared his attack.

The assault had gone perfectly, Eddie thought bitterly, if you didn't count the fact that Haskel and Bronski were dead. Haskel had been shot in the shoulder by a Raider woman with a small pistol. It wasn't a serious wound, except that he dropped the thunderbomb he had just armed. There wasn't enough left of him to retrieve, but at least the bomb took out the woman as well.

Bronski had cleared a hall, killing three armed Raiders, and was cautiously approaching a doorway, when a young boy darted from under the stairwell and drove a makeshift spear up through several of his vital organs. Bronski killed the boy as he went down, but it was a bad trade.

Eddie counted thirteen dead Raiders, including four women and the boy. As far as he could tell, he and the rats were the only living creatures in the building. He'd be dead too, but his comm-pad had deflected a slug. The bullet had probably killed him anyway, he thought, because he couldn't report in or call for a retrieval team. Haskel had been carrying the spare. His only hope was to hole up during the coming day, and try to get out at night. The chances were slim--Raiders would kill him as a stranger, Government troopers would burn him for a Raider.

Meanwhile he still had the mission. One by one he searched the dead Raiders, destroying weapons, trying to identify the chieftain. It was probably the tall bastard Bronski had burned. In the back of his mind was the hope that one would have a stolen comm-pad. No joy.

The last raider he turned over was a woman, but that wasn't what made her different. She was alive.

Eddie swung the taser-rifle to eliminate her, but held his fire. Brown eyes starred passively at him from a dirty face. Her cap had fallen off, exposing auburn hair tied up in a bun. She was young, perhaps 16, and oddly innocent looking. He twisted her arm to turn her on her side, exposing the tattoo of a snake near her shoulder. She was a Raider, of a particularly vicious tribe. No wonder they'd had trouble.

Eddie knew he should kill her, but she was offering no resistance, had no weapon in her hands. His stomach turned over. There was no sound, except her pained breathing which shifted her small breasts against the denim of her shirt. He assumed she'd been stunned by one of his thunderbombs.

"Can you move?" he asked.

"Yes."

Perhaps, he thought, headquarters would value a prisoner, though he was quite sure they would shoot her out of hand. Maybe she could help him escape from the city. Eddie stood, hauling her unceremoniously to her feet with him. She was hardly above five foot tall. He ran his hands roughly over her body, suddenly aware of her curves, and found no weapons. She bore his touch without reaction.

"Come on," he ordered. Clutching his taser-rifle in one hand and her arm in the other, he marched her toward the door. Even though she was unarmed, Eddie was careful to give her no opportunity to strike.

He selected a deserted, second-floor apartment as their hidey-hole. Eddie would have preferred to be farther away, but it was more important not to be seen. He checked the exits and observed the streets from a broken window. Nothing moved. There was no activity near the battle site. If they hadn't been spotted, they might have a chance. The girl crouched in a corner, staring at him. She had remained silent, completely passive. Eddie watched her cautiously.

"You're a Raider," he said. It was a statement, not a question.

"I am Kara of the Viper Tribe, yes," she answered softly. Survival in the city depended on speaking in whispers.

"Why? Why would a young girl join a band of killers?"

"You are a killer," she said flatly, brushing a strand of hair from her smudged face. He smiled as she tucked the wisp carefully back into her bun. It was held by a bit of colored ribbon, exposing a delicate neck. Even a Raider woman, fresh from battle, could be vain.

"I'm a soldier, Kara.," he said. "My name's Eddie," he added as an afterthought.

"And I am a tribeswoman. We are both just trying to live, Eddie."

Tears started rolling down her cheeks, and her small body shook, but she stifled the noise of her sobs, silence being the first rule for a tribeswoman. "Do you know what it's like to survive in the city, hunted by both tribesmen and soldiers? When I was eleven, three Wolf tribesmen slaughtered my mother. They were taking turns using me when a Viper tribesman found us. He killed them and the Vipers took me in. I owe the Tribe life. What do I owe anyone else?"

Eddie looked away. He didn't know.

The room grew light in a smoky dawn. "What are you waiting for?" she asked.

"Night." He explained his plan, and she promised to guide him if he would take her out of the city, away from the killing. He agreed, grateful for any hope of help.

Kara smiled, and began unbuttoning her shirt, exposing young breasts. "Since we have all day, Eddie, let us pass the time in pleasure," she said.

Eddie rolled exhausted from her heaving body, sweat coating his face. Kara had caressed his head tenderly, mewling softly in delight, while he thrust at her. Other than a whore near the base, she was his first woman. Maybe, he thought, he could hide her in a village outside the city, visit her on passes. The Service need not know. He closed his eyes, dreaming--and woke trying to scream as she drove a small knife into his throat.

Wiping the blade on his shirt, the tribeswoman tied it back in her hair with the ribbon, watching as Eddie's life gurgled out like Johnson's had. Then Kara, Chieftain of the Vipers, went to gather what was left of her tribe. The soldier's taser-rifle would be useful.

"The Service will forever honor Corporal McFee's sacrifice and remember his name," General Vartan said. Eddie's parents were crying softly as he presented them

16

with the Valor Cross. He looked at the blue ribbon they gave the families of troopers killed on missions. Napoleon said a man will fight long and hard for a bit of colored ribbon. He wondered what it was worth to a dead boy's mother, or to his girl, if he'd had one. It really wasn't much. He sighed, supposing that all women loved ribbons.

Published in *SpaceWays Weekly* #43, June 26, 1998.

Acceptable Casualties

Gunnery Sergeant Albert Feldman looked around at his Marines. Some were joking, but many looked close to tears as they prepared to board the ship that would take them away to this new deployment. Wives and parents were trying to smile bravely, but here and there a mother or sweetheart was crying. Ken Dunbar's young wife was one of the latter.

Jennifer's quiet sobbing profoundly embarrassed Ken. He glanced at his fellow Marines, all of whom were ignoring him, intent on their own partings. Two-month-old Brian caught his mother's despair and began wailing loudly. Lance Corporal Kenneth Dunbar plucked his son from his wife's arms, entirely forgetting his macho image.

"Hush, Bri, hush now." He rocked the infant, while his bride of fourteen months leaned against him for support, holding him fiercely. "You hush too, Jen," he said fondly. "Now you've got Brian upset." He dangled his dogtags for the baby, distracting him with the shiny disks.

"God, Kenny, he should be upset. His daddy's going away for at least a year, maybe...longer." She looked up at him, tears running freely down her cheeks. Her hazel eyes were puffy, hair disheveled. Distractedly she pushed wisps back in place.

Ken smiled. "You're a sight, sweetheart. Good thing I've got a picture to remember you by." His kidding didn't stop the tears, so he turned serious. "I've got to go, Jen. I'm a Marine--you knew that when you said yes. Besides, this won't be all that dangerous. It's just another peacekeeping mission--I'm not going off to war. You'll be living with my folks and, what with Mom's driving, you'll probably be in more danger in Massachusetts. Besides, I'll bet these guys put down their guns and crawl home when the Marines hit the beach. The Army outfit we're relieving has been there four months already and only had two guys hurt. I could be back in six months!"

Jennifer shut her eyes and leaned her face against his chest. "Please come back to me, honey."

"Saddle up, Marines!" Gunny Feldman bellowed. "Two minutes."

She tilted her face and kissed him, hard. "I'll write every day, Kenny. I promise." They hugged, squeezing the baby between them, until the Gunny tapped him softly on the shoulder.

Ken hoisted his seabag and kissed her lightly on the forehead. Jennifer and Brian stood alone in the crowd, watching him walk up the ladderway. He waved and went below, and she turned, unwilling to watch the gray hull that was taking her husband away.

Gunny Feldman held up his hand, and the eight-vehicle convoy stopped. They were "showing the flag" in an area that had been quiet, free from Irregular activity for weeks. Still, Feldman didn't like it--the recalcitrant rebels the Marines called the "Irritating Irregulars" had a way of turning up unexpectedly. The potholed road made a sharp left turn just ahead, then climbed a hill through a heavily wooded cut. It was a perfect place for an ambush. The troops called Feldman "Gunny Felt" because old timers claimed he could "feel" an enemy presence.

Feldman dismounted, walked carefully to the turn in the road and peered around.

47

Raising his binoculars, he slowly scanned both sides of the road. Nothing. He then scanned the pocked road surface, looking for disturbances that might indicate a mine had been buried recently. Nothing. He still didn't like it.

He waved the lead Humvee forward, indicating with hand-signals the rest of the convoy should hold up. The driver stopped the vehicle short of the turn, and passed Feldman the radio handset. He got on the horn to the convoy commander, Captain Johnson.

"Skipper, this don't feel right. I think we should dismount a couple of squads and sweep the flanks."

"You got it, Gunny. I'll send the LAV up to block the road."

While the Captain organized the flanking movement, Feldman continued to scan the wooded slopes. The convoy's light armored vehicle revved its engine and pulled out to pass the Humvees. At the noise, a clump of trees just slightly past the bend spit fire as an automatic weapon opened up, it's rattle cutting through the LAV's engine noise. The Gunny pivoted toward the Humvee, waving frantically. "Back, get back," he ordered. The driver threw the vehicle into reverse, spinning the wheels. Feldman sprinted toward the Humvee, where a stream of bullets cut across the angle of the bend, smashing the windshield. A hammer slammed into his left elbow. He knew he was hit, but felt no pain.

Several Klishnikov rifles began firing, as the Irregulars realized their ambush was blown, and tried to slow the Marine assault squads so they could escape. Feldman wrenched the door open, and Ken Dunbar tumbled out in a welter of blood. Feldman pulled him to the ground, where, thankfully, they were sheltered from the fire by the corner of the roadway. Dunbar was bleeding badly and Feldman pressed the kid's field jacket over the wound to try to staunch the flow.

"Gunny!" Feldman looked around. A scared face was peering at him from beside the second vehicle, hugging the ground. The LAV was churning forward, intent on using its firepower to suppress the ambush.

"Tell the Skipper we've got six or eight weapons firing from the right side of the road. Dunbar's hit bad--sucking chest wound. We need a Corpsman, now!" The Marine waved acknowledgment and wiggled backward.

Feldman decided to try to drag Dunbar away from the shattered vehicle. It was still drawing fire from the tail of the ambush, and if it exploded, they were cooked meat in their present position. His wounded arm was throbbing. Holding his right arm over the young Marine's chest, he started painfully crawling the ten yards to the next Humvee, pulling the wheezing boy with him.

At the command vehicle, Captain Edward "Tripwire" Johnson quickly organized a reaction force to assault the ambush. Acting on Feldman's information, he ordered them out to roll up the Irregulars' flank while Marines on the left of the road moved to cut them off. By the time the Gunny turned over his burden to two Marines who had crawled out to meet him, they were firing on the withdrawing insurgents from two directions, and the LAV was chewing up the woods. The rules of engagement for this peacekeeping mission prohibited pursuit. The short action was over.

Captain Johnson bent over the wounded Gunnery Sergeant, sweat running down his black face, despite the cold, clammy day. Johnson was a "Mustang" officer, graduating from OCS after service as a staff sergeant in the Gulf war. In addition to a chance at a commission, that conflict had given him a nickname when he'd triggered a boobytrap in an Iraqi bunker--which failed to explode. His troops started calling him "Tripwire" and it stuck.

"How do you feel, Gunny?" he asked.

"Been happier, Skipper. Arm hurts like a bitch. How's Dunbar?"

"Chopper's minutes out, but Doc thinks he won't make it."

"Damn. My fault. If I'd stopped the Humvee five yards back, their tail-end-charley couldn't have hit it. We get the bastards?"

"Three bodies, and two blood trails, so we hit a couple more. But for you, we'd been in the shit earlobe deep. There was a command-detonated mine under a rock, which could've screwed up the LAV's maintenance record totally. If you hadn't smelled them, half the convoy would've been in their killing zone. So you get a ticket home and a Purple Heart from a Grateful Congress." Both men grimaced. Like warriors in every age, they were disdainful of politicians safely posturing thousands of miles from the trouble.

"Screw that. Rather have my arm fixed. Ask the Grateful Congress what they're going to tell Ken's wife."

Johnson looked up at the sound of the medivac bird. "Hang on, Gunny. Your taxi's here."

Jennifer was watching a soap opera when the bell rang. Perching Brian on her hip, she rose to answer the door. Two men in uniform were standing awkwardly on the small porch. She went white when she recognized the Marine officer's dress blues. The Navy chaplain snatched the baby from her as she crumpled to the floor.

Nine days after Lance Corporal Kenneth Prescott Dunbar was buried, with full military honors, the White House issued an update on the latest peacekeeping mission. Progress was being made. The mission was on track. There had, unfortunately, been casualties, but they were at an acceptable level--far below what critics of the administration had predicted. The credibility of the nation was at stake. The public and Congress must support our troops in the field. Etc.

A nineteen-year-old widow in Pittsfield, Massachusetts missed the news report, so it is not known if she considered the casualties at all acceptable.

Endgame

The lot of the MacDonald is sorrow. To the sorrow that was Glencoe, to the sorrow that was Culloden, to the sorrow that was Malvern Hill and Neuve Chappelle, Lance Corporal William Wallace MacDonald had added the sorrow that was Khe Sanh.

Like so many who are innocent of gunfire, Billimac had gone to war with a sense of joy; the invulnerable myth of being young, and strong, and proud, and right. His friends of course thought he was insane when he dropped out of college in the spring of his junior year to enlist in the Marines (of all things!) and volunteer for Vietnam (of all places!). But Billimac MacDonald was a history major, with a concentration in Celtic history. Unlike most of his generation, he felt a continuity with his Celtic ancestors and a sense that the tides of history were moving against the West as they once moved against the Celt. "They canna' have a war, and no the leal heart of a MacDonald," he told his skeptical friends, "Besides, what true Celt wouldna' prefer the sword to books!" (That was a period when he was cultivating what he fondly believed was a Scots accent in honor of his heritage.)

Thus it was that Billimac found himself in the heat of Parris Island in the summer of 1966, and in the heat of Khe Sanh in the summer of 1967. It was there that he made the friendship of John Grahame, which brought him both the intense joy that only friendship under arms can bring, and the lingering sorrow that now clung to his heart like the Spanish Moss of his native south.

When Billimac met Corporal John Grahame, his sense of history naturally led him to dub John, "The Bonnie Dundee." Johnnie Grahame had no idea if he was Scottish, no idea who "The Bonnie Dundee" might have been, no interest in history beyond that of his beloved Marine Corps (where he intended to stay until he was Sergeant Major of the Corps), and no intention of finding any of this out. He did have an immediate affinity for Billimac, and understood that the nickname was some kind of compliment. And what the hell, there were worse nicknames! Together they shared everything from fear, to unlikely plans for the future, to first pick from a case of "liberated" C-rations.

Khe Sanh was a quiet place in the summer of 1967, at least as far as a combat base in Vietnam could be, but there was an uneasy sense of the storm that would break over all of Vietnam at the next Tet holiday, and that would thrust Khe Sanh into the headlines. Billimac and Johnnie were among those who knew something was coming. Bored by the deceptive quiet, they had volunteered for recon patrols, and were regularly in the hills along (occasionally over!) the ill-defined border with Laos. You did not have to be a specialist in military intelligence to detect increasing activity as the NVA 325-C division moved into place for the unfolding drama. It was on one such patrol that Billimac lost both the Bonnie Dundee and his joy at being young.

There was no premonition of sorrow when the chopper lifted Billimac, Johnnie, the Gunny and a new PFC with an unpronounceable name off the base. Billimac looked down at the Radio Relay tower as they circled out, and at the small Marine combined action platoon compound in Khe Sanh ville and decided he'd rather be out in the bush where he felt far less vulnerable to rockets and other undesirable airborne implements. It was an opinion subject to change.

It was a routine insertion and a quiet day with no contact. When trouble came, it came as it often does; at night, with no warning, and with total confusion as its companion in arms. The Gunny had the watch, and he shook Billimac awake with a hand over his mouth. The trail they were watching was alive with what looked like an NVA company. That shouldn't have been a problem--they were there to count and report, not fight--but by the luck of the MacDonald, a zip patrol walked right over them. (Flank security? Latrine detail? Billimac never knew.) He did know that the night burst into flame and noise. He did know that the Gunny took an AK burst in the chest trying to get to the new PFC, who was down. He did know that he emptied three magazines into the little rice-propelled bastards before a blast (Grenade? RPG?) knocked him down with his legs full of shrapnel, and his jungle boots full of blood. He did know that he dragged himself and his radio into some thick foliage. He did know that he lay there all night listening to the gooks hunting them, and thinking he was the only survivor, which appeared to be a very temporary condition. He knew they didn't find him, but had never been able to discern a reason. He knew one other thing; a terrifying rage and an endless sorrow, as he lay there helpless the next day and watched them march Corporal John Grahame, limping, back down that trail to become a POW. If he was fortunate.

For all the people that told him he was lucky, Billimac didn't feel lucky. They said he was lucky the enemy didn't find him, lucky the radio still worked, lucky the chopper heard him, lucky his wounds would take him out of 'Nam and back to the World, but would do no permanent physical damage. For William Wallace MacDonald, the war and his childhood were over.

Billimac returned to college on a McNamara scholarship, as the vets called the GI bill, and to a major in business administration. The joy and romance had gone out of history. History was blood and endless sorrow. The business major led to a decent corporate job, a sweet wife, a good kid, and a ranch house in the small city he called home. The sorrow led to brooding.

The brooding led to a divorce, to a small apartment, to a growing distance from friends and co-workers, to cheap scotch, to unemployment. The brooding chafed his soul the way the MIA bracelet--CPL. JOHN GRAHAME 8-19-67--had chafed his wrist every day for over fifteen years. Year after year he had inquired, and year after year there was no word of Johnnie. "Corporals aren't very valuable prisoners," they told him. "Johnnie is dead," they told him. "You're lucky to be alive," they told him. But he never believed that Johnnie was dead, even if an uncaring public and government had so declared. So over the years he brooded, built his contacts among vets, POWs, and the refugees, and hunted. Now he knew the truth that the politicians wanted to ignore. Johnnie was alive, as were four other Americans in a small camp in Laos. Now the brooding would stop. Now he would, "Follow the bonnets of Bonnie Dundee." Now the joy of a terrible anger about to be unleashed infused every corner of his existence. Lance Corporal William Wallace MacDonald, late of the 26th Marines, was going back.

Six of them, Viet Vets all, had been training for months; getting back into shape, small arms, memorizing the details of the compound that had been smuggled out of

Laos. Financing hadn't been a problem--there were Americans with money who still cared. Now they were ready, and Billimac was going back for Johnnie .

So far it was a flawless operation. It was a very small camp, really only one building. They were in position, and undetected. Billimac eased the safety off his assault rifle as the seconds ticked off to 0030, the jump off time. His objective was the guard shack and cells and every move was rehearsed and committed to memory. Time. Humming, "Let a' the clans their slogan cry . .., " he started forward.

There were only two zips in the guard room, and they were too surprised to grab their weapons. He cut the first one down, and the second raised his hands, shaking with fear. "Let's get Johnnie out" he said, and prodded the guard toward the cells. That's when it started to go sour. The cells were empty, all but the last one. The dirty, bent and old human it contained was surely American, and responded groggily when he called Johnnie's name, but that couldn't be Johnnie. Snarling, he turned towards the guard in time to see another guard enter the corridor. He was bringing his rifle around when a great numbness hammered at his chest, and the blankness washed over him.

"Just Tell me what happened, sergeant."

"I tell you, captain, I have fucking had it. I'm taking my twenty years and retiring!"

"Calm down, and tell me what happened."

"I was on the desk when this wild man in camouflage outfit busts in here with the goddamnest big rifle I ever saw--"

"--Only a Ruger 22 .. . "

--"and shoots Murphy in the shoulder. Then he marches me back to the cells yellin' he was getting Johnnie out of here. We ain't got anyone tonight but that old drunk we picked up again. I think his name is John, but everyone calls him "Old Jack." Who ever heard of bustin' a drunk out of jail? When he sees him in the cell, he gives me a look that says it's all over. I'd be dead meat now for sure if Murphy hadn't drug himself in there and put three slugs in the lunatic's chest. This is my last day as a cop, captain. It ain't worth it, it's like a war that never ends!"

Win one for old Earth

The sweat started as I hiked from Starport to the nearest Chalot den. The casino-planet Tau is temperate, but everything I had was going on the table, and that puts the wind up an old starbum. I'd even mortgaged the ship.

Tau offers every game of chance known, but Chalot was boss, because it was complex, paid big, and was loved by the Andrians, who would rather play it than kill. They wouldn't believe an Earthone knew how.

It was played like pick-up-sticks, but with odd pieces. A pair of twelve-sided dice controlled your choices, making Chalot a tough combination of luck and skill. I'd learned from a prisoner, an Andrian Chalot master left for dead in a wrecked starcruiser after the scrap at Signon II. But what secrets hadn't he told? Well, Mamma always told me not to gamble.

An Andrian gave me a hard look as I entered the den. Tau was neutral—they wouldn't violate that—but in a sector they controlled. They'd see few humans here.

I handed a bag of Bandobeast leather to the change critter, who counted out tokens from a dozen worlds and passed me a ten-thousand Taun marker. Leaving my last credit as a tip, I looked for a Chalot challenge.

To my right an Andrian female offered odds of ten-to-one. I placed my marker on her table and she gave me what passed for a grin. Actually she wasn't bad looking, if you went in for scales. Their reddish sheen told me she was young, perhaps twenty rotations of their planet. I ignored the necklace of crystal-imbedded trophies from her kills—including what looked to be a human tooth. Collecting the Chalot pieces, I dropped the pile. She picked up the dice and threw.

Eight plays later, she gave an Andrian hiss of anger, rose and waddled away. I'd thrown doubles, which allowed me to extract a blue 30-piece and a silver 50-piece, boxing her out.

I hit the button that challenged at odds of one-to-twenty on my screen, letting my eleven markers ride. Another Andrian took her place. Chalot has a strict pecking order. A hundred-odds rated Andrian would rather kiss a Bandobeast than play an Earthone at twenty-odds. Non-Andrians were always assumed to be inferior and rated at one. Sweat soaked my armpits as the next game started.

By my seventh win, letting each bet ride, I had over ten million Taun on the table. Andrians were filling the room, drawn by spreading word of an Earthone who played Chalot. Finally Admiral Sithliith of the Andrian fleet pushed into the den. If I hadn't studied his holographs, I'd still have known him by the Victor's Battle Cluster on his chest and the broad expanse of silver scales.

He stood by the table, staring intently, but I ignored him while I defeated an Andrian assault officer who'd taken me up on one-to-two-hundred odds, ruining his nest. What frightened me was but for a very lucky throw of the dice, he'd have had me. A pauper's death in the mines wasn't a joyful thought, and that wouldn't be the worst of it.

Drawing a deep breath, I hit the button offering one-to-a-thousand odds. I'd no choice but to bet. And the only thousand-odds Chalot master on Tau had to play to save face, or so I hoped.

Sithliith settled across from me, grinning savagely. "You play well, Earthone. What terms do you ask?" So I told him. He hesitated while I sweated, then nodded and dropped the Chalot pile.

I threw the dice, starting well by taking out a 40-piece. After five plays, I relaxed. Sithliith was proving no more challenge than the female I'd bested first. Probably got his thousand-odds rating because toadies let the Admiral win.

Too late, I saw his trap. Unless I threw the highest combination possible, then removed two wedged pieces without bringing down the pile, I was boxed.

I threw, and there was angry hissing from the Andrians as the dice turned double twelves. Wiping sweaty hands on my jumpsuit, I slowly tugged out a 20-piece. Nothing moved.

Sithliith's black eyes bored into me. Praying to the gods of thirty worlds, I slid the red 100-piece free. There was a chilling silence while we watched the pile, then a low moan arose and Sithliith swept the pieces from the table. Turning, he barked orders at an underling, then coldly returned my tense gaze. "The attack on your home system has been canceled, Earthone," he hissed. I started to relax, when he nodded toward the female I'd beaten earlier. "And as is our custom, you shall have my daughter Sithlaar in marriage this day."

She bared her teeth at me and I swallowed hard. Mamma always told me not to gamble.

The Identity Thief

Kelsey Hammond smiled at the Identity Thief. Finding the woman—her name was Claire—had taken a week, and Kelsey knew there'd be no second chance. Jim would be back in six days, and she'd better be finished. She'd been very lucky as it was. Big Jim Evans was a powerful and thorough man, and very intolerant of mistakes.

"I need your help," Kelsey said. "And I'm prepared to pay well for it."

Claire returned her smile, but there was no warmth in it. Kelsey knew she was dealing with a woman with absolutely no feeling for anyone but Claire Duffy. She'd learned all about identity thieves. You couldn't have a relationship—a cheap affair, Kelsey admitted sourly to herself—with anyone as high in Atlantic City's organization as Big Jim without knowing all about human perfidy.

Short of violence, an identity thief was almost the worst person an honest citizen could cross paths with. They didn't just steal your money and max your credit cards. They established a new identity as you, guaranteeing you ruined credit, endless hassles and usually a criminal record that could take years to correct. Since they often worked several identities, just when you thought your life was your own again, your evil twin would surface, and your world would unravel. In the end, they stole your good name.

Kelsey wondered how many women's lives Claire had wrecked. She'd score the IDs here, then go elsewhere to milk them. Women on vacation, having a good time in the Boardwalk casinos, could be careless. And an ID thief could work from as little as a credit card number or driver's license.

"Money's my favorite topic," Claire said. "Tell me what you want—and how much you will pay."

Kelsey realized she'd been holding her breath. If this went right, she's be away and safe with three million dollars of Big Jim's dirty money. If it went wrong...well, three million was a pittance to Jim Evans, but the kick in the old macho of a girlfriend gutting his wallet could only be eased one way. She shivered slightly, and started her cover story.

"My husband is a well-to-do, cold bastard," she told Claire, displaying the gold band she'd picked up for the occasion. "He has me locked in with an airtight pre-nup. I'm going to dump him, but I don't want to go back to being a penniless waitress. He's off on a two-week business trip Saturday, but he doesn't know I have the number for one of his bank accounts holding over eighty thousand bucks."

Claire laughed. Kelsey knew she'd assume the figure was twice as large. "So," Claire shrugged, "take it and run."

"I plan to, but I have to ease it out over several days, transferring it to my new account slowly so the bank doesn't get curious."

"And what do you want from me?" Claire asked.

"A friend at a casino said you could get me a new ID."

"Who?"

Kelsey shook her head. "Just a boyfriend. All he said was he'd heard you had a source for false identities. I'll pay you $5,000 for a new ID. By Saturday. Then the money will be out of reach under my new name."

Claire relaxed visibly, and Kelsey knew she was relieved by the lie. In fact, it had been Bennie the Forger who'd fingered Claire from among his many clients, as being close to Kelsey in age and appearance, factors she needed. The information had cost Kelsey $25,000, and she knew Bennie had to keep his mouth shut. Otherwise Big Jim would shut it permanently.

"I can get what you need," Claire said. "But it will cost $15,000." They haggled, settling on twelve. Starting with her social security number and driver's license, Kelsey dutifully gave Claire the information she claimed she needed to create Kelsey's new identity.

Claire was beaming with genuine pleasure when they parted, overjoyed, Kelsey hoped, at finding a wealthy pigeon greedy and dumb enough to hand over her own ID.

Kelsey sweated out the next two days, praying Claire was biting. She'd used documents from Bennie to set up an account for her supposed husband. Claire would have that by now, and with Kelsey's ID, the account number and $12,000 bait money, she should be drooling to take off with a stolen identity—or two.

She wondered if Claire was as nervous as she felt when they met at a pizza parlor on the Boardwalk. The exchange of cash for documents went quickly, and they didn't linger to chat.

Kelsey dropped the fake ID from Claire in the nearest trash bin. She already had new ID from a pro in Philly—not Bennie—and she knew Claire would keep copies hoping to grab the husband's money too.

By a coincidence, Claire Duffy, traveling as Kelsey Hammond, boarded a flight for Atlanta at almost the same time Kelsey climbed on a bus for western Pennsylvania.

"We found her, boss."

Big Jim Evans squeezed the phone like he could choke the life out of his treacherous girlfriend through the instrument. "Where," he demanded.

"Stayed in Atlanta. The boys down there checked around after we found out about the flight. Died her hair black, but she's registered under Kelsey Hammond—real dumb, like—and spending your money like she's playing monopoly."

"Forget the money. Tell Tony in Atlanta what to do, and I'll owe him a big one."

"You got it, boss."

Jim Evans leaned back and smiled for the first time in four days. Cross him, would she?

"What you smiling at? I'll say, Susie Evans, you're the happiest waitress this restaurant's ever had!" Kelsey put down the newspaper and grinned at her boss, enjoying the secret joke in her new name.

"Oh, I was just reading about a terrible crime in Atlanta and thinking how happy I am to be living in a small town, where I feel safe," she said.

Published in *Calliope*

The Supervisors' Tale

By the year 2071, the North America Gynocracy, founded in 2044, has eliminated crime, violence and war. Stringent laws and electronic supervision of public areas protect Women from sexual harassment or rape, which includes any type of heterosexual penetration. Patronymic family names, the remnants of male ownership of Women, have been replaced with numbers. Men have their special role in society, but their aggressive natures are finally under control. Yet not every Woman is happy in paradise...

Eddie kept his eyes lowered, but his well-honed peripheral vision—a necessary trait for male supervisors—took in the spacious office and expensive chrome and glass furnishings. He also caught the tiny smile on the Miz's face. His heart thudded and he wondered if could she hear it. Melissa 97e was a Fourth-Level Miz, the highest-ranking Woman who had ever spoken to Eddie, and adrenaline was pumping through his system. He artfully avoided looking at her stocky body. Meeting her dark eyes directly was unthinkable—giving offense to a Mother of Melissa's rank could get a male brain-corrected, maybe even changed!

"I scheduled this interview, Edward 782b, to inform you that you have done particularly well this week," Melissa said. "Only three correctable incidents."

Eddie felt his heart swell with pride. Only three dings in a whole week! At 28, he was the youngest male he knew to make First-Level Supervisor. This might mean he was on track to the Second-Level, a privileged position less than one-tenth of one percent of males in the North American Gynocracy attained. He'd surely be selected to provide breeding essence. Eddie felt giddy, fought to control himself in front of the Mother.

"Thank you, Miz," he replied humbly, flushing as he thought about the honor of being the source for Daughters. "This male works hard not to give offense to Women."

"Would you like to know your offenses?" she asked.

"Please, Miz."

"They are actually rather small, Edward. But they are all incidents that could lead to Inappropriate Contact with a Woman. Tell me why the Mothers made Inappropriate Contact Crime One, Edward."

Eddie felt a trickle of sweat run from his short hair down the back of his neck, collecting on the starched collar of his blue supervisor's jumpsuit. Could she know he touched himself at night, fantasizing about such contact? He suspected most males had some uncivilized moments of weakness—a few of the worker-level males in his unit made quite crude—and dangerous—comments when no checkvid was monitoring them.

"Please, Miz," he recited by rote. "Inappropriate Contact between a male and a Woman is the crime of Rape, the embodiment of male aggression, violence, crime and war. These evils were eliminated from civilized society when the Gynocracy replaced patriarchal barbarism in 2044. If a male has intimate physical contact with, or penetration of a Woman, it is Rape, because no Woman can freely consent to countermanding the Tenets of the Mothers."

"Very good, Edward, you know your Prime Tenets. But wrong actions speak louder than recitations, and must be corrected. On Tuesday last, checkvid tapes of your unit show you reprimanding Thelma 23a in a personal way. This could lead to low self-esteem in the Woman, setting her up for Inappropriate Contact. You understand, Edward 782b?"

Eddie thought of Thelma's angular body, matted hair and dull eyes. The only contact he wanted with Thelma 23a was stuffing her down a recycler when her clumsiness set the unit's production back a week, as happened too often. "Yes, Miz," he said. "This male recognizes his error."

"On Wednesday last, the checkvid reveals you praising Anne 14a in front of her peers. This constitutes grooming, and can be an attempt to induce a Woman to engage in Inappropriate Contact."

Anne was a tall, red-haired worker of about 40, and Eddie reflected that she had a nice smile. Perhaps he had been inadvertently grooming her. "Yes, Miz, this male recognizes his error." Sweat was soaking through from his arm pits, and he prayed the Miz couldn't smell him.

Melissa went on matter-of-factly. "Most serious, Edward, Tammy 24a reports that you gazed upon her parts in a way that made her uncomfortable. This has happened before, so there will be a double correction."

Eddie knew he would receive a short, painful shock as behavioral correction for each of his errors, administered by the Women he had offended. Even counting the double, four hits was nothing. He'd once had twenty-two. It wouldn't bother the Miz, he thought—a little discomfort for offensive males was hardly a large price for a society free of rape and violence.

"Yes, Miz, this male recognizes his error." Recognized it fully. Tammy was an earthy blond who made it a habit to leave the top three buttons of her tunic undone. Then she would bend over in front of males, slyly watching to see if they glanced at her large, swaying parts. Eddie wondered if Tammy might enjoy administering corrections. She was called to do so almost every week, usually to male co-workers, but occasionally to Eddie, or Frank 342b, his shift alternate. Regardless, Eddie knew the fault was his—he was a male, requiring firm internal control to protect Women. The Mothers said so.

He sighed softly. Tammy was the sleep-partner of a Second-Level Miz—no way to get her transferred to another unit. He would just have to govern his uncivilized eyes, and not offend her.

An amused look flitted over Melissa's sensual face, and she tossed her dark hair out of her eyes. "We expect continued improvement, Edward 782b. You may report to correction immediately, while these offenses against Women are fresh in your mind."

"Thank you, Miz," Eddie said gratefully, backing toward the portal. "This male cherishes the Tenants of the Mothers."

The door from the observation room slid open. Susan 56b smiled brightly at her mentor, though her stomach felt queasy as she entered the office and took a seat in one of the comfortable chairs facing the Mother's desk. She knew Melissa would want to make love—she always did after correcting a male. Despite the intense orgasms Melissa gave her, Susan never felt quite comfortable with love-making. Probably, she thought, because she was only 23, and her sleep-partners were much older, more experienced. Melissa was in her late 40's and Susan's first mentor, a Third-Level Miz, had been 38. She would learn.

Susan felt intensely conscious of Melissa's gaze on her petite form. She knew her mentor loved her long, copper hair, pointed breasts and slim legs. Melissa would already be moist from dealing with the male, and Susan could smell her strong need.

"What did you think of Edward?" Melissa asked. Business came first.

Susan tensed. She had only added the "b" of a First-Level Supervisor to her name—Susan NAG-56b-20756-4th Sector—six months before. Was this a test? Did Melissa know she had inappropriate thoughts about males? Perhaps all young Women did, before they were fully educated.

"He seemed civilized enough—for a male," she replied carefully.

Melissa threw back her head and laughed. "They are all barbarians underneath the veneer we paste on them, Susie-sweet," she replied. "They would all penetrate you if they could!"

Susan shivered. Penetration was Rape, still practiced for procreation, she knew, in backward areas of the world not under the civilization of the five Gynocracies. She'd been schooled to believe it was the worst offense a Woman could experience. But she thought of Edward's finely-muscled body, his boyish face, and wondered.

"I hate to speak of penetration—it gives me the heebies," she said. "Why do we let males, who carry evil, become supervisors?" Best to change the subject from male penetration.

"You know the Gynocracy needs males," Melissa replied. "Many jobs require certain types of dexterity or upper-body strength found often in males. They also provide breeding essence to allow new Women—and, of course, more males—to be created." Susan knew breeding essence was extracted from the male parts by machine, while electric pulses stimulated the pleasure centers of their simplistic brains. She thought it would be exciting to watch it being done. Melissa said males could become quite civilized when competing to be selected for the honor.

"But why make this Edward or any male a supervisor over Women?" Susan asked. At the same level as me, she wanted to add, but thought it would betray too much ambition. Susan longed to become a high-level Miz, and had the education and connections to eventually be a Mother. For an intelligent Woman—who was sleep-partners with the right mentors—a carefully-constructed career could take you all the way to the Twelfth-Level—Mother of the Gynocracy. If you didn't put a foot wrong.

"You have much to learn, Susie-sweet." Melissa smiled. "Males who are properly disciplined can make quite competent First or Second-Level Supervisors, filling a need. We've even moved a few to the Third-Level near the end of their careers, with good results. This not only gives worker males something to strive for, it allows us to identify males with the necessary combination of drive, intelligence and self-control to be valuable providers of breeding essence. You were bred from a supervisor male."

Susan knew males were necessary for breeding, and were selected based on the characteristics desired, but imaging a male contributor to her make-up was unsettling.

"So you see this Edward 782b as a breeder?" she asked. A vague image of what breeding must be like in the uncivilized world, where Women were Raped to produce children, entered her mind. She felt her belly contract, and shivered again.

"Perhaps a breeder, but also a useful tool and role-model for worker males," her mentor replied. "Once he completes a full week without offenses, he will be milked of essence. That will much encourage his ambition, while improving his behavior. Meantime, I want you to interact with him as a peer First-Level Supervisor, and report to me how he behaves when he believes a Women is his friend. You will overlook minor offenses to gain his trust."

Susan nodded her understanding, wide-eyed at the assignment. Melissa went on, "That will be the test. Taking breeding essence is always something of a gamble, and we like to be as sure as we can before we use it. Careful breeding has helped us eliminate much male aggression. But be very alert—the most civilized male carries the Rape gene."

Susan smiled to hide her concern. Interact with a male, pretending to be his friend! She hadn't known such things happened. "As you wish, 'Lissa—but males interest me only when they can boost my unit's production. I'd rather spend more time with you." She cocked her head fetchingly and wet her lips, hiding her aversion. Pleasing a mentor was vital for advancement.

"Of course you would," Melissa replied. "But learning to evaluate males is part of your training for the higher levels. Now come here for a taste. I need your sweet kiss to relax me before the council session."

Smiling, satisfied she had a firm hold on her mentor, the young Woman knelt in front of Melissa's chair.

Setting about her assigned task, Susan found herself liking Eddie, despite the averted eyes and distant formality required of a supervisor male who wished to advance—and to avoid correction. She also discovered she could learn from him. Even with the imposed limitations necessary to his gender, he was an effective supervisor, and his unit often outdid hers. She picked up several techniques from him for motivating male workers.

Gradually she drew him in, asking his assistance as a colleague. It was an intriguing game, watching him flinch at her small jokes or when she came too near, expecting to be reported for offenses against a Woman. It excited her to tease him, and he was like a puppy in his clumsy efforts to please.

This duty was becoming very enjoyable for her, though she was troubled that images of Eddie's sinewy body had begun to come unbidden into her mind when 'Lissa was making love to her. Susan suppressed her hunger, and wondered if she were some sort of throw-back to submissive Women under the patriarchy. But with each step, she wanted to know more about this male, wanted to get closer, wanted to see how she could manipulate him. It was, after all, only a game.

When, over coffee in the supervisors' break room, his leg accidentally touched hers under the table, Eddie quickly jerked it away, expecting a ding. Thankfully, it was out of the view field of the checkvid. She only smiled slightly. When no correction was forthcoming, he relaxed. Susan didn't know she had replaced Tammy in Eddie's almost-nightly fantasies, but she knew he was under her spell as much as 'Lissa was.

Two days later, she boldly initiated knee-contact under the table, feeling a thrill at the flush that crept up his trembling neck. He broke away after long seconds, making a hasty excuse to leave the small room. A feeling of power that was almost sexual rippled through her.

Edward NAG-78-2b-996235-4th Sector realized he was hopelessly in thrall to a Woman. He would have gladly traded his career, his "b" designation as a supervisor, and his private sleeping cube for another such touch. Was she deliberately tempting him? What should he do?

Weeks passed, and her touches increased, always casual, always out of sight of the checkvid, always seemingly by accident, never mentioned. According to the Mothers, the male was fully responsible if Inappropriate Contact occurred. Eddie was torn between his growing need and guilt over his contacts with her. He knew Susan couldn't be blamed for what was happening.

Not even when she initiated the Rape.

It took weeks of careful planning on her part. She had to locate a storage room with an inactive checkvid. She had to think of a pretext to get Eddie there. And she had to touch him first, boldly, intimately, finally kissing his lips as if he were a sleep-partner. Under her moving hands, Eddie suddenly found he had no control at all. The discovery delighted them both.

Before each sweaty, delicious, forbidden meeting in the storage room, Susan carefully reviewed checkvid status reports, to be certain theirs was still inoperable. But there was no way for her to know an over-worked male technician would repair the errant surveillance equipment twenty-two minutes before their fifth tryst. And so a Rape was recorded.

Susan knelt before her mentor, head bowed, taut with fear and anger. How *could* I have been so stupid? she berated herself. Her career was ruined. She wondered what would happen to Eddie, and chills shook her small body.

"You were penetrated by a male." Melissa's voice cracked like ice snapping in the cold. "I had the humiliation of watching the checkvid tape with the Sector Council of Mothers, seeing them smirk as my sleep-partner participated quite lavishly in her own Rape! Under questioning, that male claimed you arranged the opportunity!"

"I did, Mother," Susan whispered. Then she raised her eyes, heat flaming in her face. "I arranged everything. I initiated the Inappropriate Contact. Eddie did nothing—he is not at fault!" She was practically spitting, in anger at losing her career or her lover, she knew not which.

"Mind your tone, girl." Melissa snapped. "A Woman who undermines the Gynocracy may be corrected as severely as a male. The Prime Tenet of Inappropriate Contact states the male, the ever aggressive, ever violent, Rape-minded male is always at fault!"

"If Eddie is at fault, why has my status been down-graded to worker?" Susan asked, taut voice betraying her anger. "Why am I to be re-educated? Why am I to be relegated to secondary sleep-partner? Are you afraid you can't compete with a male?" She put acid into the insult.

Melissa leaned forward and slapped the kneeling Woman sharply across the face. Susan's head snapped to the right, white finger-marks on her flushed cheek. "'Tis only by favor of mine you have any kind of life left at all," Melissa spit back. "I will see to your re-education in the Tenets of the Mothers, and in return you will please me when I wish, as I wish. Otherwise, you may share the fate of your male."

"Does he live?" Susan asked softly.

"Oh, he lives, indeed, lives quiet happily." Melissa laughed, making the younger Woman's gut clench at the bitter sound. "In the patriarchy, when violent men ruled through barbarian custom, people were put to death for capital crimes like Rape. The Gynocracy has no violence, no death penalty. But crime must be mended. Yesterday, May 23, 2071, in the Twenty-eighth year of our Gynocracy, the Fourth Sector Council of Mothers decreed that Edward NAG-78-2b-996235-4th Sector be brain-corrected. Do you understand?"

"No," Susan said. She had gone pale, color draining. Her fists were clenched, and she slipped her hands behind her so Melissa wouldn't see them trembling.

"In the old patriarchy, there was a procedure called a lobotomy, done crudely with a knife in the brain, as one would expect of males. Modern brain-correcting is similar, but a more complete procedure, accomplished entirely with electronic pulses. The decree was carried out this morning. Your male's personality was disconnected, and all drive, aggression, and ambition were eliminated. He will spend the rest of his pleasant days doing small, manual tasks." Melissa sneered. "Oh, and he was changed, of course."

"Changed?" Susan asked.

Melissa smiled broadly. "A laser painlessly removed his offending parts, for the safety of all Women, especially including you."

Susan stared up at her mentor, unable to speak. Tears streaked her white face.

Melissa leaned down and licked a salty tear from Susan's ashen cheek. "You really are quite pretty when you weep, Susan," she said. "So vulnerable, I could almost forgive you. Now come to bed and try to repay me for what you've done." She straightened and turned her back on the grieving Woman, moving heavily through the portal to her personal quarters.

Susan could picture the canopied bed, the lace hangings, and Melissa's fleshy body writhing in sweaty heat while the younger Woman pleasured her. She rose and followed obediently, stomach knotted, crying quietly. Her hand slid into the pocket of her tunic, gingerly touching the blade of the small kitchen knife she'd taken from the break room when the brusque command to report came over the speaker.

The Mothers are right, she thought. Inappropriate Contact with a male leads to violence.

Pick a Winner

Alan was hunched over the mouse, staring intently at meaningless graphs and lines on his computer. I slipped unnoticed into his cubical and stared at the multicolored screen over his shoulder. I figured he was either saving the company from bankruptcy or saving the world from alien invaders. With computer geeks it's hard to tell. I'm in PR, and I use a computer strictly for word processing and email. The rest is beyond me.

It took Alan several moments to notice me. He stopped working and leaned back in his chair. "Well, Matthew, to what do I owe the honor?" he inquired. I smiled.

"You haven't quite got that British accent down, old bean. It's Friday night and, unfortunately, I have nothing on my social calendar. I thought you might like to go to the track?"

"Wagering on horse races?" he asked, trying to both improve the accent and raise his eyebrows in a humorous way. "You know that I never gamble, unless, of course, I am able to calculate that the odds are overwhelmingly in my favor. Though I have perused several computer programs designed to improve one's handicapping, I have concluded there are so many variables one cannot calculate, that betting on horses is always a gamble. I don't gamble!"

I sighed. Alan's a nerd, but deep inside, he's a very nice, boring nerd. I waved at his computer, where a cartoon figure he'd designed as a screen saver was running back and forth, chucking miniature computers out of cartoon windows. "Using computers is a gamble," I said, "your magic box here could be emitting deadly rays right now."

"Oh, it is," he said, "but you can precisely calculate the extent of the danger and thus avoid the harmful effects. It isn't gambling. I never gamble," he repeated with finality.

"Look, Alan, stick with me. Match every bet I make on exactly the same horses, and I guarantee you'll lose about forty bucks tonight. There's no gambling involved-- it's a sure thing."

"If you know you're going to lose, what's the point?"

"A few people go to the track trying to make money. Some lose the rent, just as some fools do on dice, poker or the lottery. But most people go to the races for entertainment. They enjoy the crowds, the excitement and watching the horses. It's a challenge because of all those variables--much more so than a computer game! They bet modestly, depending on their income--which for me is about six bucks a race. If I take a date, and we don't cash a ticket, the evening will cost me about $75 bucks- -about the tab at a good restaurant, but a lot more fun. Sometimes I break even, and once in a great while I come out ahead. Then it's a real cheap date." I stopped. Alan was smiling his nerd smile.

"So take a date, oh balding one!"

I winced at the double hit. At thirty-three, my slightly receding hairline was starting to spoil what I thought of as a fine set of average looks. And I hadn't had a date since I broke up with Cindy two months ago.

"I bet I can do better at the track than you can chatting on the Internet to female nerds--or female impostors!" I said.

It was Alan's turn to wince. Six months ago, he'd carried on a lively E-mail chat with a sultry beauty, until he discovered accidentally that his correspondent was really a teenage kid getting some sick kicks. He shook his head. "Face it, Matt--we're a losing bet either way." He clicked his mouse and was instantly lost in a computer fog. The world and I had vanished. I slouched back to my desk, feeling vaguely annoyed, lonely and more than a little depressed. The hell with it, I thought, I'll go to the track alone. Maybe I'll be lucky.

Collecting my change, I pushed through the turnstile and stopped to buy a program. I passed up the guy hawking tip sheets, on the theory that I could pick my own losers for free, and surveyed the crowd. It was still sparse, with almost an hour to post time. I grabbed a beer and settled down to read through all the races, familiarizing myself with the field and the jockeys, winning percentages, track condition, records and, though I hated to admit it, looking for hunch bets.

A horse in the fifth caught my eye: Love-in-Bloom, twenty to one in the morning line. Ain't it the truth, I thought. Love for me is always a long shot. Out of the corner of my eye, I noticed feminine legs passing in the aisle, and they diverted my attention. A small woman in a green top and white shorts was making her way toward the finish line. I gave up studying the first race and concentrated on admiring her. She was no more than five-one, about a hundred pounds, with supple, tanned thighs and a lithe shape. I guessed she was about twenty. Her soft brown hair bounced as she strode toward the railing, exuding presence, a kind of kinetic energy. A pacer, I thought, but definitely a thoroughbred rather than a standardbred.

I wandered back to the betting windows and put six bucks across the board on the five horse, a middle-shot called Abide-a-Wee. It was a maiden race, so who could figure. After a pit stop, I strolled out to the finish line. It's hard to see the whole race from there, but I like the excitement of the final rush. She was still there, but, unfortunately, there was a distinguished, silver-haired gentleman with her. He patted her possessively on the back. Old enough to be her father, I thought sourly, probably a high roller.

I watched her face until the race was called. She didn't look like a bimbo. She had large eyes that appeared to be green because of her top, but were probably that changeable shade of hazel. A smear of kid-like freckles softened a rather serious, straight nose. Her generous mouth was perpetually smiling, pulling out a dimple on her left cheek, exposing tiny white teeth. Not a beautiful face, but somehow compelling. Twice she caught my eye and smiled. I smiled back and we both glanced quickly away.

"They're off!" the announcer cried, and I turned my attention to admiring the thoroughbreds on the track. Abide-a-Wee abided in fourth place from start to finish, never fading, but never closing, either. Oh, well. I tossed the ticket and pulled out the program to study the second race.

"No luck?"

I looked up, startled. She had managed to edge closer. Her companion was gone. Hope lit in my chest like I was holding the first half of the double. "No, I was on the five horse."

"Me, too," she grimaced, "I thought Abide-a-Wee was such a cute name!"

"Well, there's a lot to be said for cute." I gave her my best hundred-watt smile, to see if she'd get my meaning. She flushed prettily and opened her program.

"All these numbers and abbreviations--why do they make the program so complicated? I tend to bet on horses with cute names, on hunches, or on tips. And I like the gray horses, I guess just because they're different!" she said.

Well, I thought, I hope I'm different enough to have a chance. Up close, I realized she was nearer my age, probably twenty eight or nine, which was good. Unfortunately, I'm going bald, not gray. "Hasn't your, ah, friend explained how to read the program?"

"Daddy?" she giggled, "about a million times. He thinks he knows everything about horses, but I do as well on hunches and tips." She giggled again, and a shiver went through me. Delighted to learn that the old fellow wasn't a romantic interest, I found myself wanting to make her laugh. We kidded back and forth. She said her name was Beth and I introduced myself. I saw her glance at my left hand, checking for a ring. I'd already noted she wasn't wearing one. I was finding her bubbling personality intoxicating. The horses became secondary.

Finally they announced, "Five minutes to Post Time" and we didn't have a horse.

"I think we should play Wandering Looker," she said, "because when I first saw you, you were wandering around looking at everything!"

"Gee, I thought I was mostly looking at you." She flushed again. I gently took her arm, tingling at the touch, and steered her toward the betting windows. "Wandering Looker it is--the three horse across the board!" Beth giggled again, and put six bucks on the three as well.

It was a mile and a sixteenth race, so we had a long time to cheer and jump up and down. The three stole it by half a length, charging on the inside. Beth squealed and hugged me, which, frankly was better than the fact that our horse paid $16.20 to win!

I warmed myself in her smile, content to let Beth pick the horses. I was developing this golden, hazy glow which had nothing to do with the fact that I was ahead at the races for the first time in months.

In the next race we had a $6.80 winner, but were knocked out of the exacta when a long shot grabbed second from the six horse. The race after that, we cashed twenty bucks worth of place and show tickets on a 15 to 1 shot who almost, but not quite, held off the four horse for first. Beth was proving to be as lucky as she was charming.

She insisted on buying us beers and sausage dogs. Her zest and energy must burn off those calories. We looked at the program, and she gave me a silly, sweet grin. "What do you say we bet on Love-in-Bloom, Matt?" I couldn't tell from her face if she meant anything personal, but I hoped she wanted to bet on more than a horse race.

I glanced at the tote board. Love-in-Bloom was listed at 34 to 1. "I don't know, Beth," I protested. "She hasn't run in four months, and the last time out, she finished way back--pulled up! They're probably only tuning her up, not trying to win."

"Come on." She grabbed my hand and pulled me toward the paddock. We watched the horses parade out, hopeful, proud, lovely. Going to the paddock is fun, but I always want to bet on them all, just to encourage them. "There she is," Beth squeaked. "She's a gray, too. Come on Matty, we're ahead. This is a sign, we just have to! Let's bet thirty bucks each across the board. Please?" She stood on her toes and kissed me lightly on the lips. My world went golden and unfocused.

"Sure" I said, totally bemused. We marched firmly back to the windows and put twenty to win, twenty to place and twenty to show on the two horse, Love-in-Bloom. It's a good thing she didn't ask me to bet my house and car, I thought.

Walking slowly down to the finish line, Beth held my hand. Her soft, warm touch kept me from reflecting that I'd just put down my biggest bet ever on a horse race. I thought I was falling in love, but I hoped it was with Beth and not with betting, because if she asked, I'd have given them my Visa card. The two dropped to 22 to 1 by post time. We weren't the only foolish punters. Vaguely I hoped the barn knew something.

"They're Off!"

It was only a six furlong race, and Love-in-Bloom broke last in an eight horse field. We couldn't see the pack behind the tote board, but it didn't matter. Beth had her eyes squeezed shut, like she was praying, so she couldn't watch. She was breathing deeply, her hand squashing mine in a tight grip. She really cared about this race. I couldn't take my eyes from her face. I decided she really was beautiful, after all. I was willing to go on betting on long shots, rocking horses, or turtles as long as she'd hold my hand and let me watch her animated face.

The crowd roared and broke our spell. All we could see on the turn was a tight pack of horses. The tote board flashed the order. The two was in fourth place and it was tight! Beth began screaming and I was cheering hoarsely, "Bring her up, baby. Bring that two horse up!" They swept by us, the three lead horses in a line across the track, the two pounding up the outside, her gray flank blotting out the others. The red neon "Photo" sign flashed on, and we held our breaths--along with every punter in the place.

It was only a few moments, but it seemed like hours, no, years. Looking into Beth's eyes, I desperately wanted her horse to win, not for the money, but to make her happy. The crowd roared again when they flashed the winner--two! Beth was crying, hugging and kissing me, and trying to jump up and down at the same time. I think I was crying with joy. Love-in-Bloom, oh, yes.

Over her shoulder, I saw Beth's dad come striding up. She'd told me he usually hung out with friends in the club house, while she preferred to be close to the track. He didn't look mad at catching some stranger embracing his daughter. A wide grin split his face. "I see you've made a friend, Bethy" he said. Then without pause, "Did you see the Love charge up the outside? Wasn't she beautiful? Jimmy was right, she was ready, more than ready!" Beth flushed again. I was starting to enjoy how easily she blushed.

"Daddy, this is Matt. Matt, this is my know-it-all daddy, Arron Duncan. Matt and I went partners on the Love!" Suddenly, it hit me that she knew this horse. I must have looked bewildered.

Mr. Duncan laughed. "Has she beguiled you, Matt? I saw she had her eye on you and bolted for the club house--I hate to watch a lamb being led to the slaughter!"

"Daddy!"

"I bet she gave you her famous innocent act. Did she tell you that her Uncle Jimmy is Love-in-Bloom's trainer? Of that she sometimes rides that filly in workouts? Or that she could read a racing program when she was five? You should be honored, lad--this girl picks winners!"

Beth stamped her foot. "Matthew is a gentleman, daddy, and not at all boring like you. He likes hunch bets too, don't you Matty? He doesn't bother with the boring old records! Now he's going to buy me dinner, aren't you Matt?"

Overwhelmed, I stared down into those hazel-green eyes. I decided that, if I could keep her smiling at me, I didn't care about anything else in the universe. "Anyplace you want, Beth. Anytime you want. As often as you want."

Beth beamed and her father shook his head, pretending to look sad. "Another victim!" he groaned. I shook hands with a grinning Arron Duncan, and let her drag me to the windows to cash in on the Love horse.

We've been going to the track at least once a week, and I've met Uncle Jimmy and the rest of the family. A framed picture of Love-in-Bloom in the winner's circle hangs in my cubicle at work. I discovered that Beth's second cousin was the jockey who rode her the day we met. I've even taken a hand helping in the stables once in a while, which isn't all that romantic, despite Beth's presence.

Mr. Duncan's offered me a PR position with his company. Beth and I aren't sure that's a good idea, but we promised to think about it after the wedding. Oh, yes--we've invited Alan, just so he'll know that I can pick a winner without using a computer.

Published in *Texas Thotoughbred* and *Romantic Hearts*

The Loser

I ordered a round of drinks and nodded for the barmaid to include the boys at the Thursday night poker table. "Thanks, Jim," the usual suspects sounded off. Drinks are cheap at the VFW, so buying rounds is SOP.

A former sailor we called Doc limped over to collect their beers. He has a ruined leg, but the other guys let him hobble for the drinks. Doc takes offense if anyone helps him. Foolish pride, I think, but it's not my business.

The other players were Eddie O'Leary, a Marine Vietnam vet originally from Southie who owns a small printing company over in Worcester, and two retired brothers, Tony and Sol Tomasino. Like me, the Tomasinos are World War II vintage Army types. They had family money from cranberry processing someplace near the Cape. The game was too rich for me, and I wondered how Eddie afforded it, since it wasn't that unusual to see him drop four hundred bucks, pretty steep for a friendly game in a small town.

I knew Doc mostly lived on his disability pension, but he didn't have to sweat the cost of poker, because he always seemed to win. Usually the game was these four guys, with occasionally a couple of others. Once a smart guy from Boston dropped by to play, eager to take the hicks. The local boys picked him clean.

Setting the beers down, Doc wrenched himself into his chair, wincing at the pain. The other players pretended not to notice.

There was a large stack of ten dollar chips in front of him, and I surmised Doc was having a profitable night. Eddie complains about his bad luck, but in poker only skill wins consistently. Which is why I don't play with Doc. My pension from the Commonwealth doesn't stretch to dropping a couple hundred bucks a week.

Doc picked up the cards and dealt seven stud, with a Jack up for Tony, a trey for Solly, a seven for Eddie, and a King for himself. He flipped a chip into the pot. Tony and Eddie called, Sol folded.

In the next round, Doc caught another King. His bet drove Tony out, but Eddie raised. He had two clubs, probably chasing a flush. Doc eyed him and called.

On the following two rounds, Eddie caught red cards, while Doc paired up sevens. Eddie couldn't have the flush yet, but he continued to bet against Doc's strong hand. The pot was almost two hundred dollars.

Doc dealt the final round, and Eddie peeked at his last card. "Busted!" he said disgustedly, while Doc raked in the chips. I shook my head, thinking dumb Marine.

So it went, Doc winning, Eddie and the Tomasinos losing. Then Sol dealt Jacks-or-better. Doc opened, both brothers dropped, and Eddie raised. Doc called, and they each drew one card. I could see Eddie's hand over his shoulder—two pair, Queens and nines. And he drew another Queen for the full house. I figured he had this one.

Doc bet ten dollars, Eddie raised ten, Doc raised back, and Eddie, to my surprise, called. Doc laid down a heart flush. "Damn!" Eddie swore. "Beats two pair." He showed only his original hand, hiding the third Queen, then quickly shuffled the cards. I almost fell off the barstool.

An hour later the game broke up. Doc bought a round of drinks and headed off, painfully climbing the stairs. Eddie put the cards on the bar and sat beside me. I picked them up and shuffled through.

"I always knew Marines weren't the brightest bulbs on the tree, Eddie, but you're the first guy I ever saw cheat himself," I said. He looked at me funny, then glanced quickly around as I tossed three Queens on the bar.

"You got to keep this quiet, Jim," he pleaded. "It's like this. Doc was our company corpsman at Dong Ha. What you Army guys call a medic. Anyway, our patrol got caught in a rice paddy by a machine gun. Three of us were hit, pinned down and hurting. While the other Marines fired at the VC, Doc ran out and dragged us in, and we all came home alive. I was the last guy, and his luck ran out. The machine gun caught him just as he got me to cover, and he was hit worse than any of us."

I tried to interrupt, but he went on, angry now, face hard. "You know what he got for it? A Navy Cross, a stinking little pension—and a body so tore up he can't work much. That leg ain't the half of it."

"And the poker?" I asked.

"One of the guys whose butt Doc saved is now a banker in Providence, the other's got a construction company in Vermont, and I'm not doing bad either. Thanks to Doc, we got kids and families and good lives. He's too proud to take any help from us—but he's always loved to play poker with dumb Marines. So the other guys send me betting money every month."

"How'd you do tonight?"

"I lost over three hundred to Doc, but I took seventy off the Tomasinos," he said. "So for a dumb Jarhead everybody thinks is a loser, I think I did okay."

Eddie finished his beer and left, after getting my promise to keep his secret.

I ordered another Scotch, thinking the dumb Marine had done pretty good, at that.

Trial by Fire

The venerable law firm of Habner and Smith--fully seven months had passed since the founding--was having a drink. More specifically, the firm was conducting their regularly-scheduled Friday afternoon review of the week's cases in their conference annex, known to the public as "Pete's Pub & Grub." Given their all too-light case load, the senior partners--Howie Habner and Alan Smith--had developed the habit of retiring to Pete's by three p.m. on Fridays to grouse about the lack of adequate financial remuneration for bright young lawyers and--both being divorced--check out the talent coming in for happy hour. There were no junior partners, no law clerks and only one over-worked secretary in the firm.

"Damn it, Howie, someone has to be responsible!"

Howard Habner turned from his contemplation of the leggy--if somewhat shopworn--redhead sitting at the bar, to regard his partner. "Why?" he inquired.

"Because it's the American way, for God's sake. The guy was injured. His car was badly damaged. He lost time from work. Throw in pain and suffering, mental anguish, loss of consortium..."

"He wasn't married, Alan--who'd he lose consortium with?"

"...Possible loss of consortium, psychological damage, fear of driving, night sweats, and some things I haven't thought of yet, and we're talking a major settlement, with at least 40% to us. Not to mention the possibility of punitive damages."

"Maybe Freddie's responsible for his own accident. Guy's a horse's ass anyway." Howie took a sip of cheap Scotch, wishing the budget allowed Glenlivet.

Alan looked at his partner with pity. "Honest to God, Howie, sometimes I wonder how you got through law school. If Freddie's responsible for his own accident, who we gonna sue?"

"Sue Freddie!"

"Number one, Freddie's pockets are even shallower than ours. Number two, if he had any cash, he wouldn't pay us 40% to get it away from him just to give it back to him. Old Fred may be a couple burgers short of a happy meal, but he isn't that slow."

"Maybe it's Freddie's fault and there's no case."

"This is America in the twenty-first century. No one is responsible for his own accident or his own problems. If you get hurt or go wrong, it was your parents, or big business, or labor, or the government or society or air pollution or junk food. That's a fundamental of modern American jurisprudence, for God's sake. Our whole system of law, the livelihood of tens of thousands of attorneys, judges, court employees, insurance salesmen and mental health workers depends on it. If people start being held responsible for their own actions, the whole Goddamn system would come crumbling down!"

Howie looked back at the redhead, who smiled and recrossed her legs. Things were looking up, and he thought about inviting her to join them. He decided to wait until she'd had another drink or so and perhaps something to eat from the happy hour buffet. That would keep the cost down, though there was always the risk of someone else scooping her--he wasn't the only semi-desperate young professional who frequented Pete's. "So who you gonna sue?"

"Unfortunately, Freddie was sober when he hit the mailbox, or I'd sue the tavern, the distributor, the distiller and on up. If he'd hit a phone booth, I'd sue the phone company. Can't go after the post office--they'd just lose the documents in the mail. I'd sue the construction company, but that highway is straight--no previous accidents for miles. Freddie's model Honda has an excellent safety record and I can't find a mechanic who will testify that there was a flaw..."

"Other than the nut holding the steering wheel."

"I thought about suing his parents for not teaching him to drive, but his father's dead and his mother's in a nursing home. No deep pockets there."

The redhead took a route unnecessarily close to their table on her way back from the buffet. She was carrying a miniature plate piled with chicken wings, greasy cold meatballs and carrot sticks. When Howie met her gaze she held it briefly, wetting her lips in what he took to be a hopeful gesture, then teetered back to the bar, failing to notice the meatball that rolled from her plate and bounced under their table.

Howie figured if she had one more drink he could afford to entertain her for the evening, and if he had one more, he'd want to. He caught the waitress's attention and circled his finger in the air. "Maybe," he said, "we should sue God."

Alan put his feet on the table pedestal and leaned back in the captain's chair favored by Pete's, a habit that had led to his public embarrassment at least twice in the past. "What do you mean?"

Howie looked closely at his friend. Alan's face betrayed no hint that he realized Howie was joking. The hazel eyes stared intently from his puffy face, waiting for elaboration. The waitress set another Scotch and water in front of Howard and switched Alan's empty glass for a full draft. Howie glanced at the bar, noting approvingly that the redhead had ordered another drink, then turned back to his partner.

"Only that if none of us is responsible for our actions or conduct, it must be the manufacturer's fault--or the designer's, have it how you will. I mean, if I hurt someone you sue me, but since I can't be responsible, someone else must be at fault. Ultimately, the evidence chain leads to God," he said.

"Suppose you don't believe in God?"

"Then it's fate, kismet, random chance--but fate doesn't have deep pockets."

"And God does? How do we attach assets in heaven?"

"Hey, God has major assets right here on Earth. Look at all the property owned by the Catholic church. And the Protestant churches. And the Jews. And all the other religions. They all claim to hold their property in God's name. If you get a judgment against God, and it's his property, it could be used to satisfy the judgment."

"What grounds do we sue God on?"

"Well, God made man, right. No problem proving that mankind..." Howie paused and politically-corrected himself. "...humankind is all screwed up, flawed, full of bad habits. Put friend Freddie on the stand as exhibit A and you're home free on that one. If you accept that God is the designer and maker of this flawed product, you have a case for product liability, probably false advertising, maybe even malpractice, since God should be perfect and produce perfect works--which we ain't."

Howie broke off expounding on the topic when he noticed the redhead leaving, and not alone. The old devil with her had one arm around her waist, his hand dangerously close to cupping the buttocks that were churning provocatively under her tight green skirt. Shit. She looked better going out than sitting at the bar. There went the evening.

"We may have a case," Alan said.

With a despondent sigh, Howie gave his partner his full attention. "It's a goof, buddy. You can't really sue God."

"Why not? If He's responsible, then He should pay."

"Well, first of all, you'd probably go to Hell."

Alan laughed. "You know what Mark Twain said--Heaven for climate but Hell for society!"

"Secondly, no judge would hear the case."

"Frumpner might. You know how the crotchety bastard loves publicity and this would beat suing the president. We'd be breaking new legal ground. Our names would take their place in legal annals alongside the guy who thought up the Twinkie Defense!" Alan waxed enthusiastic.

Howie began to panic. "You're a wild bear when you get the bit between your teeth. This could wreck the firm."

Alan laughed, ignoring Howie's scrambled metaphor. "This could make the firm. We could be the top kook law firm in the state."

"Exactly."

"Not to worry. Some kooks have money. We send the poor ones on their way and represent those who can pay. A few high publicity cases and you'll be able to make support payments to your ex. Besides, God, or his vicars here on Earth, may settle out of court. That could be worth big bucks."

It was Howie's turn to laugh. "Forgive him, Lord, he knows not who he sues!" He drained the whisky and rose. "Let me know where to send the subpoena."

Alan watched his partner depart. He signaled for another beer, pulled a legal pad from his briefcase, and began making notes. Ten minutes later he was delighted to look up and note that the redhead was back at the bar. He smiled and gestured toward the chair Howie had vacated. She slid off the bar stool, picked up her drink, and headed toward the table. Howie's problem, Alan thought, was that he missed the big chances.

The Boss clicked off the VCR he'd been using to review the tape of Howie and Alan's conference and turned to his computer, calling up their records from the database. This had real promise. He buzzed his secretary, waited and buzzed again. There was no response and he cursed softly. His workforce grew daily, but it was almost impossible to get anyone with a decent work-ethic.

"Well," he muttered to himself, "they probably wouldn't be here then." Pushing open the door to his air conditioned office, he yelled "Delores!"

A busty bleached-blond in a short skirt rose from where she was bending over an accountant's desk, displaying generous cleavage to go with her tanned legs. "Ya want me, Mr. L?"

He did, but it could wait. "Send in Snyder." He went back to the computer and ran print-outs on Howard Habner and Alan Smith.

Snyder was sweating when he approached the Boss's office, but then he was always sweating. One hell of a way for a lawyer to work, he thought, and chuckled at his little joke. In a previous life, Snyder had prosecuted the conspirators who tried to kill Hitler. Lately his demons had been bothering him about that case, but it was still his proudest legal moment.

He read the brass plate on the Boss's door: "B. Lucifer, CEO and President, Institute for the Morally Impaired." Always changing names to keep up with the times, Snyder thought, and imprudently rapped directly on the plate, burning his knuckles.

"Come."

Gingerly Snyder pushed open the door. The Boss was studying his computer screen. "You sent for me, Mr. L?"

The Boss waved him to a chair. Snyder was grateful for the rest. The cool air made his shirt stick to his body under the wool suit all the attorneys were required to wear, regardless of the heat.

"We got an interesting possibility here. Couple of desperate young attorneys thinking about suing the Big Guy. Bright fellows--I expect they'll work in your section some day. Meantime, I want you to give them all the help you can."

"How do we know about this?"

"One of our agents reported with a tape. Redheaded hussy named..." he paused to consult the sheet, "Gloria Greenbaum." Snyder winced. Given his past Nazi association, he was uncomfortable working with Jews. The Boss didn't like them much either--they were hard to recruit, being distressingly free of the finer vices, a fact Snyder discovered to his surprise. Apparently this Greenbaum broad was an exception--or maybe she wasn't really Jewish?

The Boss hit the VCR clicker and the screen filled with the table in Pete's, taken from a miniature camcorder at the bar. The Boss narrated. "Big guy on the left is Alan Smith. He's 33, six foot one, 210 pounds, divorced, no kids. Likes beer and women. He's the flamboyant one of the pair. Good talker, ruthless in the courtroom. Will cut your nuts off--our kind of guy. Greenbaum says he's athletic in the sack, but not imaginative. Women seem to like him despite the flab. He's the one running with the ball on the potential suit against our competition."

"The short, balding guy is Howard Habner. He's 31, five foot seven, 143 pounds, divorced, two kids. Likes Scotch and women--doesn't do too well with either. We should bind him if we put one of Greenbaum's pals in his bed. He's the brains of the outfit. It was his logic that pointed out what we've been saying all along--if the World's a mess, who made it?"

The Boss leaned back, his eyes dreamy. "If we can get an official ruling that the Big Guy screwed up, who knows..." he trailed off and thought. Then he swiveled around and slapped the desk. "I'm sending you into the field, Snyder. Be a nice vacation for you. Maybe make a few female converts? Your job is to run this operation. Help these guys. Top priority. Put some resources in their way--cash, booze, Greenbaum and company. Keep this ball rolling. Frequent reports." He paused to fix Snyder with the gaze that had shaken human hearts for thousands of years. "And Snyder. Don't screw this up. Lots of talented attorneys here would like your soft job-- and I have other jobs."

Snyder rose, shaking--but the Boss was used to humans shaking. "Sure thing, Mr. L. You can count on me."

"Of course I can, Snyder. Of course I can." He waved toward the door and Snyder left, trying not to scurry. He failed. As the door shut, he heard the Boss start to laugh. Other than the Boss's air conditioning, that laugh was the only chilling thing in the place.

Howie was startled to see a media mob when he arrived at the office Monday morning. He dodged a TV van and double parked behind some SOB whose Volvo was in his spot. Probably a postal employee had gunned down his co-loafers at the branch office next door, he thought. Howie had a low regard for postal employees, having once lost a case when "overnight" mail took two weeks to arrive. In his view, the crazy thing was that it was always postal employees shooting up post offices when by rights it should be irate customers.

He crossed to the front of the building and fought his way to the front where a cop was keeping order. The badge barred Howie's progress. "No one gets in until after the press conference."

"Press conference?"

"Ain't you heard? Some numbnut lawyers are suing God!" The cop snorted, a deep, resonant snort that fully communicated his contempt for the entire race of attorneys and the folks who spawned them.

Oh, shit, Howie thought. "You'd better let me in. I'm one of the numbnuts."

Alan was in conference when Howie unlocked the office door and stomped in. An ancient bald man stopped speaking in mid sentence. Howie thought the guy must be pushing ninety-five. He looked like one off those walking sticks you buy in craft shops--shiny on the top, twisted and skinny all the way down. He glanced around the table and was startled to see the redhead from Pete's sitting close--too close, he thought--to Alan. To her right was a plump woman who seemed to consist entirely of badly dyed, blond hair and enormous breasts. At least they were taking up a lot of table space and were only partly hidden by the bleached tresses hanging over them. The firm's elderly secretary, Helen, completed the motley quintet. Bloody wonderful, he thought.

"Howie!" Alan jumped to his feet, almost knocking over the redhead, "Thank Go...er, glad you're here. We are rollin'. Frumpner's agreed to accept the case. Mr. Snyder here has volunteered to back us." He waved toward the old man, who smiled like he'd just outlived his last enemy. "Gloria and Delores are going to help with paperwork and coordinate publicity. I'll argue the case--and you'll write the briefs!"

"What in the living hell is going on?" Howard asked. Snyder flinched and stared at the floor.

Alan had the grace to look sheepish. He glanced around his coterie for support, drew a breath, and announced, "We're suing God. It was your idea. Using Freddie's case, we're starting a class action suit on behalf of flawed mankind. We're going after the resources of all the churches. We expect thousands of less-than-perfect humans to join in the case!"

Howie slumped in the vacant chair and put his head in his hands. "Oh, Jesus," he whispered.

"Him, too, Mr. Habner," Snyder said, "Him, too."

Howie got through the press conference only because Delores--the blond--propped him up by putting an arm around his waist and bracing her left breast under his armpit like a flotation device. Calling the conference a zoo would probably generate libel suits from animals everywhere, he mused.

The mainline media thought it was a hoot. The newspapers ran it on page one as a human-interest sidebar. TV news ended their evening broadcasts with shots of Alan and his merry little band of legal blasphemers.

The local tabloid, on the other hand, played it as a straight story. Of course, it ran next to another straight story about a two-headed woman who was pregnant with Elvis's love-child. Alan was in glory, rising to heretofore unrevealed rhetorical peaks as he excoriated the Almighty for all the flaws and failings of humankind.

Howie managed to make it to his office before collapsing at his desk. Delores brought in a bottle of Scotch, which he noted with surprise was Glenlivet. She rubbed his neck, occasionally brushing the back of his head with her chest, and brought him up to date. It seemed that Alan had hooked up with Gloria--the redhead--after Howie'd left Pete's. During a night of carousing, he'd told her about the idea of suing God. She'd been enthusiastic and introduced him to an "old family friend," Mr. Snyder, who was wealthy and had a grudge against heaven. Interestingly, Snyder used to be a lawyer in Switzerland, or someplace, so he could provide both advice and cash. Anyway, Gloria was her roommate, so she--Delores--had become involved because "it sounded like a real goof!"

Howie leaned back and felt her bosom envelope his head. Maybe, he thought, there would be compensations for having Alan ruin his career.

By Tuesday, Howie's world had degenerated far beyond the power of any psychology term to describe. Thousands of religious protesters were picketing their office, their apartments, the court, the TV stations, and the homes of people named Smith or Habner for seventy miles. The phone was totally blocked with death threats and obscene calls. Howie's mother called to disown him but, luckily for his peace of mind, was unable to get through. They put in an unlisted line and some fundamentalist at the phone company blew it to the media within thirty minutes. Helen quit.

The mail brought a flood of threats and condemnation--but, to Howie's surprise, at least a rivulet of contributions from individuals who wanted to join the suit because, in their estimation, they'd been short-changed by their Creator. Howie was convinced they were correct. At the peak, at least $5,000 per day was rolling in.

There were also counter-protesters. A handful of morons from the unfortunately-named Atheistic Studies Society made an appearance, but their presence--as well as the acronym on their signs--so outraged the pro-God forces that the atheists were forced to retreat in disorder.

Howie, Alan, Gloria, Delores, Snyder and a succession of Snyder's startlingly-young girlfriends were living and working in a three-bedroom luxury suite Snyder leased a block from the courthouse. The doors were guarded by hired thugs who, Howie thought, bore an uncanny resemblance to Nazi storm-troopers in the old war movies. With a steady diet of fast food, Glenlivet and Delores, Howie found he wasn't doing much of the work. He also found he didn't much care.

"What about the Jury?" Alan asked.

"Maybe you should go for a bench trial?" Howie suggested.

"Frumpner's far too smart politically to rule for us. We need to convince a jury. Who should be on it?"

"I believe we should certainly challenge anyone with a religious bias," Snyder said.

Howie looked up from where he was petting Delores's soft thigh. "Problem is," he said, "if a juror believes in God, he may vote against us on religious grounds. If he doesn't believe in God, he'll vote against us on legal grounds. No God--no defendant."

Alan said the "F" word, causing Gloria to stop typing and look hopeful.

After much struggle, the court managed to impanel a jury, all but one of whom believed in God, but none of whom was, in Snyder's phrase, "dangerously religious." There were three men and nine women, including one working prostitute, known in the trade as Sister Mary. It was a jury that gave both sides hope, a politically correct jury of seven Christians, two Jews, a Muslim, a Buddhist and one agnostic who avowed that, if it were proven that God was at fault if He existed, he'd be willing to find God guilty in case He existed. With that, both sides had to be satisfied.

The case opened with Judge Frumpner making a pious speech about how everyone, even the Lord, deserved his day in court to defend himself against possibly-scurrilous charges. Attorneys for the major religions moved to dismiss, but Frumpner, wallowing in the media lights, demurred. Alan got to make his case.

He called a historian to cite the dismal record of human folly: wars, slaughter, bigotry, murder, blown Superbowls. He called a philosopher to testify that man knew right from wrong, and a psychiatrist to claim that man was incapable of choosing right. He called Freddie to show just how inferior a product the "average" guy was.

His arguments, devised more by Snyder than Howie, sparkled. How could God be advertised as perfect when his greatest creation--humankind--was so clearly defective? If you, ladies and gentlemen of the jury, created something one tenth as destructive and hateful as humans, the courts would take everything you owned to compensate the victims of your negligence--your malfeasance. Should God, the creator of the universe, be held to a lower standard than you? Surely damages were in order, substantial damages, punitive damages. Alan strode the courtroom, beat on the jury box, begged, pleaded, cried, howled and laughed. "What the devil's got into him?" Howie asked Delores. She smiled and rubbed his leg under the table.

If his performance impressed his friends, it mesmerized the opposition, the judge, the spectators...and the jury. The defense was feeble and dispirited. The case went to the jury with the press openly speculating about the size of the award. Snyder boasted that he would open a billiards hall in the nearest church. Then they waited.

It was Sister Mary, the aging prostitute, who turned the jury around. Man wasn't God's greatest creation, she declared. She knew men--they laughed--and man was far down the list. A kitten, possibly. A rainbow or a daisy, quite probably. A beer and a pizza, definitely. All were better creations than man. "Besides," she asked, sweetly, "when you meet God--and you will--do you want to tell Him that you were on the jury that decided He screwed up when He created you?" Even the agnostic blanched.

In a unanimous decision, Freddie lost. Snyder, Gloria and Delores departed abruptly, taking the last bottle of Glenlivet. The agnostic juror entered a seminary. Alan and Howie went home, took their phones off the hook, and slept for a week-- giving the media, and thus the public, ample time to forget all about them.

Snyder cringed when he entered the Boss's office. He knew it was going to be bad-very bad. The room was changed completely. Gone were the corporate-executive trappings. Instead there was a towering throne, with a sinister figure attired in a black cape. Sulfur vapors stifled the atmosphere. Water dripped from the stone walls.

Snyder glanced at the walls and licked his very dry lips. Damn, he thought, he's back to the "Earl of Hell" bit bestowed on him by the old Scottish divines. It'll be millennia before I taste water again.

The Earl gestured toward a large shovel leaning against the foot of the dais. "Please take this when you go, Mr. Snyder. I have a small job for you. It should take between nine and thirteen hundred years. The penalty of failure. Now go!"

Snyder snatched up the tool and bolted for the door, where his supervising demon waited, face white with anger.

"I think this calls for a celebratory drink, Patrick," the Big Guy said, "how long have you had Sister Mary in place?"

Saint Pat crossed to the bar, poured a Jamison's for himself and a rare Islay malt for Him. "She's been working as a hooker for about fifty years," he replied, "saving a soul here, reporting a problem there. She was our closest agent."

"Damn fine work, too," the Big Guy replied, savoring his malt. "You Celts can be troublesome, but you do make excellent whisky! What do you recommend we do now?"

"Well, you could counter sue?"

The Almighty heaved a sigh that would have been a worldwind on a hundred planets. "And where," he asked, "would I get a good lawyer?"

Published in *Gateway Magazine*

Wheels of Love

A burst of laughter interrupted Norman's thoughts. Turning, he saw a wheelchair tilted over the curb, one wheel wedged in a storm grate, on the verge of tipping into the street. A young girl laughed as she struggled to free herself. Norman ran to help.

Without being asked, he grasped the armrest and wrenched the chair free, easing it back on the sidewalk. Smiling, he bowed gallantly. "Your servant, ma'am."

"Thank you, kind sir." Norman looked up, surprised. The voice was that of a woman, not the child he expected. She was in her mid-to-late twenties, and startlingly lovely--a pixie who couldn't dance. He realized her small size--she couldn't have weighed a hundred pounds--had led him astray. Looking into her crinkled, hazel-gray eyes, he flushed, aware she was now laughing at him.

"I'm sorry," he said, "I thought you needed help, though you seemed to think it was funny."

"Indeed I did, need help that is. And I thought it was funny. I'm always getting this thing stuck and having to be rescued by some hero." She wrinkled her small, straight nose at him, and the dimple in her left cheek winked. "My mom thinks I do it just to meet guys.

"Well, I'm a guy," he extended his hand, "so it worked fine this time. Norman MacLeod."

She gave him a delicate hand, aware of his dark, curly hair and the solid build under his tailored suit. "Pleased to meet you, Norman MacLeod. I'm Amber Eisenhower, no relation to the president." She held his blue eyes and her smile beamed again. "Can I buy you a cup of coffee to thank you for my rescue?"

Norman felt his breath catch. He glanced at his watch, deciding Frank Wilson could wait. "I'd be delighted."

Taking the handles with her consent, he steered the chair toward a small cafe while she chatted, asking about his work. He admitted to being an attorney.

"A lawyer! I hope you're not like those pests who called my parents after the accident?"

"I'm afraid I'm much more boring, Amber. I practice corporate law, trying to keep clients from getting their socks sued off. No personal injury work. On the other hand, maybe we could sue the city over storm grates constituting traffic hazards!" She laughed with him.

They reached the cafe, and Norman maneuvered her to a table. There was some awkwardness rearranging the chairs, but Amber didn't seem to notice. He pulled his cellular phone from a coat pocket and dialed the office, giving instructions to delay the Wilson meeting for an hour.

"I'm not making you miss something, am I?" Amber asked.

"Not at all. There's a certain businessman who didn't take my advice. Now he's in the soup. A little wait will allow him to develop a properly contrite attitude." Norman extended his leg, displaying a black wingtip. "While he's begging, I believe I'll have him shine my shoes."

"Boy," she said in mock seriousness, "you charge more for some rescues!"

They exchanged life stories. "Norman's not a common name nowadays," she said.

"It is among MacLeods," he replied. "Half the MacLeods in the world are named Norman--and that's just the women!"

Amber told him about the drunk driver who took away her ability to walk at eighteen. "I cried for a year. Then I decided that he could put me in a wheelchair, but I was damned if he could make me unhappy the rest of my life." Norman revealed he was divorced, but didn't mention his hobby. One cup of coffee stretched into three. By the time he walked her to her specially equipped van, they had set a dinner date for the weekend.

Norman found Amber constantly on the fringes of his mind as Saturday drew nearer. There was something fetching about her, something richly appealing. He hoped his sudden affection wasn't based on pity.

Concerned about the wheelchair, he made reservations at a private club where his firm maintained memberships for the attorneys. The food would be excellent, the service attentive and discreet--and there was an elevator. Dealing with wheelchairs was outside his experience.

Amber was radiant in a green cocktail dress, setting off the reddish highlights in her sandy brown hair. Where earlier she'd looked like a child, now she appeared more sophisticated than her twenty-eight years. At thirty-five, Norman was acutely aware of their age difference, and gratified by her display of maturity.

The waiters were charmed. Amber accepted their attentions like a benevolent princess on a throne, paying them with musical laughter and soft smiles. By dessert, Norman was holding her hand across the table.

"MacLeod," she mused, "So you must be Irish, right?"

"Scots!" Norman pretended to bristle, smiling to show he was teasing. "From Clan MacLeod on the Isle of Skye." He told her about his three vacations in Scotland. Amber listened, eyes shining wetly.

"Maybe someday," she said softly. He squeezed her hand.

"Maybe."

"So, have you ever worn a kilt?"

"Aye, lass--all the time." Norman had been dreading this point. "When I'm not helping some executive escape the consequences of his feckless ways, my hobby is Scottish Country Dancing." Amber winced and looked away briefly, then smiled at him, eyes glistening. A huge hand squeezed Norman's heart.

"I used to love to dance. Tell me about Scottish dancing. You do the Highland Fling?"

Norman found himself explaining the difference between the individual, competitive sport of highland dancing, like the fling and sword dance, and the jigs, reels, waltzes and slow-tempo Strathspeys of country dancing. "It's social dancing, usually in four-couple sets, just for fun."

"Will you take me some time, to watch? I want to see you in a kilt, in fact I want a picture for my desk. And you have to tell me, Norman MacLeod, what does a Scotsman..."

"...Wear under his kilt?" Norman laughed. "That's easy, lass--shoes, socks, and a wee bit of talcum powder!" He told her there were Scottish dance classes in most American cities, and promised to take her the following week.

When he kissed her goodnight outside her parents' ranch house, Amber's soft lips sent a small electric current from his mouth to his chest. Norman wondered if he was falling in love. The tingle lingered on his drive home.

Norman began to devote his free time to Amber, neglecting even his workouts at the gym, and some research projects. He took her to dance class several times, though it made him uncomfortable dancing while she watched. She didn't seem to mind and studied the dance formations in the manuals. A graphics designer by profession, Amber quickly grasped the basic moves, and devised a dance for him she called "MacLeod to the Rescue." The other dancers were delighted with Amber, quickly making her part of the group.

Three months after their first date, they were sitting on her front porch, enjoying the first cool evening of Fall. Norman handed her a Scottish postcard, with a picture of a worn scrap of cloth. "That's the MacLeod Fairy Flag at Dunvegan Castle. It's the most sacred relic of my clan, and I want you to have a copy. Even today, MacLeod men carry that picture into battle to keep them from harm. I always have one in court." He smiled at his Celtic superstitions.

"Will it keep a Pennsylvania Dutch girl safe as well?"

"Aye, it would lassie--if she was Mrs. Norman MacLeod!"

Amber's face twisted in quick pain, and Norman felt his chest constrict. He couldn't breath. "I love you, Norm, but I can't marry you."

"Won't have a lawyer in the family, huh?" He tried hard to keep the pain out of his voice. His palms were sweating, cold, and he wiped them on his jeans.

"Oh, Norman, look at me. I'm what the politically correct call differently abled." She waved a hand at her ever-present wheelchair. He'd never heard her sound bitter before. "I can't marry a dancer!" She put her head against his chest and let the sobs come. He held her close, fighting back his own tears.

"Don't say no now, sweetheart. Let's just keep negotiations open."

For the next month they avoided the topic of marriage. On the weekends, Norman took Amber on long scenic drives, stopping at romantic inns for dinner, hoping that love would win her over--love and a plan. When the plan was ready, he invited her to his townhouse for salmon poached in the microwave, his one culinary specialty.

After dinner, he wheeled her into the living room, and left, promising a surprise. When he returned, he was wearing a harness made by a friend, and carrying a similar device. Amber started to question him. Placing a finger over her lips, he hushed her. He strapped the second harness over her cotton top. Bending over, he clipped the harnesses together at shoulder height. "Put your arms around my neck, lass" he ordered.

Amber complied, clutching him tightly. Norman stood easily, holding her in his arms, her feet floating six inches off the floor. Though she was light, he was grateful he kept in shape.

Using a remote, he cued the CD player. The rhythmic strains of a Scottish waltz filled the room, and Norman began to glide over the rug, whirling slowly with Amber in his arms. She cried softly, kissing his neck and ear, hugging him desperately. The waltz finished and was followed by a reel. Norman skipped the length of the room and back, the harness distributing Amber's light weight, making it easy. Finally he stopped, panting only a bit. "You're a fine dancer, my love--you follow very well!"

Amber pulled back her head and looked into his questioning gaze. Her shining eyes were puffy. "You win Norman MacLeod. I'll join your clan. Whither thou goest, I will go." Then she kissed her fiancée. Norman's world went hazy and golden, and he cued another waltz. They went on dancing, eyes glistening with happy tears.

Norman made a kenspeckle groom in his MacLeod kilt, with a yellow, black and red tartan plaid sweeping down from his left shoulder. Amber's chair was decorated in matching tartan as her dad wheeled her down the aisle to the Lewis Bridal Song. Under his formal Prince Charlie jacket Norman wore a harness, which matched the one waiting for Amber at the reception.

On the Isle of Skye, where the bonds of clanship are strong, a two-hundred-year-old hotel was scrambling to make sure key areas were wheelchair accessible for a honeymoon.

Published in *Cappers Magazine.*

Merry Christmas, Snake

A Vietnam Christmas

Eddie wrapped a length of C-ration baling wire around the trunk of Aunt Thel's tree, and wedged the end between the bunker's crumbling sandbags. That corrected the starboard list caused by a bent stand. Considering that their mail had been air-dropped from a C-130 cargo plane, the two-foot artificial tree had come through remarkably well, with only the bent leg and one broken limb. At Snake's suggestion, they had turned the "bare spot" to the wall and trimmed the tree with the surviving decorations and local crafts: a tin star cut from a C-ration can, a pair of lance corporal chevrons with the black coating worn off so they glittered, some brass M-16 shell casings.

Eddie would have preferred canned peaches from Aunt Thel, but he thought the tree looked right cheerful in their bunker. He twisted the tin star to catch light from the radios and began softly singing:

"Jingle bells, mortar shells, V. C. in the grass--
You can take your Merry Christmas and shove it up..."

He sensed "incoming" and ducked as Snake's boot banged into the wall, safely away from the precious tree, sending a trickle of sand dribbling through the slats of the wooden pallets that served as the bunker's floor. Eddie turned and saw Snake smiling at him over a can of C-ration ham and limas. You couldn't get pissed at a guy who would trade you beanies and weenies for ham and "slimies," which every reasonable person hated the way Santa's point-deer Rudolph hated clear weather.

Eddie wiped his eyes to get rid of the stinging caused by grit from the sandbags. It didn't help. "Since when did you get the Christmas spirit?" he asked, "I thought you were a Black Muslim?"

Snake had announced his new religion several weeks ago, the fourth in seven months. Though he maintained a devout facade, his "conversions" were a standing joke in the platoon. Eddie had reasonably pointed out that while he, himself, was black, Snake was a white dude—an awkward start for a Black Muslim.

Snake's response was that Eddie was an Uncle Tom; and, that since there was no other black dude to be the radical on their radio relay team, he would have to do it himself, "Just like every goddamned thing else around here."

"Can't be a Muslim on Christmas Eve," Snake smiled, and continued dropping pieces of John Wayne crackers through the floor planks for the rat. He's been trying to kill the rat just last week, but, following the lead of the Viet Cong, had declared a Christmas truce with it yesterday.

Eddie picked up the jungle boot, and turned it over, observing that it was nearly new. He looked down to his left boot, where the electrical tape holding it together was coming loose. The sides had rotted and he hadn't been able to scrounge replacements from supply's limited stock.

"Hey, Snake, how about giving me your extra boots? We're the same size, almost."

"Certainly, my man," Snake promised, "As soon as the Sear's catalog comes and I can order something more stylish. We might, however, barter--I do admire that K-bar knife on your belt." Snake rose and headed to the bunker door, which hung precariously from the hinges of shell boxes. "I'll go switch generators."

He went into the night, taking only a small flashlight, to carry out the regular task of alternating the 400-cycle generators that powered their AN/TRC-27 radio relay unit.

Eddie was re-taping his boot when the first mortar round exploded in the small perimeter. "Christmas truce!" he spat, lunging for the door, "Little rice-propelled bastards!"

By the time the corpsman had checked the flow of blood from Snake's mangled leg, and closed the flap of open flesh on his right cheek, the painkiller had taken hold and he was babbling happily.

"Lucky break, Eddie," he said, laughing, "I tripped over the goddamn antenna guy wire and couldn't make the hole. Now I'm going home for Christmas, buddy. I'll be dancing in Time's Square on New Year's Eve while you're still stuck in this shit hole, man."

Eddie glanced at Snake's leg and winced as they loaded him onto the stretcher. "Nail one of them hippy broads for me," he said.

Snake laughed again, almost a giggle. "Hey, Eddie," he said, "You can have those boots." He gave a weak, cheery wave. "Merry Christmas, man."

"Merry Christmas, Snake," Eddie said, then he impulsively pulled the K-Bar from his belt and laid it on the stretcher, knowing that some rear-echelon pogue would probably steal it from Snake. "Take that home as a souvenir of this slice of paradise."

Snake waved again as the corpsmen hefted the stretcher and struggled carefully up the muddy slope toward the med-evac LZ. "Merry Fucking Christmas," Eddie whispered to himself.

He turned to go check the radios. The grit was bothering him again. *Now*, he thought, *who the hell can I trade ham and limas to?*

Published in *Calliope*.

The Lock

I hesitated, tapping a blue chip on the blanket covering the poker table we'd made out of shell boxes. Then I tossed it in. "Ten bucks to see my aces," I said. In fact, there was only one ace. Chasing a flush at five card stud was a fool's play, but Vietnam tended to make you foolish. Catching the seven of hearts had left me with only an ace high for a hundred dollar pot.

I'd decided it was time to bluff, just so my fellow Marines wouldn't think I always played tight and ban me from the game. With six months to go in-country, poker had already put almost five thousand bucks in the bank account my grandmother was keeping for me. I was hoping to make it ten, unless Charlie Cong sent me home early with my third Purple Heart. Which would be most excellent, if I got the Purple Heart, and not my grieving family.

Everyone folded except Alex Murphy, our squad's red-haired blooper man, who grinned and tossed in his chip. "Call," he said confidently, "I think you're bluffing, Sudden."

"Caught me, buddy." I turned over my hole card, the three of clubs. Alex laughed, and flipped a seven, showing a pair. He raked in the pot, smiling broadly. I tried to look disconcerted, but smiled inside, pleased with my investment. Alex had already contributed a lot of his combat pay towards my mustang convertible fund and I hoped I'd just set the hook for more.

Alex was probably my best friend, you understand. Two patrols back he'd saved all our asses, using his blooper to drop grenades on a VC machine gun that had us sucking paddy water. It was Alex who nicknamed me "Sudden" after I'd I shot an NVA officer at 400 years with an M14 we kept around for distance work. When asked, I told the Skipper the guy was "suddenly dead." But friends are friends and poker is poker. And we had lots of money with nothing much to spend it on.

The game went on. About an hour later I was up over three hundred. Then Alex called five stud, and proceeded to deal me wired Jacks. Since he was showing a King, I bet gently until I paired up fours on the last card. Only Alex and I were left in the pot, which was about two hundred bucks. Since he still had only a King high, I had a lock. His best hand was a pair of Kings against my two pair.

I tapped a blue chip on the table, sending the bluff signal I'd started to develop last game. Then I tossed it in. "Three fours bet ten."

Alex laughed. "See your ten, Sudden, and raise twenty." He was raising into my lock—beautiful! Bam, I saw his twenty and hit him with five more blue chips—our max raise—like an oh-five battery firing for effect.

I'll say this, he never flinched, pushing ten blue chips right back. "Raise another fifty, buddy," he drawled. I felt euphoric. Almost giggling, I maxed him back. And he did the same.

This craziness went on until he'd gone light three hundred bucks, from a pot of at least a thousand. Finally tapped out, he said, "You're bluffing, Sudden. I'll put up my R&R next week in Bangkok against the pot."

"Call," I said. Alex flipped the King, smiling. His smile died when I turned the Jack. "Never bet into a lock, buddy."

He shook his head. "But you always tap a blue chip and bet ten when you're bluffing!"

"Didn't old Sergeant Sudden teach you to watch out for ambushes?"

I climbed down from the chopper, memories of Bangkok's gold Budda and golden women making my slight hangover well worthwhile. Gunnery Sergeant Edwards came out to help the new lieutenant who'd flown in with me. "Welcome home, Sudden. You missed a hot firefight. You hear about Murphy?"

Sharp, cold fear grabbed my chest. "He okay?" I asked.

"Better'n okay. He saved the Skipper's life, dragging him in under fire when Hornsby was shot in both legs. They put him in for a Silver Star."

"That little son-of-a-bitch," I laughed, relieved. "Where is he? I want to tell him about the women in Bangkok."

"You missed him, son," the Gunny said. "He picked up his third Purple Heart pulling Captain Hornsby out of the shit—just a crease from an AK-47, but he's on the freedom bird back to the World, if he ain't home already. Said to tell you sometimes it pays to bet into a lock. Said you'd understand."

Edwards picked up the lieutenant's seabag, and they walked off toward the headquarters hooch. I stared after them, wondering where I'd be right now if I hadn't caught that second four.

Marine terminology:

Blooper—M-79 Grenade Launcher
In-country—in Vietnam
Utility Uniform or Utilities—Fatigue or Combat Uniform
VC, Charlie, or Charlie Cong—Viet Cong
Purple Heart—Medal given American troops for being wounded, or their families if they were killed
Oh-five battery firing for effect—Six 105mm howitzer cannons firing maximum fire to destroy a target
Gunny—Gunnery Sergeant, E-7
AK-47: North Vietnamese combat rifle
Freedom bird—plane out of Vietnam
The World—the USA, home
Seabag—duffel bag
Hooch—Bunker or hut

The Target

The Fed-Ex envelope came while Sally was grinding hazelnut flavored beans for her morning coffee. With the House not in session on Fridays, she'd decided to take the day to herself, perhaps drive up through the southern New Hampshire countryside, and think through the disturbing change in her relationship with Allen. She'd canceled her one scheduled meeting with a town board of selectmen, and slept late.

When the doorbell rang, she belted her tartan robe tighter, checked the peep hole, and signed for the package. As the delivery van pulled away, she walked out on her secluded lawn to retrieve the Boston Globe. The trees shielding her small house from the road were starting to turn, and she shivered against the slight September chill. Sally loved the autumn, and decided to stay over in New Hampshire. There was nothing on her calendar until her speech at the VFW Saturday night.

Inside, she glanced at the oversized envelope. It was formally addressed: The Honorable Sally MacPhearson Birdwell, State Representative, 45th Middlesex District, Commonwealth of Massachusetts. She shrugged, pitching it on the kitchen table. Probably some desperate group lobbying hard for a bill.

Deciding her 33 year old hips could stand a bagel, she popped one into the toaster oven. Returning to the oak table with juice and coffee, she glanced at the Globe, then pulled the envelope closer. She didn't recognize the return address.

Tearing off the seal, Sally pried it open and spilled its contents on the table. There were several photographs and a thick sheaf of legal papers. She stared at the top picture in shock, recognizing the inn near Lake Winnipesaukee where she and Allen had stayed three weekends ago. In the photo, they were coming down the front steps, hand in hand. She had her head tilted back, laughing happily. Her short brown hair was touching her favorite sweater, catching highlights from the morning sun. Allen looked serious.

Quickly, she riffled through the other pictures. All were of Allen and her that weekend: kissing in a restaurant, walking through the field behind the inn, even cuddled on the couch in front of the fire, her head on Allen's shoulder, asleep. In each photo, he looked depressed, almost pained. Sally tried to remember a moment during the weekend when he hadn't been smiling, tried to recall anyone with a camera. She couldn't. Someone nasty had been very clever, very careful.

Dreading what she would read, she picked up the legal brief. It was a deposition charging her with sexual harassment. Sally skimmed the pages, fighting tears of anger and frustration. Allen detailed how she had made advances, how he feared for his job and reputation; how, at 26, he didn't know how to deal with the pressure for a sexual relationship, how she'd forced him into an affair. There were fourteen pages of smear, lies and innuendo. Reading it made Sally feel dirty, soiled. Half way through anger overwhelmed her. She hurled it across the kitchen, pounding her fist on the table, splashing cold coffee on the Globe.

"Damn him," she said. Then she put her head down and really began to cry.

After several minutes, her misery abated, leaving only a white-hot rage. Her cat rubbed against her bare calf, and she scooped him protesting into her lap, petting him fiercely. His broken purr, and the way he cocked his torn ear, made her feel inexplicably better.

"I hope you can still catch mice, Scruffles," she told him. "Momma is probably out of work." Unconcerned, he started cleaning his paws. Sally watched him without really seeing, her mind rapidly turning over options.

Abruptly, she dumped the cat on the floor, and searched through the debris on the table for her cell phone to call Barb. Barbara Collero had been her roommate in college, had stood by her through the divorce from John, had been there when Sally's mother died of cancer last year. If anyone could help, she would know what to do.

She caught Barb at her job in the Federal Building. After a short conversation, Sally re-packed the incriminating envelope and drove carefully to Barb's condo, keeping her anger under tight control.

Barb read through the deposition, twice, while Sally quietly sipped a glass of wine.

"That bastard," Barb said. "Tell me how you got involved. Start at the beginning."

Sally took a long breath. "When did I last see you, early May? Well, just as we were starting work on the state budget, Annie quit, leaving me without a legislative aide. Thank God this isn't an election year. I put the word out around the State House, and brought in the usual resumes—kids eager to change the world, or political hacks whose goal in life is to have lobbyists spring for lunch at Locke-Obers."

Barb nodded, letting her continue.

"The week Annie left, Allen walked in, asking to see me. I couldn't believe my luck." Sally smiled ruefully, "I know, if it seems too good to be true, it's probably not true. He seemed perfect—bright, older without being jaded, and with political experience working for a legislator in New Jersey—or so his resume said."

"We'll check it out," Barb noted.

"He told me he was working on his master's in public administration, and would need Tuesday and Thursday nights free, unless it was an emergency. Barb, he has this sunny disposition that just attracted me to him. He'd done his homework, too. He knew I was in my second term, that I'd served as a town selectman before being elected to the House, the issues I was involved with. Once he started in the office, I found his charm worked wonders on whining constituents—five minutes on the phone and they were ready to elect him governor."

"Sounds like his charm worked on divorced legislators, as well."

Sally drained her glass, and Barb refilled it.

"Too well," Sally said. "I figured it didn't hurt he was terrific looking. That shock of blond hair and those blue eyes could really melt you." She shook her head. "I can't believe I was so stupid."

Barb laughed. "Honey, if we weren't stupid about men, the human race would have died out like the dodos. Tell me how the relationship turned personal."

Sally took another sip of wine, and resumed talking. Even if Barb couldn't help, just telling the story made her feel better. She started with the night they first went out.

The Speaker banged his gavel, declaring the House adjourned to meet tomorrow at 1:00 p.m. Sally glanced at her watch. Ten fifteen. Wonderful, she though, there's a committee hearing at eleven tomorrow morning. Maybe she should just get a room at the Parker House. She gathered her papers. Turning to leave the House floor, she was surprised to see Allen standing at the rail in the rear of the chamber.

"Congratulations on your amendment, Representative—it should carry you through the next two elections." Allen smiled broadly and reached out to take her papers.

"You know the political rule, Allen: What have you done for me lately?" Sally shook her head. "The local selectmen and papers will love this tomorrow and forget it by next month—never mind by next year's election. Besides, I'm not sure our beloved Senator has the clout to help us keep it on the bill in the conference committee. What are you still doing here?"

"I had to get those letters on the gun bill out before thousands of your armed constituents descended on our office. No class on Mondays, so I thought I'd stick around and watch the boss in action. Quite impressive, too—you're not just another pretty face, Representative Birdwell."

Sally flushed slightly at the compliment. Allen had been a Godsend. He was organized, turned out quality work and had a way with people. "No flirting with the boss. Remember my last opponent called me 'That Birdwell Bitch!' How about if I buy you a drink?"

Sally and Allen went out by the police desk and crossed Bowdoin Street to the Twenty-First Amendment, a tiny pub catering to legislators, staff and lobbyists. It was close enough so legislators could have a drink while the House was in session and get back if there was a roll call vote on the floor.

Both the pub's small rooms were crowded. They stood at the bar, where Sally ordered a beer for Allen and white wine for herself. When a small table opened, he grabbed it.

They talked shop for half an hour. At one point she knocked over his beer, waving her hands to make a point. He mopped up while she ordered another.

Allen told her about a constituent—a man well into his eighties—who'd called and insisted he wanted to file a bill putting the gray squirrel on the endangered species list. In Massachusetts, citizens have the right to file bills under "free petition," a right they exercise often enough to be a nuisance to legislators and an expense to the taxpayers. Sally laughed loudly when he described convincing the gentlemen a bill of this importance should be filed by the state senator, not a lowly representative. She wiped away tears, impulsively reaching out and squeezing Allen's hand.

"Senator Anders isn't exactly an animal rights activist," she laughed. "I'd love to see his face. I hope he doesn't find out you set him up."

"Not to worry. I explained the bill couldn't be filed until the next session, and convinced our mutual constituent the good senator would kill it if he knew you were involved—political jealousy."

They ordered another round. Allen was easy to talk to. Unlike the common run of men at the State House, he really listened, asking questions to draw her out, rather than jumping in with his own opinion every time she took a breath. Sally found herself talking about her personal life, finally about the divorce from John her first year in office.

"He was fine when I ran for the board of selectmen. That was part time and, I guess, he thought part-time government was woman's work. He seemed okay when I started my House campaign, kidding about my little hobby, putting up yard signs, shaking hands. After I won, it changed overnight."

"Two months after taking office, I found out he was having an affair with a 23-year-old secretary from his company. We divorced as soon and as quietly as possible. The only thing I kept was his silly name. I'd go back to MacPhearson, but Birdwell is how the voters know me."

"It's not anyone's fault, Sally. You're bright, attractive and, to use an old-fashioned word, nice. When you became locally famous as well, I suspect his ego just couldn't take it. He had to prove he was still Mr. Macho. You just need to find a man who can match your abilities and accomplishments. You should manage fine."

Sally shook her head. "It's not easy, Allen. There are four single women in the legislature under, say, forty-five. We talk. It's hard to find a guy who isn't intimidated by a woman with a title. Plus, we have to be extra careful about scandal. It's not fair, you know. The single guys up here are cutting a wide swath. Even some of the married legislators flaunt their little bimbos, and nobody seems to mind. Me, I'd better stick with my cat!"

Allen touched her hand. Sally liked the tingle, but swiftly withdrew it to sip her wine. "You deserve a personal life, Sally. Getting elected, passing bills, that's not everything. As you said, it's forgotten next month. Don't pass up happiness for political glory—it's not worth it."

A little alarm sounded in her head. Allen was too damned attractive. Did he find her attractive as well? She knew she was pretty, but sometimes felt plain, and dressed conservatively. She changed the focus of the conversation.

"What about you, Allen? Special girl? There are lots of college interns in legislators' offices who would love to date an aide." Sally stopped, stricken by the sad look in his eyes.

"I was engaged, Sally. She dumped me seven months and two weeks ago. I'm not interested right now."

"I'm very sorry, Allen." She rose. "I'd better get down to the Parker House if I want a room." They left the bar. Outside the night was cooling, but still humid.

"If you don't think it would create a scandal, I have a pull-out sofa. It would save you the cost of a room."

Sally knew Allen had an apartment on Beacon Hill, a few blocks away. He'd explained he had independent income from stocks his grandmother had left, which allowed him to live well on an aide's salary.

She shrugged, ignoring her misgivings, eager to spend more time with him. He would hardly attack his boss.

"Maybe a scandal would help my image. If you'll let me buy breakfast, it's a deal."

Allen let her collect her emergency overnight bag from her car, and met her discreetly on the corner of Hancock Street, on the Beacon Hill side of the State House. They walked three blocks to his small, second-floor apartment, where they talked over Red Zinger herb tea for another hour, before retiring. Sally was careful to keep the conversation away from their personal lives. He was, as she expected, entirely proper.

That evening changed her relationship with Allen. She'd quickly come to depend on him in the office. Now she found herself depending on him for emotional support as well. She told herself it was only a friendship, putting her growing attraction out of her mind. They started having dinner two or three nights a week, ostensibly to talk business. Once Allen drove out to her district to attend a political function, staying in her guest room. Several evenings after the day's House session adjourned, they walked through the Boston Gardens, while Sally talked out her political—and personal—problems. Allen listened and offered supportive, nurturing advice.

"I don't know if you're my employee or my therapist," she told him.

"I'm your friend, Sally. If that conflicts with my employment, I'll quit. Being your friend is more important. You need friends—aides are two a penny."

"Not aides like you, Allen. You're priceless—or, at least, worth more than the Speaker will let me pay you."

Twice more she stayed at his apartment, sleeping on the couch. On the third time, she slept with him. She could not be sure who initiated the physical relationship, it just seemed to happen. In the morning, he apologized.

Sally laughed. "I'm the boss—it's probably you who was taken advantage of. Besides, I haven't felt happier in years—didn't you tell me happiness was the most important thing?"

If anything, Allen grew more proper in the office. They made a fetish of never touching in public. In front of others, Allen always addressed her as "Representative." The nights were different. Sally would meet Allen at his apartment, using the key he gave her. On weekends, he would come to her house, carefully parking his BMW out of sight in the garage. She was grateful for her home's secluded location.

Sally knew the relationship was dangerous, knew it couldn't last. Allen was, after all, her employee and seven years junior. She postponed thinking about it. He was efficient in the office, attentive after hours and sweet in bed. Sally wanted all of that, wanted it to go on. Tomorrow would have to take care of itself.

Then Allen suggested a weekend get away. He made reservations at a New Hampshire inn where it was unlikely anyone would recognize them—few state representatives are known outside their own districts. The weekend was exquisite— Sally could not remember being happier. They laughed and played, and made love. She knew then this was more than friendship, more than physical attraction. Sally Birdwell, nee MacPhearson, was falling in love.

Sally entered her office after the short Thursday House session to find Allen wanting to talk. He followed her to her desk and plumped into the old leather chair facing it.

"We're getting calls about Senate Bill 4810," he said. "It's up in committee next week, and you're probably the swing vote."

"If I'm the swing vote, it's dead. You know I've never voted for a gambling bill."

"You should think about supporting this one, Sally. It means a lot of revenue for the Commonwealth. It could also mean some powerful political support if Anders retires and you run for the Senate next year."

"We'll find the revenue in better places than bleeding gullible poor people through gambling, Allen. That bill has an odor about it. I'm a solid No."

"Damn it, Sally, you need the support of the people behind this bill," Allen pressed his point. "Stop being Mary Poppins just once and think about your political future."

"I'm not in politics for a future, Allen. I'm here to make a difference for people now."

"You could at least vote for it in committee, so it gets a favorable report to the floor," he retorted. "Then you can be Miss Priss and vote against it."

Sally was hurt and angry. Allen had never taken a position on legislation before. Now he was not only lobbying for a bill, but a bad bill—and lobbying hard. It disturbed and confused her. "Forget it!" she snapped, and stalked out of the office. No mention was made of plans for the weekend.

The next morning the envelope came.

"Let's find out what we're dealing with," Barb said. "Call Allen and ask him what you have to do to get him to drop the charge. I doubt he's gone public yet."

To Sally's amazement, Allen was at her office. Apparently, he wanted her to be able to reach him. He refused to discuss the situation over the phone, but requested she meet him and his counsel at a bar in Summerville late that afternoon. Alone.

Barb insisted Sally should go. They had four hours to prepare.

Sally was surprised to find the lounge selected for their tryst was rather upscale, though dim and almost deserted. Allen was sitting in the back with an older man. He looked to be short, though neither stood when she approached. He was balding, pudgy and florid.

Allen introduced him only as Tony, his counsel.

"Pleased to meet cha, Representative. Make sure she ain't wired, Al."

Allen smirked and rose, holding out his hand for her purse. Sally hesitated, but handed it over, feeling violated as he rummaged through it. Then he stepped toward her, running his hands down over her hips and thighs, then insolently up over her crotch and belly, lingering slightly at her breasts. Furious, she fought to control her shaking, feeling sick and dirty.

"She's clean."

Tony waved at the empty chair. "Have a seat, Representative. What'll you drink?" She asked for a light beer, and they sat in silence while Allen went to the bar.

He put the beer and a glass in front of her. Ignoring the glass, Sally took a long swallow from the bottle, setting it down in easy reach.

"I'm sorry, Sally," Allen said, "it didn't have to be this way."

"Sorry! You're sorry? That's at least true, Allen—you're a sorry son of a bitch. What about me? What about my life?" She waved her hands toward her chest, catching the beer bottle and knocking it into her lap. They all jumped as the beer foamed out, soaking her summer skirt. Sally looked at their snide smiles, back down to her skirt, and burst into tears. She knew Allen was thinking about that night at the

Golden Dome, and bolted for the woman's room.

She was back in five minutes, damp but composed. Calmly, frostily, she asked what they wanted. Tony did the talking.

"Look, no need to ruin your career over a little roll ina hay, Representative, right? Here's the deal. S-4810 will be up in your committee come Wednesday. You should have a change of heart. You should vote for the bill and say nice things about it. Everybody knows you're a Girl Scout, should grease the skids when it comes to the floor. Allen here, you kinda took advantage, but he's a reasonable boy. Smart girl like you helps out his friends, he's gonna forget all about the way he's been hurt."

"And the next time you need my vote?"

"Look, Representative, get smart. We can't use you again. Besides, we won't need you. Just you're in the right place, this one time. We get your vote, bill passes the House, you get the pictures, deposition and Allen resigns—unless you want him to stay on?" Tony leered, and Sally's stomach turned over.

"When do I have to decide?"

"Vote's on Wednesday. You let us know Monday, or this'll be in Tuesday's Globe. Might be a fine idea, you hold a press conference Monday afternoon, announce your support for the bill. Allen don't look good. He'll be out sick Monday. You call him at his place before ten—you got his number, right?"

Sally rose. "I've got his number."

On her way back to Barb's condo, Sally had to stop the car to throw up. A man named Jim let her in. Barb and another guy she'd introduced as Robert came in ten minutes behind her.

She was still shaking when Barb helped her undress, carefully removing the tiny microphone from her bra.

"God, Barb, I was sure someone was going to come in the damn ladies room while you were putting this thing on me. Then I was sure they'd search me again, and probably shoot me."

"No danger—they wouldn't want the publicity," Barb said. "You did fine. We've got the conversation clear as a bell. We'll get you some coffee, or maybe a drink?"

"Tea, please. I need to settle my stomach."

"And you'll need to give a deposition to Robert and Jim, on tape. They're waiting in the living room. Don't sweat a thing. The Bureau has been interested in your friend Tony for a long while. We have a lot on him, and were really close, but this nails him down. He and Allen and probably a few others will be in custody by Monday." Barb smiled tightly, "I plan to cuff lover-boy myself—he's a new one on us. This is a bigger public service than any bills you've passed, Sally. The publicity should be positive— Honest Legislator Risks Life to Nab Blackmailing Mobsters! Maybe you should run for governor."

Sally started to cry. "What would I have done?"

Barb hugged her. "You'd have voted against their damn bill and lost the next election. You're not the type to roll over for dirtballs. Next time they target a legislator, I'll bet they check to make sure she didn't go to school with an agent on the organized crime strike force."

Essays

Soon it will be spring.

We are entering the days of anticipation; in just a few short weeks, it will be spring. The air will be soft and. warm and the sun will shine. Hearts will lighten as this annual miracle of reawakening comes to pass. But Julie Cunningham and Georgeann Hawkins won't be there to share our joy.

As spring spreads over our land, snows will melt in the mountains and streams will run in spate. The flowers, nature's promise to our hearts, will begin to push out and bloom. But Susan Rancourt and Brenda Ball won't notice the flowers.

The planting will begin as our farmers, on whom we all depend, seek to again fill the cornucopia of good things for our tables, preparing the harvest for which we will give thanks in the autumn. But Janice Ott and Carol Valenzuela won't be there to enjoy those good things.

Bees will buzz among those flowers and crops, gentle spring winds will kiss them, and birds will add their songs to our joy. But Kimberly Leach and Denise Naslund won't be there to hear those songs.

In Tallahassee, azaleas will spread their scarlet cloak on every block. The townsfolk will welcome the season with the annual parade. Mothers will stroll in the park with their babes to watch the parade and savor the fine weather, the sparkle of life and the laughter of children. But Lisa Levy and Margaret Bowman won't be there--will never walk with children in the park.

We who remain have had the happiness of a dozen springs denied these and others who are gone. They will not be with us again this year. But this spring will be a bit different. An old, all-too-familiar face will not be with us. When the earth reawakens this year, when the window is thrown open to the first gentle spring breeze bringing nature's flowered perfume and the songbird's call, when the first truly spring sunbeam enters that window, Ted Bundy won't be there either.

Published in the *Tallahassee Democrat* on January 25, 1989. (With apologies to Judge Roy Bean, "The Law West of the Pecos.")

Riding Along With Officer Al

Eight fourteen p.m. My partner and I left the station house to patrol zone 8A. My name's Friday. No, wait, my name's Bob--the day was Friday, and I was starting a 10-hour shift as a "citizen observer" (they call them "ride alongs") with Officer Al Jarvis of the Tallahassee Police Department. The hours that followed might not have been "One Adam Twelve" but they sure weren't "Car 54, Where Are You?"

You start with a criminal record check--they apparently missed the fact that I had a successful political career in Massachusetts. You then sign a form agreeing that if you are shot in the head several times, you, your heirs, and your lawyers won't be the slightest bit annoyed.

I reported to the station and Al took me down to the "Check-on Room" where the squad is briefed before duty. There was a rush when the sergeant dumped keys on the desk - apparently not all patrol cars are created equal. The squad indulged in much good natured banter. Most of it was at an intellectual level that would startle folks who have a negative stereotype of police officers. The banter stilled considerably when the sergeant announced that I was a "reporter"--cops are as reluctant to have their humor publicly misinterpreted as are politicians.

In the patrol car, Officer Jarvis explained the rules. I could get out of the car unless it looked like trouble, in which case he would leave me locked in to enjoy the fun. "In the unlikely event (oh-oh, the airline phrase!) that what you might call a 'running shoot-out' should develop, I'll put you behind a lamppost, and you'll stay there until someone comes for you--at which time you'll express a wish to stay married to that post," Al said. Well, I was a bit insulted. I am, after all, a Marine Vietnam Veteran. No one has to tell me when to hide.

Much of the night was routine--8A is a "quiet" zone. Of course, any of those routine calls--for which rookies get $20,515 per year--could have resulted in gunfire and dead officers. We checked out an empty building, looking for a white Camaro. We kept kids moving out of local parks and parking spots ("No, officer, that's not my empty beer carton!"). We came in as back-up for an officer checking out a report of "shots fired." (I'm unarmed and in a car that's hurrying toward a report of a shooting?!) We answered a false alarm at a beer distributor, costing them $25 and the taxpayers much more in police time. We interviewed some college students, one of whom alleged he had been slammed through their splintered apartment door by a weight-lifter who thought they had parked in his space. Al remarked that, "It was a long time since he had a victim assaulted with a house." Between 2:30 a.m. and 4:30 a.m. we quelled four noisy parties--one of which was the answer to the question "Where did the Sixties go?"

Most interesting (read "dangerous") was a 3:00 a.m. "domestic dispute." The police had been called three times the previous night for the same folks. The large (former?) boyfriend refused to leave the area. and wound up arrested. The small girlfriend wanted a "trespass warrant" against him--but cried when he was cuffed. The older man she was staying with alleged that the boyfriend had beaten her and dragged her down the street. She refused to sign a battery complaint. The boyfriend alleged that she was "soliciting." She wanted to know why I was looking at her "like that?!"

("Me? I'm just looking for a lamp post!") I decided they were all off my Christmas card list.

The night ended with us helping to surround Tallahassee Community College. One person had been apprehended leaving the building and it was thought another might be inside. I suggested it might be a student arriving early. If so, he cut the class.

Maybe Al was trying to impress me, but I didn't notice any time--the whole 10 hours--for sitting in a donut shop drinking coffee, let alone lunch. He did relent when I mentioned that a men's room would be a welcome sight.

I recommend trying the "ride along program." It'll be interesting--and will make you grateful you don't earn your living that way. And even more grateful for those who do.

Published in the *Tallahassee Democrat*, May 22, 1989

Developing Influence. By Robert A. Hall
March 9, 2014

I'm starting this article as I'm ~~incarcerated~~ admitted to the VA Hospital in Madison for some repair work on the new lung I received on December 23, 2013. I can't say enough about the staff here, as all of the nurses, doctors, health techs and other professionals have been wonderful. I've developed friendships with several, including an excellent nurse, Jason Govia, RN. In between running to poke other patients last night, Jason, aware that I'm a recovering politician, said he had become interested in how people obtained influence. We tossed around ideas, and I concluded that since having influence with others is strongly correlated with career success, getting my thoughts in this essay would be a useful addition to my Tiger Tooth Mountain Resume Service.

What is influence?

Influence, like whisky, comes in many variations, good and bad. Most people are influenced by money out of need for a paycheck or business income to feed their families and survive. Too many are influenced by greed. Six senators I served with later switched from Brooks Brothers to Orange Jumpsuits, and I think greed was a factor in every case—though I did think one Democrat got a raw deal. He took a $1,000 check for consulting before he was a senator, and claimed it on his tax return, so he thought it was legal. If you take what you know is dirty money, you ask for cash!

Many people who contribute to political campaigns on both sides do so because they believe the candidate deserves to be in public office based on character, ability and support for issues. My two largest contributors, at $500 and $1,000 each, never asked me for anything, not even a vote on an issue that I recall. Others—far too many in today's world, alas!—expect something in return, and hope their contributions buy influence. I discovered that two of my contributors in 1974 (whose names I still remember!) gave $50 or $100 both to me and to my opponent. Clearly they didn't care who won, but just wanted the senator to feel obligated. Personally, I'd have helped someone who only supported my opponent before I would have helped either of them.

Coercion and fear can also be an influence. If a druggie steps out of an ally and sticks a 9mm Smith & Wesson auto in your stomach, you are going to be strongly influenced to hand over your wallet and pray.

Influence is also a form of power, and, as you may have heard, power corrupts. People have understood hubris for thousands of years, but the cure escapes us. So entertainment and sports stars with few credentials, little knowledge and limited education, but enough opinions and certitude to outfit a progressive university, pontificate on global warming, foreign affairs, crime and economic policy. And the great uninformed lap it up. Influence, like any power, may be abused. More on this, below.

And, of course, every teenager is required by law to have one "bad influence" in his or her circle of friends. My family thought it was my best friend Charlie. His parents thought it was me. Both were probable right.

So we need to define influence as discussed here. For the purposes of this essay, I'm talking about the ability to change people's minds, attitudes, ideas and behaviors in (what you believe) is a positive way, through your influence.

Influence, in fact, is a variation of positive leadership. In 1966 on Okinawa, I was a Corporal and my outfit sent me to NCO Leadership School, doubtless hoping I'd learn to be like the senior NCOs. But the Corps preaches that "Persuasive Leadership" is better than "Authoritarian Leadership." Unfortunately, four of the five NCOs who outranked me were strict authoritarians. The exception was a SSGT Russell, a black NCO, who was a fine Marine and a good leader, from whom I learned much. Unfortunately, the others tended to marginalize him. Maybe it was envy, but from remarks I overheard, I suspected racism.

Putting what I was taught into practice got me into even more trouble. But since I finished first in a class of 57, they could hardly court martial me—so they shipped me to the 26th Marines, a better outfit bound for Khe Sanh.

Most of the areas where you can develop influence through leadership, below, come from the Corps' "Traits of a Leader," because they apply strongly to exerting influence.

And let it be said that these influence factors apply differently to different people in different situations. Almost without exception, something that gives you influence with one person will cost you influence with another, because of differing circumstances, values, personalities< or world views.

Factors you can't control

But first, there are factors that give people influence, over which you will have little control:

Appearance: Studies show that people who are considered more attractive are more successful in life. (I've been successful, but I had to work extra hard to make up for this vicious type of discrimination!) Far more than 50% of presidential elections—though not all—have been won by the taller candidate. In 1960, people who heard the debate on radio rated Nixon the winner. People who saw it on TV thought Kennedy won—appearance counts. It's known that employers discriminate, often unconsciously, against obese candidates, thinking they are lazy, unmotivated and likely to be out sick a lot, despite little evidence for that bias. The best you can do here is to keep your appearance as presentable as possible, within the limits that Providence has provided for you.

Ethnic and Racial Heritage: Again, this can cut both ways. People are more likely to listen to "one of their tribe," (Marines in my case) than to those viewed as outsiders. People who are able to overcome this, and treat other folks as individuals, awarding trust or caution based on individual merit, rather than as members of a group, have lives that are richer and more successful—and this all gives them more influence. But even for the best folks, this always remains a challenge, as I don't believe any person is free of biases in this area. Every culture has such biases and children are inculcated with them and must fight to rise above the bias. Changing your ethnic heritage is harder than changing your shirt. There was a perennial city council candidate in Boston who decided he was losing elections because he had an Italian name, so he had it legally changed to an Irish sounding name. He was soundly and appropriately defeated in the next election, as both groups voted against him for obvious reasons.

Age: Some people and cultures view older folks as wise and experienced (and we are—witness this essay), giving them more influence. Others view them as out of touch and unable to adapt. (And we are—I'm having a struggle using Word 10 on my wife's laptop as I write this. Curse you, Bill Gates!) You cannot change your age, but if you are young, you can work to present a more mature appearance. If you dress like a kid, you'll be treated like a kid. And if you are older than dirt, which according to Google is 22 months younger than I am, you can work to keep in shape and dress more up to date. This was always a challenge for someone like me, because my wardrobe has come mostly from places like Goodwill for years. I recently told my brother I had picked up a couple of sweater vests there. "Hang on to them," he said, "They may come back in!" I tend to be the non-conformist in the family, wearing what I like, but it hasn't always helped my career or my ability to project influence.

Religion: You can, of course, change your religion. But if you did so to exert influence, or do better in your career, I think you'd get the same results as the faux Irish candidate I mentioned. And I'm not sure God would approve. Still, religion is a tribe thing too. People are more likely to trust "one of our own," than "one of them." And in many places, they are still killing "them." But there is a reason that so many of Bernie Madoff's victims were coreligionists. As with ethnic heritage, working to rise against your biases in this area (including those who have a secular bias against the religious) is not only the right thing to do, but will pay dividends in a better life, more success and expanded influence. Still, if you want to loath Jihadist extremists who murder gays, young girls and their coreligionists who hold slightly divergent doctrines, or to despise members of the Westboro Baptist Church, who spew vileness at soldiers' funerals, who am I to gainsay you?

Gender and Sexual Orientation: Without repeating much of what is covered above, people have preprogrammed biases in these areas, for or against. Remember that individuals matter, not group membership. (I follow a couple of gay, conservative Republicans on Twitter.) Serving in the Marines and the Senate, I absorbed the lesson that there are good, honest, decent people in every ethnic, gender, age, political orientation, and religious category. And there are bums in every category. Judge individuals by their character and abilities. Otherwise, you cut yourself off from many interesting, talented, and good people, a loss to your life.

Factors you can develop

Since I'm taking the time to write this, the least you can do is become highly proficient in each of these areas in, say, the next month. I haven't over almost 68 years, of course, but my failings are no excuse for you. The fact is that no one is close to perfect in any of these areas, and no one is likely to be above the 50th percentile in a majority of them. Perfection is impossible to achieve or even define. But constant improvement is in the reach of every person and every organization.

In most of these areas you wouldn't make the effort to improve just to become more influential. But all of them will pay dividends in your career, family and social life—while increasing your ability to be a positive influence on others.

The Marines' "Traits of a Leader"

The stronger you are in each of these areas, the more other people will respect and admire you, increasing both your success and your influence. Keep in mind that they will have to be applied differently in different situations and for different people. One size does not fit all. Perhaps the three people who have influenced me the most in my life are my Marine Drill Instructors from Platoon 273 at Parris Island in 1964, Sergeants William H. Harris, Michael P. Martin, and the late Ezekiel Owens, Jr., who I was distressed to learn had been transferred to Marine Security Guard, Heaven on December 16, 2013. The self-discipline they gave me has been the source of my success in life, and they have been with me every day for 50 years. But "tact," from the list below, didn't seem to have a high priority with them that I can recall.

And, of course, there are others who have had a great influence on my life, using different approaches and traits: my parents and other relatives, teachers like Ben Mark, my high school economics teacher, John McLaughlin , a college history and government professor, colleagues in government and association management, Marine officers, two former pastors, Alison Bucklin, DMinn and Rev. John Zingaro, and my current one, Rev. Jeff Vanden Heuvel, fiction writers like Robert Heinlein and Tom Kratman, and writers like the brilliant economics professors Dr. Thomas Sowell and Dr. Walter Williams. (Note that Rev. Jeff influences me in religion, not so much in politics, where we hold divergent world views and values. The lesson is that different folks are influences in different areas.)

All these people influenced me in positive ways, in different ways and using different factors. And of course, I learned a lot about leadership and exerting influence from bad examples like the NCOs I mentioned above or political or management colleagues who lacked ethics, tack and much else. When I have a dilemma, I often ask myself, "What would Sergeant R. do?" Then I know what not to do.

People who have these traits have influence over others. So, here we go.

Justice: If you treat people unfairly, or differently due to the biases already discussed, the folks discriminated against will lose respect for you, diminishing your influence. Oddly, so will many of the folks discriminated in favor of, because you will have revealed your character. The same will apply if you have "teacher's pets" in a classroom or at work who get special treatment based on their likeability, attractiveness or what they can do for you. Being "just" pays dividends for you, for other folks and for the organization—which doesn't mean it's easy, just right.

Judgment: They say good judgment comes from experience and experience comes from bad judgment. Wise people learn from their mistakes, but the really wise learn from observing the mistakes of others, and avoiding making them in their own lives. If you know someone does drugs, steals, loses jobs by inappropriate behavior, smokes, drives recklessly or makes frequent bad, even if small decisions, will they have much influence over you in other areas?

Dependability: If you don't show up when you are supposed to, don't keep your word or honor your promises, don't complete tasks you accept, and let people down, you will not have credibility or influence with them. Everyone drops the ball sometimes, but some people couldn't hold the ball if it was made of glue.

Initiative: Who will have the most influence at work—the person who does just enough to get by and does only what he is told, or the person who seeks out new ways to do things better, takes on new responsibilities without being ordered to, and finds ways to help colleagues and the team without being asked? And who will have a better job in five years?

Decisiveness: Not making a decision is a decision—usually the worst one. And if you wait until you have every bit of information to make a perfect decision, it's very likely too late. Yes, hasty decisions can be disastrous, but no decision can be worse, and will destroy your credibility and influence in the bargain. The trick is balance. See judgment, above.

Tact: Compare this approach: You say to your wife, "Sea World called—they want you for the whale act," or to your husband, "We got a notice from the Post Office—they've assigned your beer gut with its own Zip Code." With this one, "Honey, I'm getting a little concerned that our diets may be having a negative impact on our health. I'd like to keep you around for a while and me with you. What say we look into eating healthier?" Which would be most likely to influence your snuggle bunny and have positive benefits? Unfortunately, many folks can't see how tactless they are, or don't care. The funny thing is, they are often the same people who make a hobby out of being perpetually offended by small, perceived slights.

Integrity: Few things will destroy your standing in the eyes of others, and thus your credibility and ability to influence them like having folks discover that you play the edges. I once took over an association, with hidden financial problems, where the executive before me used to take one of the two or three favored staff members (out of 14—see "justice," above) out to lunch at a very expensive restaurant about twice a week, on the association's dime for "team building.". The deficit didn't stop him from treating himself royally in other ways, too. It was a "turn-around" situation, which I had not detected, because the board didn't know and the books had been at least warmed over. Imagine the influence he had with the staff who knew what was going on, but had to keep their heads down with the boss and board. Not the least of the problems was the chaos and infighting created through such policies. It was a difficult fix, but they survived. I've never been able to spend other people's money lavishly, on myself or fancy items that were not mission-critical. My frugality has been a running joke in some of the associations I managed, but my ability to influence the boards on fiscal policy was always high.

Enthusiasm: Compare, "I don't know if this is going to fly—we'll do the best we can and let the chips fall where they may," with, "We are so going to nail this—I'm just delighted to be working with this team because this project is going to have a huge impact on our organization!" Who will have the most career success, the most influence on coworkers and be the happiest at work? This applies, again, to the other parts of your life as well.

Bearing: "Bearing" is how you carry and present yourself, and it seems to come naturally to some folks. The rest of us have to work on it, but people with bearing exude confidence, and thus have more influence on others. When I was in the Marine Reserves, I was at an Army base and a guy asked me, "Where'd you get that tee shirt, Marine?" I told him, then, since it wasn't a USMC shirt, I asked how he knew I was a Marine. "By your bearing," he said. I walked around for the rest of the training period like someone gave me a medal. So he surely had an influence on me—that was in 1979!

Unselfishness: Self-centered people have little influence and suffer for it, because other folks don't care that much about them in return. Other-centered folks have great influence on others because they care. (See doctors, nurses and health techs, Madison VA hospital, for excellent examples.) Put the needs of your family, friends, coworkers and especially subordinates first, and your needs will be taken care of. Share the credit for success and take more of the blame for failure yourself. Suppose I asked the board of my association for a 10% raise and for a 3% raise for the rest of the staff? Do you think they would not know? Or that they would work extra hard to make me look good and to make the organization thrive, to my career benefit more than theirs? Would I be able to influence their performance? The big hog at the trough is seldom respected by the piglets.

Courage: We think of physical courage, which in mostly-safe America we are seldom called on for. We have police, firefighters, EMTs and troops on the parapets of freedom for that. (Freedom is not free, but the U.S. Marine Corps will pay most of your share. --Captain J.E. "Ned" Dolan.) But moral courage is always needed and too often in short supply. If you pass the blame for your mistakes and duck challenging the boss on a hot issue, coworkers will not respect you—and your influence will decline. If you stand up, you might lose your job, of course, especially if the boss hasn't read this, but you'll retain your self-respect—and your influence with others.

Knowledge: My surgeon, Dr. Jim Maloney, is highly respected, has a great success rate and presents to and trains new doctors. He told me he was undecided on a certain procedure, and I said, "Doc, if you added all I know about lungs to what you know, we wouldn't know any more. I have unlimited faith in you. You look at it and use your best judgment—I'm fine with that." Sure, there may be problems beyond anyone's control, which is why the five-year survival rate on lung transplants is 50%. But his reputation, skill, and knowledge gives him great influence with me. And not only in his field, but because of his intellect, I'd listen carefully to his opinions on other areas. Of course, you have to be careful of "bright guy" disease, as I called it in an article, where the successful person in one field comes to think he knows more than professionals in other fields. That diminishes his influence. There's a difference between knowledge and narcissism.

Loyalty: If your wife finds out you have a girlfriend, your boss finds out you've been bad-mouthing the organization, your friend finds out his wife is your girlfriend, and your coworker finds out you took credit for his work, you might have a funeral—but not much influence.

Endurance: Though partly the luck of the gene pool draw, everyone can build up their endurance, because as with most things, attitude and mental toughness is 80% of the battle. I had pulmonary fibrosis for six years. For the last three, I pulled an oxygen tank behind me to work—and everyplace else. It got especially challenging when my lungs took a big hit six months before I retired. But in the last ten years, though I was out for doctors' appointments and tests, I didn't miss a day because I felt too bad to work. (Thank you, Sergeant Owens.) That I had the endurance to persevere gave me added respect and influence with colleagues and my bosses.

Other Influence-Enhancing Factors

Example: Albert Schweitzer said, "Example is not the main thing in influencing others. It is the only thing." I don't agree it's "the only thing," but it may be the most important thing. Not to belabor the point, but see the numerous examples of the different impact created by the good and bad examples presented above. If you don't set the example, people are unlikely to be influenced by what you say.

Communication Skills: Having strong writing and verbal skills, thus being able to express yourself clearly (so the average person can understand) and concisely (I know—my communication weakness!) is a priceless career advantage for most people. And it's hard to have influence if folks don't understand your points. Presentation can make all the difference. Going through the transplant process, we became close to a black couple from Louisiana, John and Donna Payne. John is a brother Marine who saw a lot more action in Vietnam than I wanted to see. His new lung came through five days before mine and he's doing very well. (Update--We lost John on June 2, 2016)

Donna retired as a CNA and CNA Supervisor, where she worked in a mental hospital. One of the patients was an old southerner who had slipped off the rails. His racism had intersected with his mental disability, and vile slime spewed from him—I won't repeat what she told me. Donna was the only staff member willing to work with him. Finally she said to him, "You know the difference between you and me? I've got the keys. (Cue dangling keys.) I get to go home at night, while you have to stay here. And you will until your attitude changes." And his attitude slowly changed. "By the time he left, we were the best of friends," she said. She found a way to calmly influence him in a way that helped him and, one hopes, everyone he came into contact with. She's a no-nonsense person, but she's other-centered, cares about people, forgives the unforgivable, has courage and good judgment, and has great communication skills. This gives her lots of influence. Both John and Donna have influenced me to want to be more like them, because the of the example they set.

Stature and Status: People who have high status because of career, celebrity, money or family usually have more influence, though they often squander it by acting like jerks. I would not suggest that you try to increase your influence by becoming famous or prominent, but if your goal is high success, it might be an interesting byproduct. I come from a middleclass family of great lack-of-wealth. When I wanted to get into politics, folks thought I was aiming too high running for the state senate for my first campaign. On the other hand, Teddy Kennedy was elected to the US Senate never having held a job, but his family was in the wealthy one-percent folks now complain about—unless they agree with them politically. And it didn't hurt that his brother was President.

When I became a candidate, people were more likely to listen to my opinions, and I influenced a slim majority to vote for me. (Some folks my opponent influenced to vote against him.) Once I was a senator, people sought out my opinions on government, politics and policy. Public office gave me influence.

The problem is that the public is often so over-awed that they are influenced by famous people with limited credentials, experience, or knowledge on a variety of subjects outside their fields, who are often wrong but always convinced. I would likely be influenced by a pro football player's views on going for it on fourth down, or if I cared about such things, a famous entertainer's thoughts on pop music or current movies, but if I wanted foreign policy input, I'd go to Dr. Condi Rice, or if on economic policy to the nationally known economists Dr. Thomas Sowell or Dr. Walter Williams. But since famous, wealthy and high status folks often have undeserved influence in areas where they have limited knowledge or credentials, we must be aware of the fact.

Hopefully, this essay has impressed you enough that it increased my influence with you. Maybe it decreased it. But influence is never static—it waxes and wanes daily. Like any asset, guard it carefully and spend it wisely.

A Lung for Christmas
(Publlished as: Local VA helped extend my life)
May 25, 2014

I had a right lung transplant Dec. 23, 2013 through the Veterans Administration hospital. So I took more than academic interest in your May 15 article "Two new lungs mean new lease on life."

Like Seth Melde, I believe without the transplant I'd be dead now because my pulmonary functioning was failing fast. But the excellent article missed some valuable points.

While diseases such as cystic fibrosis and emphysema require a double lung, my problem was pulmonary fibrosis. PF patients can do very well with a single lung because PF does not spread to the new lung.

PF is not smoking related — my next cigarette will be my first. Pulmonary fibrosis kills as many people as breast cancer each year but gets only a fraction of the research funding.

Lung transplants are extremely complex, with thousands of variables, many beyond the medical team's control or understanding. Going in, the UW pulmonologist warned me 20 percent don't survive the first year — and that even if I did everything right, I could be in that group.

I did great the first six weeks and was climbing 10 flights of stairs a day. Unfortunately, my new lung has developed "issues," so I'm back on oxygen and breathing very hard with limited exertion.

I have been back in the Veterans Hospital twice for three more surgeries through a bronchoscopy and also for pneumonia, and I am scheduled for more. It now looks like, through the luck of the draw, there's at least a 50 percent chance I will fall into the 20 percent who don't survive a year. (Update: I came very close to the edge the day after this was published, but thanks to prayer, Parris Island and the VA, I pulled through. I have been off oxygen since August of 2014, and as of this book still have complications but am doing okay.)

But I and everyone at the VA are still in there pitching. I stress this is no one's fault — these things happen.

Regardless, I know that at 68 (now 70), I've lived longer than 99 percent of the people ever born. Because I was born in a modern, free-market society, I've lived better than 99 percent as well. So I have no complaints if I'm not able to stretch to 99.2 percent!

I read in the *State Journal* every day of people who are less fortunate that me.

There is no chance for a second lung transplant. The prognosis would be poor at my age, and lungs are in short supply. Many people die on the waiting list. This underlines the need for more folks to list as organ donors.

Getting a lung or lungs depends on your evaluation score. The trick is to be sick enough to get to the top of the list, then to hang on and be well enough for the operation if the right lung comes along. If they don't get a match in blood type and size, in time your score won't matter.

I've been reading a lot of bashing of VA health care due to the Arizona situation.

I can only speak for myself, but the care I have received at the Veterans Hospital and UW in Madison as I went through the lung transplant process has been beyond superb. There is no medical professional there, from the surgeons and other doctors to the nurses and assistants who I would not want to care for me or a loved one in the future.

I hope the community recognizes what a great resource we have in these providers.

In addition to becoming an organ donor, the VA needs volunteers. They say that "freedom is not free." At the VA, you can help folks who paid most of your share.

Published in the *Wisconsin State Journal*. A version was also published in the *Philadelphia Inquirer*.

Eight Books Every Presidential Candidate Should Read. (But won't.)

Advice to War Presidents by Angelo Codevilla

If they would read it, I'd be delighted to buy copies of this well-researched book for President Obama, Secretary Clinton and all the GOP Contenders. It's a must read for officials and everyone interested in foreign policy. It can hardly be described as a liberal or conservative book. Dr. Codevilla eviscerates all sides for their blunders and lack of seriousness: Bush and the "Neo-cons," the CIA, Kissinger and the "Realists," and every liberal internationalist from Wilson on. After reading it you will never again put complete faith in what the CIA or FBI says it "knows." He uses historical examples from ancient Greece to the War of Terror to illustrate his points. There is something here to offend every viewpoint. Some Quotes: "For European Governments and the U.S. State Department, calling a conference is the 'school solution' to any problem." (P-86) " Today as ever, in public life as in private, leaving no favor unrewarded and no offense unpunished is the key to respect and a rule of life that you neglect at your risk." (P-159) "Nor are the shopping malls and college campuses that characterize modern American 'consumer society' apt to produce the human capital of soldiers any more than of people to make and fix things. America's producers and soldiers come from the less favored parts of the economy, while the uncalloused hands and undisciplined habits at its apex are as foreign to making and fixing as fighting." There were things that made me uncomfortable and that I disagree with, but I'm willing to concede that the author has both more experience and has thought more deeply than I have about the subject. This is a book that will challenge your viewpoints and make you defend them. It may, and should, change your views of both war and statecraft.

The Hundred-Year Marathon: China's Secret Strategy to Replace America as the Global Superpower by Michael Pillsbury

This is a terrific but frightening book, well written and well documented. China places a very high strategic value on deception and making us believe they are weak and have no intentions of surpassing the US. He cites a Chinese proverb from the Warring States period that China's military and civilian leaders often use: Wai ru, nei fa--"On the outside, be benevolent. On the inside, be ruthless." He believes that all recent presidents--Republican as well as Democrat, have been fooled by the benevolent outside, as have most China experts, himself included until he started reading things he wasn't supposed to read. The book details how China has stolen technology and IP, built up it's cyber-attack forces, developed "Assassin's Mace" asymmetric weapons to counter our much more expensive weapons, and is working on all fronts to replace us. The military buildup, in their strategic thinking comes last, so as not to alert the "old Hegemon" to their intentions. Very scary read by one of the US government's leading China Experts for about 40 years. Pillsbury speaks and reads Mandarin, and has had access to top Chinese leaders, hawks as well as moderates, and Chinese defectors, as well as obscure books and documents that most westerners never get to see.

Cyber War: The Next Threat to National Security and What to Do About It by Richard A. Clarke, Robert Knake

This article was originally, "Seven Books Every Presidential Candidate Should Read." After reading this frightening book about the vulnerability of our military and economy, from the power grid to the financial structure, to cyber war, I added this book. Clarke is a recognized expert, and is not a partisan hack. He has served as an adviser to Reagan, the Bushes, Clinton and Obama on these topics. Though this was published in 2010, I've seen nothing to suggest we are less vulnerable today, and some articles suggesting we are more so. Worth reading, and not just by computer geeks.

Coming Apart: The State of White America, 1960-2010 By Charles Murray

Despite the subtitle, this is a book about class, not race. The author is looking at a lot of data that suggested the upper class that runs the country, which he calls the Narrow Elite and the Broad Elite, is increasingly wealthy, increasingly takes in both liberals and conservatives with high IQs and is increasingly isolated from the experience of the rest of America. He focuses on whites because that Narrow Elite is overwhelmingly white. He also focuses on the white lower class, so the comparison will not be between a white upper class and a minority lower class. He looks at a lot of data suggesting the white lower class is being destroyed by several trends: decreasing industriousness and ability to hold jobs among males, decreasing participation in civic organizations or churches, decreasing marriage rates, decreasing rates of trust and neighborliness, and sharply escalating non-marital birth rates, all trends that suggest the destruction of both happiness for these folks and what he calls the "American Project." Interestingly, after detailing the rolling disaster that is over-taking the white lower class, he presents data that suggest the minority lower class is not much different, contrary to what many might expect. This reinforces my long-held belief that race doesn't matter, culture matters a great deal. I do not think this is a "liberal" or a "Conservative" book. He says he is neither, but is a libertarian, rare among social scientists. He carefully points out in what I think is a balanced way how liberals or conservatives might draw differing interpretations from the data than he does.

The New Class Conflict by Joel Kotkin

I rate this excellent book as a "Must Read" for open-minded, intelligent people. (Not so much for polemists of the right and left who haven't entertained a thought beyond the current talking points of their "team" in years.) It is neither a liberal nor a conservative book--I can imagine Bernie Sanders and Ted Cruz sitting side by side in the library mining it for facts and talking points. Well and widely sourced (footnotes make up about 35% of the book) Kotkin quotes favorably from Marx and Elizabeth Warren among others on the left as well as many conservative thinkers. The book deals with the rise of a new oligarchy of tech billionaires and the clerisy who support them to replace the old oligarchy of energy and industrial barons. He goes into depth about the growth of income inequality and the decline of the middle and working classes in ways that will resonate with both progressives and conservatives. He spares neither party in his apportionment of responsibility for the current state of economic affairs. Kotkin weaves solid economic history from the fall of feudalism to the rise of the middle class into the narrative. Minds that are open to learning cannot fail to learn from this book. Some of the quotes that stuck with me: "Increasingly, American politics resemble not so much a rising democracy as an emerging plutocracy, with dueling groups of billionaires right and left determining most political choices." "Middle-class taxpayers have been transformed into unwitting underwriters of over $20 billion in bonuses paid out in 2013 by Wall Street." "The tax system penalizes the Yeomanry (his term for the low and middle income earners) but rewards the oligarchs." "In the absence of a focus on how to grow economies more rapidly and broadly, both political philosophies (liberal and conservative) fall short." I highly recommend this book to those with the cognitive ability to understand it, open minds, and a concern about the direction of this country.

Basic Economics by Thomas Sowell
I learned more from this book than any other book I have ever read--and I had economics in high school and it was covered in my college political science classes. Sowell is not only brilliant, but writes well for the average reader explaining concepts that can seem arcane. It has been translated into six languages and is a required text in economic courses on hundreds of campuses. If you don't understand basic economics you can do little good as you don't understand what is possible and what is wishful thinking.

Race & Economics: How Much Can Be Blamed on Discrimination? by Walter E. Williams
Dr. Williams, like Dr. Thomas Sowell, grew up poor and black (Williams in the Philadelphia projects) to become a nationally-known economist. They both have put a lot of focus on the intersection of economics, race and culture. This well researched and documented book contains his data-driven conclusions on the subject, and details how government interventions, sold as benign, have too often disadvantaged blacks and other minorities, while protecting white racists in unions and in the trades and professions. It also offers alternate possibilities for what is seen as racism which are thought provoking. I highly recommend it.

The Righteous Mind: Why Good People Are Divided by Politics and Religion. by Jonathan Haidt
I suppose the best compliment is that throughout this insightful and well-written book, I kept wishing the author was present so I could discuss, and often argue points with him. (And I suppose he was glad to be far away.) To be fair, many of the points I wanted to argue he addressed and resolved further on. Haidt is a self-described left-wing academic and atheist, though of Jewish heritage. He is a Kerry and Obama supporter, a bias he is very open about and references throughout this work. But he is also an intellectually honest man and—so rare on today's campuses—open to diversity of thought, the only kind of diversity that really matters. A "Moral Psychologist," Haidt makes a very solid academic research effort to understand the moral foundations of both conservative and liberal political thought, as well as why

religion is important in human societies. The book held my interest throughout. IT will be of great value to thinkers on both the right and the left of our political divide, who will gain understanding of why they hold the views they do, and why others hold different views. Shouters and haters, not so much.

Sowing the Wind: The Seeds of Conflict in the Middle East. **By John Keay.**
I've recommended this before, but given what is going on there, if you and Obama and Clinton haven't read it, now might be a good time. A broad look at an area we will be engaged with for a long time. This is an excellent one-volume history of the Middle East, from 1890 through the Suez crisis in 1956, with an epilog to bring us up to date. The catalog of crime and invasion, contention, execution and insurrection, siege and betrayal of Hashemite vs. Wahhabi, Sunni vs. Shia vs. Kurd vs. Turk, Allies vs. Ottomans, Britain vs. France, Zionists vs. Muslims, and other groups great and small would give a tourist pause, never mind a diplomat or soldier.

Published in the *American Thinker* November 7, 2015 (Updated with an additional book)

Fifteen Tips for Being the Indispensable Employee

Some employees are more valuable than others. And in this time of economic dislocation, the more valuable you are as an employee, the more likely you are to be retained.

Sorry if I've hurt your self-esteem and bruised your feelings. It hurts my feelings that the New England Patriots pay Tom Brady millions and won't even give me a try-out. Okay, so I'm a LOT older than Brady, in lousy shape compared to him, and lettered in chess in college. Every human being is unique and equally valuable, right?

No. Tom Brady fills the stands and puts millions of fans in front of the TV on Sunday, providing an excellent return on investment for his large salary. The only entertainment value I'd provide would be for the lynch mob of fans hunting me after my first appearance on the field.

However valuable you may be to your family and friends, that doesn't make you valuable to an employer.

All employers need employees who provide value. Those who provide the most value are the least likely to be cut in a downsizing, and the most likely to receive raises and promotions, because the powers-that-be want to keep them around.

That's obvious, right? Then how come so many employees act like their job is a right, and that they must be catered to?

The really successful and valuable employees are always trying to make themselves indispensable. Here are fifteen tips on becoming the indispensable employee.

1. Commit yourself to constant improvement. Perfection doesn't exist, but every organization and every individual can be better tomorrow then they are today. Look at your job every Friday and ask yourself, "How can I do a better job next week?" Then do it.

2. Commit yourself to life-long learning. Take courses and read books and journals that will help you do better in your area of specialty. But, equally important, expand your horizon. Read widely in other areas as well. Study the field that your employer operates in, so you understand the customers/clients and their problems. Study the jobs of your colleagues, so you understand—and perhaps can help with—their problems. And study trends outside your industry that may impact the organization and the customers. Yes, you can't read or know everything. But you can always read and know more.

3. Banish, "That's not my job" from your vocabulary. Everything that helps advance the mission is your job. The more you contribute in other areas, the move valuable you will be.

4. Banish, "We've always done it that way" from your vocabulary. Nothing is more constant than change. I was ten years into my professional career before I had a computer, fifteen for a fax, over twenty for e-mail and the Internet. If I was still doing things the way I'd done them then, I'd be unemployable.

5. Avoid gossip, drama, and back-biting with your colleagues. It seems like every office has a Drama Queen or King, who is constantly involved in small feuds, has problems with colleagues, and is generally high maintenance. "You know who" has to

be tiptoed around. And the boss is dreaming about how nice life would be if only that person could be moved on. Don't let it be you.

6. Pitch in. Look for areas where you can help your colleagues with their challenges. Do more than your share, especially of the unpleasant tasks, the "dirty jobs," that are present in every employment situation. Don't work in a silo.

7. Banish Busy Work. Look for ways to be more efficient, so that time-consuming, repetitive work can be eliminated from your schedule. Can data-entry be computerized directly from the Web, or out-sourced overseas? Having lots of busy work to do doesn't make you valuable; it makes your job fungible. There is always more valuable work available to fulfill the organization's mission. Getting rid of busy work will allow the boss to assign you more valuable work.

8. Make the boss's life easier. What skills can you apply, what can you learn, what can you take on that will solve a problem for your supervisor? Solving a couple of the boss's problems every year will make you seem pretty indispensable.

9. Be the "Go To" employee. If there's a problem, and they think first of getting you to work on it, they won't think first of you if staff census needs to be cut.

10. Keep a cheerful attitude. Sure, we all have problems. But people don't like to work with those whose hobby seems to be whining and complaining. Your boss doesn't either.

11. Go the extra mile for the customers. Don't have to be pushed to do what needs to be done to keep the customer happy. When you provide out-standing customer service, the customers will mention it to your boss, who will appreciate you all the more.

12. Share the credit. When your supervisor says you did a great job on a project, saying, "Well, I couldn't have done it without Mary's research" reflects well on you, and makes you a star for Mary. Sincere compliments cost you nothing and mean a lot to your colleagues.

13. Don't try to outshine your colleagues. Say you have a great idea as to how the sales department could increase return sales. At a staff meeting, in front of everyone, you could pipe up and say, "Well, I think WE could have increased return sales by...." Or you can go to the Director of Sales privately and say, "I have an idea I was wondering if you'd thought about, that might help our return sales rate...." Which will serve you better in the long run?

14. It's your organization too. Yes, we are fond of saying, "It's the owner's business." But it's also your business. And not just your little piece. Take ownership. If your area is doing well, but your company is floundering...your area is NOT doing well. It's like folks on the Titanic saying, "Well, the BOW may have hit an iceberg, but we're nice and dry here in the STERN!"

15. Be the most dependable person around. Under-promise and over-perform. If you say you will do something, your supervisor should be comfortable forgetting about it, because she knows it will be done well, AND on time.

If you noticed, there is nothing on this list that you and I cannot do as well as Tom Brady. And following these rules will make you an indispensable employee.

Racism in America

The election in 2008 of a bi-racial president who self identified as black, and who was seen as black across the political spectrum from professional race mongers to white supremacists, held the golden promise of a post-racial America. The highest color barrier was broken. I was bemoaning what I feared would be Obama's destructive collectivist policies to a friend, a brilliant surgeon of centrist political leaning. He responded that there was a great upside--a black president could say things to the black community that a white one would be excoriated for, moving that part of lower-class black culture beyond the social pathologies and sense of victimhood that hurts blacks economically and socially to integration with mainstream cultural values that would advance blacks as other ethnic groups have advanced. (I paraphrase the conversation.)

Alas, the promise has proved to be a chimera. Beset by Republican and conservative attacks on his leadership, foreign policy, economic policy, healthcare policy, energy policy, broken promises, and his policy of growing government, it has proved far more effective for Obama, fellow Democrats and their media and academic allies to defend the administration by charging that all opposition is based on racism, rather than policy disagreements. The need to mobilize the base has produced a situation where political discourse is infected by race issues more than ever before. Rather than a post-racial society, the election of Barack Obama has created a hyper-racial society. His supporters say this is because of the racist attacks. Opponents, stung, react furiously, often over-reacting to their detriment. Attorney General Holder claims with a straight face that no president and no attorney general have been so badly treated, implying it is because of race, despite a simple Google search turning up numerous leftwing pictures of President Bush as a monkey, calling for him to be murdered, and equal or worse slanders of GOP Attorneys General. (http://www. zombietime.com/zomblog/?p=621)

But it is also true that, while the vast majority of criticism of the Obama administration I read is policy based, there is still a virulent streak of racism in some of the opposition to and dislike of Obama. People who read my blog assume that I will appreciate them and send me racist jokes and cartoons about him, or make snide references to, "That lawn-jockey in the White House." "I'm not racist--I hate his white half too," goes around frequently. They are not only morally repugnant, but stupid, as they provide ammunition to his defenders who wish to picture all opposition to Obama's policies as racist.

Blacks are mobilized by convincing them that both they and President Obama, and they are being held back only by racism. Environmentalists are mobilized by anti-job green programs. Political contributors like Solyndra's investors by government payouts. Government unions by generous benefits. The poor by Obama-phones and Obamacare. Teachers by killing the right of poor black parents to send their kids to charter schools or other good schools through vouchers. But worse is the culture of deliberate victimization created in black people, who are taught that only big government can help them. In my view, nothing is more destructive of black futures than creating the disincentive to do anything on their own. And as Obama's poll numbers have fallen, the charges get increasingly shrill, with every policy criticism being discovered to be a hither-to-unknown racial code word, along with the claim that an America where more white people voted for Obama in 2008, than voted for Kerry in 2004 or Gore in 2000, is a hopelessly racist society.

Thug is now a racist code word. I always thought of the Klan, the skinheads and the Aryan Nation as thugs, and I'm not aware they have strong diversity programs.

Race is no longer an issue, a concern, or a problem. Stripped of spin by both sides, it is now just one more tool politicians of every stripe use to fustigate the opposition in the pursuit of power. I'm sorry to say that, in my view, the NAACP is no longer a civil rights group, just another Democrat Party special interest group like teachers, trial lawyers, or government union employees, supporting the party line in hopes of largess regardless of the impact on blacks, just as Republican special interest groups support the GOP in hopes of a payoff. (Some, of course, support both sides!) I hate that they have made me feel this way, because, as Thomas Sowell points out, the NAACP has done great service for black Americans in the past. (*Ethnic America*) But now they have, for example joined the Democrats condescending and racist view that blacks, not being as smart or competent as whites, can't get photo IDs. Nothing is as ironic as the NAACP requiring blacks to have photo IDs to get into a rally in North Carolina to protest photo IDs for voting, because blacks can't get photo IDs. . (See "NAACP requires marchers protesting North Carolina voter ID law To Show Photo ID") Republicans also have special interest groups as part of the base, organized for the same reason--obtaining power to obtain favors. We all belong to several such groups. I'm a senior, veteran, home owner, etc.

We are often told that we need to have "a conversation about race." Increasingly, these "conversations" consist of liberals shouting "racist" at any conservative who dares to criticize Obama, and conservatives shouting infectively back, "Am not! Some of my best friends..." Race is not something to discuss, but to beat down the opposition with. It is hard to find people, especially across the color line, with whom there is enough trust and good feelings to allow you to openly and dispassionately discuss race. Except, of course, when the other folks are already known to share your views on these issues. Then it's an echo chamber, not a conversation.

This made a recent conversation on race I had with two black friends both remarkable and memorable.

Going through the lung transplant process at the Madison VA, we became close to a black couple, John and Donna Payne. John is a brother Marine who saw a lot more action in Vietnam than I wanted to see. They are from Louisiana, so were stuck in a hotel here in Madison without a car. We started taking them shopping, out to eat and for drives. I would have wanted to help a fellow Marine in any case, but we quickly came to like and know them, then, it's not too strong to say, to love them as family. They are different folks from us, but very bright, good conversationalists, well spoken, hard working, and very good people who are right with God. There's not a lie in either one and I think they'd starve before they'd steal, I would trust them with anything.

John once told me, "Bob, if you don't forget, you can't forgive."

I said, "I know John, but there is a lot I have trouble letting go of."

"'Well, Bob, you're not hurting them, only yourself." I replied I was going to ask God to make me as good a person as he was--but maybe not yet!

John was drafted in the Marine Corps, put in the infantry, lost a lot of "the best platoon anyone could ask for" and mourns those fallen brothers, black and white, every day. He has the Purple Heart and scars to prove he was there. And he's still a patriotic American, despite the war and the racism he dealt with growing up in the South in that era. "Bob, there's a lot wrong with America," he said. "But if you don't like it here, if it's not working for you, why wouldn't you go somewhere else to live?" There were a lot of racial incidents in the service in the 1960s, but John confirmed what other combat vets say; the animosity and occasional violence were in the rear areas, often out of Vietnam on Okinawa or in the states. Out on the front lines, there were only your brothers, regardless of color, and the bad guys trying to kill you every day.

John likes big bands, John Wayne movies and cowboy novels; not much to feed a stereotype there. And if I had candid photos of Donna's face when he was singing country songs on Karaoke Night, I could market them for home decorations at a good price.

His new lung came through five days before mine and he's doing very well, so much so that they returned to Louisiana, alas to rebuild their home which burned a few days before they left. But at least they were not in the fire, and no one was hurt. We miss them and talk frequently. (Update: We lost John on June 2, 2016)

A week or so after my lung transplant, Donna came to visit me in the hospital while John was impressing them in physical therapy with Marine determination. In the course of the conversation, I asked her about racism when she grew up in the South. Having the comfort level to discuss race with her and John was a gift. She told me that a cross was burned on her lawn when she was five. I know worse things happen ever day, but this happened to a person I care about, when she was a child. It made me tear up--but then, a lot of things did then with the drugs I was on.

Klan thugs used to sit in a car at the end of her street to monitor the white people consorting with blacks, who needed reminding of the way things were, and to see what was going on. Nails were thrown in the driveway to give them flat tires.

She had a white great grandfather, whose genes show up. One family-born cousin has blue eyes and blond hair. Needless to say, this does not mollify the racists.

"Bob," she said. "You have to understand. This was just the way it was for us. I hold no animosity."

"That's okay," I said. "I'll hold it for both of us."

She said she had lived in Chicago for five years, and preferred to live in the South. "You know who the racists are there, because they tell you. In Chicago, they're sneaky."

"Well, I lived in Chicago for five years too. That's not the only thing they are sneaky about!"

Like my wife, through ambition, self-education, ability and hard work, Donna held very responsible positions without the opportunity to earn a college degree. She retired as a CNA and CNA Supervisor, where she worked in a mental hospital. Her best story was about one of the patients, an old southerner who had slipped off the rails. His racism had intersected with his mental disability, and vile slime spewed from him. "I used to kill niggers like you," he told her. "And for all I know, he did," she said. Donna was the only staff member willing to work with him.

Finally she said to him, "You know the difference between you and me? I've got the keys. (Cue dangling keys.) I get to go home at night, while you have to stay here. And you will until your attitude changes." And his attitude slowly changed. "By the time he left, we were the best of friends," she said. She found a way to calmly influence him in a way that helped him and, one hopes, everyone he came into contact with. She's a no-nonsense person, but she's other-centered, cares about people, forgives the unforgivable, has courage and good judgment, and has great communication skills. This gives her lots of influence. Both John and Donna have influenced me to want to be more like them, because of the example they set.

We continued the conversation when John joined us another day. He talked about the Marine Corps and racism, as I said above. His best friend at home is white, so he is used to having relationships across the color line. He had to drop out of college to work after he married for the first time. Before he retired, he built a good career in the skilled trades, running a skiving machine. (Yeah, I didn't know what it was either. Wikipedia says, "The process is used instead of rolling the material to shape when the material must not be work hardened, or must not shed minute slivers of metal later which is common in cold rolling processes." I'm not good with hand work, poor fine motor skills, so I could not have competed with him. I ranked high in my electronics school class, but was probably the worst tech in the bunch when it came to actually fixing the radios. One can't help wondering, with their intellect, what a racially-level playing field would have done for their lives.

The conversation with Donna and John focused my thoughts on the problem of race in our society. With a BA in Government/Political Science (shouldn't it be a BS?) and a masters in history, I still do a lot of reading in economics, politics and history. Naturally the problem of race is entwined in all three areas.

But I began to think more deeply and read more widely, trying to get beyond the shouting points of the polarized political divide. When I decided it would help me focus by getting my thoughts in this essay, I began to compile the "For Further Reading" list of books and articles at the end of this essay. Unless noted, I have read all of them, and recommend them--which should not be taken to mean I agree with everything in them. In fact, many conflict on points, but the points are worth considering. Many of them are from my recent reading, but they go back as far as 8th grade for me. When I am drawing on one of them for a statement in this essay, I will put it thus: (*Book Title* or "Article Title").

I did not write this essay to convince you my views were correct, but to provide you with tools to think more deeply about these issues.

You will note that the nationally prominent black economists, Thomas Sowell, PhD and Walter Williams, PhD, feature heavily on this list, because their writing over the years has greatly influenced my thinking. I find their research impeccable, their opinions cogent and nuanced, and their thinking deeper than the polemics of either side.

Both men grew up poor, in the Jim Crow era, before affirmative action. Both overcame poverty and racism to work their way to doctorates in economics and became respected academics and well-published authors. (Despite a grounding in the subject, I learned more from Sowell's *Basic Economics*, which has been translated as a college text into six languages, than any other book I have ever read.) Both have devoted considerable research and effort to understanding the intersection of race and discrimination with economics, culture and politics. (*Race and Culture* and *Race and Economics*.) Their inspiring autobiographies are on the list. (*Up From the Projects* and *A Personal Odyssey*.)

I, too am a minority. I belong to two minority groups: Americans whose ancestors came from Britain, only 15% of the population in 1981, probably smaller now. (*Ethnic America*) and Germany (13%). And my grandmother claimed that granddad was one-quarter Cree, making me, if true, twice as native American as Sen. Elizabeth Warren. (As with Warren, there exists zero verification of grandmother's claim, perhaps because it was a family secret--race mixing wasn't bragged about a century ago!)

Despite my (snort) "minority status," I am a white, male, middleclass American. This makes me ineligible to talk about race in some eyes--silencing dissent is a popular sport on both the left and right. ("We're going to have a conversation about race--you shut up and listen!") It certainly means that Black, Asian, and Hispanic Americans are almost certain to have different, more intense views on the subject. In fact, everyone has different life experiences and world views, meaning that everyone sees these--like many issues--differently. I had a black friend and roommate at U-Mass, Joe Fergusson, who was devastated when Muhammad Ali lost to Joe Frazier in 1971. Since I couldn't care less about boxing, I asked him why. "Because Frazier is white folks idea of a good nigger," he replied. The distinction had escaped me. I had never thought of either one of them as being good or bad on race issues. Different experiences produce different perspectives. Joe held no racist animosities--but he had friends who didn't like me much and wondered why he was rooming with a white guy.

As a small digression, we must consider if anti-Semitism and Islamophobia are racist. My political answer is "Well, yes and no." No, because anyone can convert to Judaism or to Islam, in the latter case, simply by making the Declaration of Faith, "There is no god but Allah and Mohammad is his (final) prophet." But while it is an odd race you can voluntarily join, there is certainly a racist component and the affects of bias pretty much fit my definition of racism, below, and thus are morally repugnant. Certainly, Jews are a culture as well as a religion, and usually seen as a distinct ethnic group. (*Ethnic America*) And Anti-Semitism is deeply rooted within Islamic scripture. ("Islamic Anti-Semitism"). As to race, the majority of Muslims are third world people with skin color of various shades of brown. Islamophobia is certainly real--there are people who look at the daily murders carried out by Islamists since 9/11 and conclude that all Muslims are evil and should be expiated. But far more often, some Muslims cry "Islamophobia" to deflect criticism of that large percentage of Islamic Supremacists who wish to murder or subjugate all non-Muslims under Shari'a Law, just as some politicians cry "racism" to deflect criticism of their policies or conduct. The Islamists are not, in my view, close to a majority of Muslims, but they are a couple of orders of magnitude larger that that "tiny minority of extremists" their apologists depict them to be. Using Islamophobia to shield murderers does a huge disservice to Muslims most of all, as the vast majority of those murdered in the name of Allah are fellow Muslims. So I include both in my discussion of racism.

In fact, we talk about racism with no agreement as to what it is. For the purpose of this essay, I define "racism" this way. "Racism" is when someone holds a person in either contempt or higher esteem, or considers another person inferior or superior, or disparages or praises a person, or tries to disadvantage or advantage another person based on that person's membership in an ethnic group, rather than on the person's individual merit. Period, as our president might say.

It is just as racist for me to assume that someone is a good or smart person because of ethnicity as it is to assume the opposite, because it assumes inferiority on the part of other ethnicities. (Though you get few complains from those who benefit from that version of racism.)

Here's a little test to see what you think is racist (some you will recognize). Read the following quotations and decide which speakers are racists. All of them? Some of them? Or does it depend on who said it, not what was said?

1. The steady expansion of welfare programs can be taken as a measure of the steady disintegration of the Negro family structure over the past generation in the United States.

2. Now, let me talk about the Spanish people. You know I understand that they come over here against our constitution and cross our borders. But they're here and they're people – and I've worked side-by-side with a lot of them. Don't tell me they don't work, and don't tell me they don't pay taxes. And don't tell me they don't have better family structure than most of us white people. When you see those Mexican families, they're together, they picnic together, they're spending their time together, and I'll tell you in my way of thinking they're awful nice people. And we need to have those people join us and be with us.

3. Today, more than 150 years after the Emancipation Proclamation, more than 50 years after the end of Separate But Equal, when it comes to getting an education too many of our young people just can't be bothered. Today instead of walking miles every day to school they're sitting on couches for hours playing video games, watching TV instead of dreaming of being a teacher or lawyer or business leader they're fantasizing about being a baller or a rapper.

4. I want to tell you one more thing I know about the negro. When I go, went, go to Las Vegas, North Las Vegas; and I would see these little government houses, and in front of that government house the door was usually open and the older people and the kids…. and there was always at least a half a dozen people sitting on the porch. They didn't have nothing to do. They didn't have nothing for the kids to do. They didn't have nothing for the young girls to do. And because they were basically on government subsidy – so now what do they do? They abort their young children, they put their young men in jail, because they never, they never learned how to pick cotton. And I've often wondered are, they were better off as slaves, picking cotton and having a family life and doing things? Or are they better off under government subsidy? You know they didn't get more freedom, uh they got less freedom – they got less family

life, and their happiness -you could see it in their faces- they were not happy sitting on that concrete sidewalk. Down there they was probably growing their turnips – so that's all government, that's not freedom.

5. I'm talking about these people who cry when their son is standing there in an orange suit. Where were you when he was two? (clapping) Where were you when he was twelve? (clapping) Where were you when he was eighteen, and how come you don't know he had a pistol? (clapping) And where is his father, and why don't you know where he is? And why doesn't the father show up to talk to this boy? ... 50 percent drop out rate, I'm telling you, and people in jail, and women having children by five, six different men. Under what excuse, I want somebody to love me, and as soon as you have it, you forget to parent. ... Are you not paying attention, people with their hat on backwards, pants down around the crack. Isn't that a sign of something, or are you waiting for Jesus to pull his pants up (laughter and clapping). Isn't it a sign of something when she's got her dress all the way up to the crack...and got all kinds of needles and things going through her body. What part of Africa did this come from? ... Everybody knows it's important to speak English except these knuckleheads. You can't land a plane with "why you ain't..." You can't be a doctor with that kind of crap coming out of your mouth. ... These people are fighting hard to be ignorant. There's no English being spoken, and they're walking and they're angry. Oh God, they're angry and they have pistols and they shoot and they do stupid things. And after they kill somebody, they don't have a plan. Just murder somebody. Boom. ... Five or six different children, same woman, eight, ten different husbands or whatever, pretty soon you're going to have to have DNA cards so you can tell who you're making love to. ... What is it with young girls getting after some girl who wants to still remain a virgin. Who are these sick black people and where did they come from and why haven't they been parented to shut up? ...

6. What shall we do with the Negro? I have had but one answer from the beginning. Do nothing ... Your doing ... has already played the mischief ... If the apples will not remain on the tree of their own strength, if they are worm eaten at the core, if they are early ripe and disposed to fall, let them fall! I am not for tying or fastening them on the tree in any way, except by nature's plan, and if they will not stay there, let them fall. And if the Negro cannot stand on his own legs, let him fall also.

7. I was in the WATTS riot, I seen the beginning fire and I seen the last fire. What I seen is civil disturbance. People are not happy, people is thinking they did not have their freedom; they didn't have these things, and they didn't have them. We've progressed quite a bit from that day until now, and sure don't want to go back; we sure don't want the colored people to go back to that point; we sure don't want the Mexican people to go back to that point; and we can make a difference right now by taking care of some of these bureaucracies, and do it in a peaceful way.

8. We have got this tailspin of culture, in our inner cities in particular, of men not working and just generations of men not even thinking about working or learning the value and the culture of work There is a real culture problem here that has to be dealt with.

9. I'll have them niggers voting Democratic for two hundred years.

10. If you are taught bitterness and anger, then you will believe you are a victim.

You will feel aggrieved and the twin brother of aggrievment is entitlement. So now you think you are owed something and you don't have to work for it and now you're on a really bad road to nowhere because there are people who will play to that sense of victimhood, aggrievment and entitlement, and you still won't have a job.

11. I ceased to advertise my mother's race at the age of twelve or thirteen, when I began to suspect that by doing so I was ingratiating myself to whites.

12. ... it bothers me that the America I know and love I feel like is being destroyed by a black man.

13. The purpose of the American Baby Code shall be to provide for a better distribution of babies... and to protect society against the propagation and increase of the unfit. ... Give dysgenic groups [people with "bad genes"] in our population their choice of segregation or [compulsory] sterilization. ... Birth control must lead ultimately to a cleaner race.

14. Uncle Sam has developed a sophisticated poverty plantation, operated by a federal government, overseen by bureaucrats, protected by media elites, and financed by the taxpayers. The only difference between this plantation and the slave plantation of the antebellum South is perception.

15. President Obama "does not even have the basic appearances of a human being. . . . It would be perfect for Obama to live with a group of monkeys in the world's largest African natural zoo and lick the bread crumbs thrown by spectators."

The speakers: 1. Daniel Patrick Moynihan, liberal Democrat US Senator. 2. Cliven Bundy, Nevada Rancher who became a flashpoint between the right and left over a dispute with the BLM. 3. Michelle Obama. 4. Cliven Bundy. 5. Bill Cosby. 6. Frederick Douglas, freed slave and black statesman in the Civil war era. 7. Cliven Bundy. 8. Rep. Paul Ryan, R-WI. 9. Attributed to President Lyndon Johnson in Inside the White House, but disputed. 10. Condaleeza Rice (Un-sourced--quoted from a speech on November 5, 2012.) 11. Barack Obama, *Dreams From My Father*. 12. Dr. Carol Swain, (a black) professor of law and political science at Vanderbilt Law School. 13. Margaret Sanger, founder of Planned Parenthood. (See Reading List for most sources.) 14. Star Parker, black writer, in *Uncle Sam's Plantation*. 15. North Korea's Central News Agency.

I'm not going to tell you which quotes I think are racist. In fact, in some cases, I'd have to know a lot more about the speaker's views to make up my mind. For many people, these statements will be racist or not depending on who made them. It's not what was said, but by whom. The short media sound-bites here are not enough to reveal it in many cases. I present it to help you think about the gradations of racism and thought that can be so described.

Below are more quotes from Blacks that might be considered racist if made by Whites. Some reflect Rep. Paul Ryan, though they rightly focus on both the pathologies in the black inner city community and in white lower class America as well. (*Coming Apart*.)

"I don't think it's about more gun control. I grew up in the South with guns everywhere and we never shot anyone. This [shooting] is about people who aren't taught the value of life." --Samuel L. Jackson, Actor.

"So not only are women 'easier,' they have become well-conditioned to take care of a guy; be the bread winner.... Now I'm not getting after men who are stay at home fathers or those who have made the decision to support their wife's career. I'm talking about the Liberal guys who connive to have a woman take care of them; they wear that like a badge of honor.." --Kevin L Jackson, Blogger

"The government is not your salvation. The government is not your road to prosperity. Hard work, education will take you far beyond what any government program can ever promise." --Mia Love, Black Mayor and GOP Congress Woman. (More quotes from her: http://www.brainyquote.com/quotes/authors/m/mia_love.html)

It is, if course, more politically effective for liberals to use the media to dismiss all policy criticism as coming from racist (if from whites) or from Uncle Toms (if from blacks). Shouting "racist" or "Uncle Tom" has immediate impact. Paul Ryan allowed himself to be boxed in ("Paul Ryan Laments Inner-City Culture Of Not Working") by using "inner city," which liberals pounced on as a "racial code word," despite evidence that lower class whites have the same pathologies in the city (See "Fishtown" in *Coming Apart: The State of White America, 1960-2010*). Discussing policy results for real people in depth takes nuance, time and reveals trade offs of both positive and negative results. It is hard to enflame the base with that. The conservatives, of course, have their own shouting points to stir up support without going into depth.

Though I grew up white and rather sheltered from race issues, I have seen racism. For about eight of my twelve years of school, I was in racially-mixed schools. But they were segregated as well, in that black and white kids tended to hang together and have little to do with the other group. In 6th grade, however, we had a teacher, Mr. Miller, who was a snide jerk. One day he ripped into Eddie Bink, a nice, quite black kid who had not done his homework. (Neither had I!). Eddie gave Mr. Miller the same excuse that the teacher--a nasty piece of work who loved to trick us on tests--had just praised a white "teacher's pet" kid for, lauding his honesty. I don't think I knew the word racism then, but I knew that's what it was. I ran into Eddie that summer at a local shopping center. Miller had failed him. I think that Eddie was at least average bright, and with a family focused on education, and some opportunity, would have been at least an average student. Miller missed a great opportunity to be a mentor in favor of pettiness. Worse things have happened in this world, but I felt bad for Eddie, and it stuck with me.

Also in 6th grade, two large black girls a few years older took a hate to me, and whomped on me three or four times, once sticking a pin in my leg. Uncomfortable, but no real harm done. Their lightening hit and run raids would have made Guderian green with envy. As far as I know, I had never exchanged a word or glance with them, and I assumed they were just beating on a white kid. I suspect now they mistook me for some kid who had offended them. The attacks stopped. Not everything can be explained by racism, though first appearances may suggest it when you are the "victim."

Joining the Marines in 1964, at age 18, was my first real experience of living with black people--and of overt racism in the south. When I went home for Christmas leave that year, we had to change busses in Rocky Mount, NC. Since there was a layover, I hefted my sea bag to grab a hamburger in the snack bar. There I discovered I was invisible.

The waitress passed me by several times, not even noticing my wave. Other patrons came in after me and were served. It took about five minutes for the penny to drop. Every other person in the snack bar, waitresses, cook and customers, was black. I was white. Quietly I picked up my bag and slid out. On the other side of the bus station was a very large, very modern restaurant with a larger menu--and white help and customers. I had my burger and fumed inside that I was going to come back with some black Marines and bust up the place. Of course, I never got to that backwater again.

One of the reasons I was so incensed was because of Sergeant Ezekiel Owens, the first of three black men who were mentors in my life, and who had a profound effect on me for the better.

The morning we arrived at Marine boot camp Parris Island, we took some tests. Then three hard-looking Marines in Smokey Bear hats came in, stared at us for a minute, then began screaming, "Get Outside, GET OUTSIDE!"

While in high school, a classmate who had a cousin in the Marines had told me there was only one black DI on Parris Island, and he was the worst, toughest, SOB on the island. And one of my DI's was black. Ah, hell, I thought, just my luck.

It turned out to be a myth. Most platoons had at least one black DI, I assume by design to avoid charges that the many nasty things that happened were based on race. Actually, they treated all of us equally as badly as possible. And Sergeant Ezekiel Owens, Jr., our black DI, was the easiest-going of the three. We'd get him laughing at our ineptitude and his tough-guy image would slip. Owens' favorite name for recruits was "Goony Bird," which was almost a compliment compared to the other things we were called. Thanks to the priceless gift of self-discipline that Sgt. Owens, Sgt. Harris and Sgt. Martin gave me, I've had a very successful and happy life, and I can never pay that debt. It is hard to believe that we only spent three months with them. As I type, it was 50 years ago, and the many incidents and lessons are clear in my mind. But I can't tell you what I had for lunch today.

I suppose it is a stereotype, but the black DIs usually had the best sing-song marching cadence, and once we learned right foot from left, we loved to march with Owens calling the beat. Yes, Owens thumped me a few times, entirely against regulations, and at risk to his career. But not brutally and not unless I deserved it. Called into court, I would have testified under oath in the face of video evidence and a hundred nuns testifying to the contrary that it never happened.

A few years ago, I located Sgt. Owens through the Internet.(Guys named "Ezekiel" are not thick on the ground.) He was a retired Gunnery Sergeant and had a locksmith business outside Camp Lejeune. He'd had several platoons as a DI, with 70 or 80 "goony Birds" in each, and there was--deliberately--nothing memorable about me. But I told him that I owed every success in my life to him and to Sergeants Harris and Martin. I kept in touch, added him to my Holiday Newsletter list, and sent him copies of two of my books, *Old Jarhead Poems* and *Eddie Grabowski's Gift,* which were dedicated to him and four other Marines. Last Christmas, his newsletter came back. I was in the hospital from my lung transplant, but thinking he had moved, I did an Internet search, and was distressed to find his obit. He died December 16, 2013, at the age of 73. I'm thankful I had the opportunity to tell him how much he meant to me. I will always grieve and always be grateful to him. In the obit, I learned his friends called him "Zeke." To me he was always "Sir" and always will be. So, okay, he thumped me--he's beyond their reach now. Semper Fidelis, Sergeant Owens--he taught me that, too. Go with God, Sir--*Kyrie Eleison.*

The second Black Marine who had a profound influence on me was Staff Sergeant Russell. I regret I don't know his first name--we were not equals.

After a year at Radio Relay tech school, I was assigned to an artillery battery at Camp Lejeune, which had no Radio Relay gear--go figure. They were using me as a forward observer. Calling fire missions was fun (as long as no one was shooting back!), but I was fast losing the little I knew about Radio Relay. The outfit was going on a six-month cruise of the Caribbean, but I got out of that. I volunteered for Vietnam. The Colonel figured I was nuts, but gave me corporal stripes as a going away present.

On Okinawa, they put me with a Radio Relay Platoon in a rear supporting unit, probably to learn Radio Relay again. Unfortunately, it was, in my opinion, also a dumping ground for poor NCOs. The Lieutenant was good, but there were several layers of worthless NCOs between him and the troops. That included the gunnery sergeant, the white staff sergeant, and one of the sergeants. The other sergeant was toxic as well as worthless, but a great example. I have rarely had a personnel problem in my career that I didn't ask myself, "What would Sergeant R. do in this case." Than at least I know what not to do.

The best senior NCO in the outfit was Staff Sergeant Russell, a black Marine. Unfortunately, some of the other senior NCOs were racist as well. There was discord in the outfit over the troops having mustaches. (I had one, with the Lieutenant's permission, though when he left, Sgt. R ordered me to shave it.) It was remarked that SSgt Russell had a mustache. The Gunny said, "That's okay, it makes him look almost human." This in front of the troops. Being a corporal, I had to keep my trap shut, but I fumed. They marginalized the only good NCO.

I was on light duty one time, due to being hit by a jeep trailer that left a lump on my leg larger than a goose egg. That meant I missed the Physical Readiness Test (PRT) for the outfit, avoiding lots of unpleasant exercise.

Of course, the senior NCOs accused me of malingering. The week after I got off light duty, our new officer, Lieutenant Smith, another mustang officer up from the ranks, decided we were going to do a 21-mile hike, over the center of the island and up the coast. With rifle, helmets, cartridge belt, and so on.

This wouldn't have been a big deal for an infantry outfit, but our guys weren't in shape for it.

We did it in seven and a half hours, plus an hour break for lunch. Not bad for a comm outfit used to riding in Radio Relay vans. Lieutenant Smith walked the whole way. Staff Sergeant Russell walked the whole way. I was the next senior man to walk the whole way. The Gunny, the other Staff Sergeant, and the Sergeants all took turns riding in the radio jeep or the ambulance. So did some of the corporals, half of whom were equally worthless—not surprisingly the ones who rode were the ones favored by the higher NCOs. One of the basic principles of leadership is the leader sets the example. So you know what kind of leaders they were.

When we had six miles left to go, over the center of the island, the Navy Corpsman ordered me into the ambulance to ride the rest of the way, to protect my just-recovered leg. I refused. He told me if I injured my leg, I'd be court marshaled. I told him I was walking in with the guys. Luckily, I had no damage other than the blisters we all had.

SSgt Russell came over and whispered, "Good man, Corporal Hall." It remains one of the best compliments of my life. He didn't care if I was white, black or green. I was a Marine, he was my leader, and his job was to motivate and encourage me. I have never forgotten him, though I'm sure he has no idea of the impact he made in the months I benefited from his example.

The Marines taught me it wasn't about race, it was about individuals. I had black friends I loved and admired and there were black Marines I couldn't stand. And, yes, some of the latter were racists, in my book, with a hostile attitude towards whites. Some folks feel black racism should be excused because of white racism. But they are no more justified in hating me because of the actions of other white people, some long dead, than I would be in hating Dr. Thomas Sowell or Dr. Walter Williams because black gang-bangers in Chicago murder children in drive by shootings.

The third black mentor who shaped my life was US Senator Edward Brooke (R-MA), the first black elected to the US senate in modern times--and in a VERY Democrat state with a black population of just 5%. Brooke was a liberal Republican, but when I ran for the state senate in 1972, he was the only prominent Republican who acted like he thought I had a chance. He not only helped my campaign, and endorsed me, but sent a team of workers to help with my recount. Without their help, I would not have squeaked through. He was an example and advisor to me.

Unfortunately, the more conservative elements of the GOP didn't stand by him, as he did other Republicans, a few years later, when liberal Democrats had no "racism" problem using smears to savage a black Republican, to replace him with a Democrat. (Power motivates politicians on both sides. Race and other issues are tools to get power, not problems to solve or principles to stand by.) After he was defeated, he was cleared of the charges (*Bridging the Divide*), but it was hardly front page news, and too late for his political career. I treasured his friendship, though we disagreed on many issues.

Citing these three men does not mean that many other black people have not had a positive influence in my life, from black Marines to black doctors in the associations I managed, to John and Donna Payne since last October, just as black writers from Booker Washington to Thomas Sowell and Walter Williams have. Nor does it mean that black folks have had more impact in my life than the far larger number of whites I have interacted with, for good or ill. But Owens, Russell and Brooke loom large in the forces that shaped me, and I'm grateful to have had their guidance. I would be a different person and have had a poorer life without them.

And because of them and others, I learned to see people as individuals, not as members of an ethnic group.

Long ago, I concluded that Race doesn't matter at all. Culture matters--which is why those desperate to keep racism alive as a tool to get power have started to define "culture" as a racist code word. So if you think that the culture of rural, mostly-white Wisconsin is better (or worse) than the culture of increasingly-white and Asian San Francisco as green initiatives have made housing unaffordable for blacks ("Liberalism versus Blacks"), you must be a racist.

The idea that a particular ethnic group isn't as intelligent as yours is an inbred racism that is hard to eradicate. Almost all groups are targets at some times. Business with "No Irish need apply" signs hired freed slaves. They were considered smarter, worked better and so on. It is well documented that blacks today score below whites on IQ tests. Both sides argue theories that support their preconceived views, liberals that this is due to racism, racists that it is due to innate intelligent differences between the races. Actual study of the problem is not politically-correct, thus is off limits to all but the bravest of scholars. ("Race and IQ, Parts I, II & III") But black orphans raised by white families score at or above the national IQ average, (*Ethnic America*) not because they are racially different, but because they are raised in a different culture. In Britain, poor black kids are doing better than poor white kids. ("A Challenge to Our Beliefs.") Are the black kids smarter as a group? Are the white kids victims of black racism? Hardly.

Dunbar High School in DC during the Jim Crow era drew on poor black students, was poorly funded and segregated, but it out-scored two of the city's three white high schools on tests and produced a generation of outstanding black leaders. The culture of the school and the parents was different in those days. ("Will Dunbar Rise Again")

Eastern European Jews arrived here as the most destitute and illiterate of immigrant populations, and were shunned and despised by even the German-ancestry Jews already established in America. Jewish soldiers in WWI averaged some of the lowest scores on mental tests of any numerous ethnic group. Yet within a decade, they had IQ scores above Americans in general. Jews were subject to heavy discrimination. Yet today they score above the national average on IQ tests, are over-represented in the professions, academia and among Nobel Prize winners, and are economically far better off as a group than other Americans. But Sowell also notes that Jews, so successful in urban life, business, and the professions, were pretty much flops as farmers. When it comes to economic advancement, he notes that "Cultures are not 'superior' or 'inferior.' They are better or worse adapted to a particular set of circumstances." (*Ethnic America*)

Japanese and Chinese immigrants on the west coast suffered violence and discrimination that was often far worse than that suffered by blacks in the old south. The Chinese in particular, arrived illiterate and impoverished. Most west coast Japanese Americans lost everything when FDR forced them into resettlement camps at the start of WWII, despite often being American citizens, a move supported by the ACLU. Yet today, they are over-represented in the professions and academia, and economically better off than the average American. (*Ethnic America*) So much so that Asian applicants to politically-correct universities often no longer list their race, because of racial discrimination against Asians in pursuit of "diversity," just as universities once had a quota for Jews so they wouldn't be over-represented.

Neither group is today considered a disadvantaged minority needing government care and intervention. Both groups had a huge advantage--a culture that was focused on education, family and a solid work ethic. If we could somehow transpose those cultural elements to other ethnic groups, including native-born white Americans, I think in a generation poverty would be a non-issue.

Thomas Sowell postulates that the pathologies of the inner-city black culture (touchy about honor or being "dissed," a work-only-if-necessary-to-get-by work ethic, violence, alcoholism [now drugs], promiscuity and a tendency to violence) is actually the culture of poor southern whites that the freed slaves picked up from them, then brought north to the cities where this transplanted "cracker culture," is defended as authentic "black culture." (*Black Rednecks and White Liberals*). I don't know. He draws on a lot of examples, but there is, of course, little hard data. Read his essay and make up your own mind. But certainly these pathologies are not present in the majority of hard-working, decent folks in the black working class, or the black middle class who have acculturated and share general American values. One of the tradeoffs for ending the injustice of segregation was the ability of black professionals and middle class--the folks who wore suits to church on Sunday--to move out of black neighborhoods. This was to their advantage, but left the poor black kids with no role models except drug dealers and gang bangers, to their hurt.

The leaders of black America have been disproportionately drawn from two groups or their descendants. One group was the "free persons of color," that is blacks who were free before the Civil War. The great black leader W.E.B. Dubois was born in Massachusetts to a free black family. This is sometimes attributed, by blacks and whites, to the fact that a high proportion of them were "mulattos," bi-racial people with both a white and black parent. They assumed, as did whites and other blacks, that their white ancestry made them smarter and superior to run-of-the-mill blacks. The majority of the 3,000 black slave owners in New Orleans in 1860 were Mulattos who considered themselves superior to their "property." ("Black Slave Owners ") That inter- and intra-ethnic group racism is of course now known to be false, however "clean and articulate" Joe Biden thinks the President may be. In fact, they had a head start on the freed slaves. They were far more acculturated to free society, far more educated and far more skilled in life and work than the freemen. Naturally, their families have prospered in relation to those of freed slaves. (*Ethnic America*)

The other group are American blacks from the West Indies. Though they are descended from slaves and racially very similar to descendents of American slaves, their culture is very different. Given they are a small elite group leading the black masses, folks like Shirley Chisholm don't advertise their West Indian Heritage. (*Ethnic America*)

I have long maintained I'd rather have a beer with a black Marine veteran, than with any number of white Harvard academics, Hollywood celebrities, or European socialists. Marines are my culture, my "tribe" if you will, the others not at all.

I have also concluded that individuals and character matter, not groups. "Character, not circumstances, makes the man," said Booker T. Washington. Ethnic groups have different characteristics, usually based on culture, not ethnicity, though it would be hard to argue that blacks are not more athletic than whites. If that were not true, whites could sue the NBA, NFL, ABL and NBL for racial discrimination under the disparate impact theory.

But it doesn't matter. If you have an Asian guy who can play better basketball than Michael Jordan, he deserves to play. But every team should not be required to have enough whites, Hispanic, Jews, and Asians to match their proportion of the general population out of concern for diversity. That would constitute racial discrimination against the better black players at the alter of diversity, just as it constitutes racial discrimination to pass over better qualified Asian and white students with "race sensitive admission policies" in homage to "diversity."

So, having come this far, we need to ask, "Who is a racist?" Alas, like beauty, pornography, and racism itself, it's in the eye of the beholder.

There is a theory that all whites are racists (except the thinkers and their progressive co-believers) and that only whites can be racist, because they hold the power. I suggest any whites who believe this, in the face of limitless historical evidence, check their "white privilege" by taking a stroll through a south Chicago poor black neighborhood at 11:00 pm in July. Doubtless their "power" will protect them from any racist attacks. Though to be fair, they would be in little more danger than local black teens walking the same streets.

A while back, a well-educated liberal friend of great accomplishment I'd sent something to read by Dr. Thomas Sowell, disagreed with it and described Sowell, who is black, as an "asshole." Sowell has a PhD in the history of economic thought, has taught at several major universities, and has several dozen books on economics, race, culture, and politics in print. His *Basic Economic* has been translated into six languages and is widely used as a college textbook. A pretty accomplished "asshole." But let a conservative disagree with any policy of President Obama, even absent profane name calling, and you are a racist. The left's double standard is so broad and breathtaking they don't notice it.

The long body of evidence is that there is unlikely to be a person alive over the age of ten who is free of racial, ethnic, or religious animosity. It's not in our DNA, but inculcated with our mothers' milk.

We are all products of our times and cultures. Henry Mayer (*All on Fire*) says that today Americans "are all abolitionists." (I think there are exceptions!) It's hard to remember that the before the Civil War, the majority of northerners may have despised slavery, but saw no alternative, fearing the impacts of millions of freed uneducated slaves on society. I'm a staunch union man. My great, great grandfather, Sgt. Oliver Vernal, fought through the Civil War with the 6th Connecticut Volunteer infantry (which went into Fort Wagner next to the 54th Massachusetts, but didn't make it into the movie *Glory*.) He was badly wounded twice. Had he died, I'd have lost my life as well, putting down the slave power.

But had you or I been born on a southern plantation to a white planter family in, say, 1840, we would have been very likely to have been rabid defenders of the south's "peculiar institution" and rallied to the Bonnie Blue Flag in 1861. Sgt. Vernal wouldn't much like the thought of me in Rebel Gray, serving under Lee or Longstreet.

Certainly white racism was a necessary component of American slavery. Its hard to sleep at night if you can't convince yourself that holding these "inferior people" in slavery was better for them. Certainly, white racism was a feature of colonialism, not that the societies they took over had any claim to moral superiority as we understand it in the 21st century. They were often busy subjugating and enslaving their neighbors when the colonial powers arrived. Given how bad these things were, would the Third World be better today if western powers had stayed home, and built not one school, road, or hospital there? Would America be a better place today absent the stain of slavery, if not one African slave had been brought to these shores? The slaves themselves would have been likely to be sold by their fellow Africans to Arabs instead, where the harsher conditions meant there is no black population today (except some mixed blood in the population from rape in the harem), so their descendants would not be around today at all.

Few cultures are as racist as Asian cultures. The Chinese and Japanese consider each other, white people and pretty much everyone else racially inferior barbarians. The rivers of blood they have spilled over this conceit dwarf by several orders of magnitude any racial violence directed against blacks, native Americans, Asians, Hispanics and in some cases whites in North America. Given Asian tensions in current news stories, they may not be done.

Russians, who saw no downside to encouraging their Communists Chinese and Koreans allies to fight Americans during the Korean War, called the Asian soldiers "Lemonski," which the excellent history *Small Wars, Faraway Places* translates as "yellow-skinned cannon fodder."

And the "Overseas Chinese" in many Asian countries consider themselves racially superior to the locals, who return the animosity in spades, and often in violence. Then there are the million people who died in ethnic violence when India and Pakistan were partitioned after Britain granted independence. One wonders if any of the dead would have preferred to live under the racism of British colonialism to ethnic murder.

You and I might not be able to discern at a glance the ethnic difference between Tutsis and Hutus in Rwanda, but the Hutus could, well enough to have slaughtered upwards of a million Tutsis and moderate Hutus in a genocide the world only bemoaned after the fact.

I could belabor the point for another thousand words, but I suggest you read *Race and Culture: A World View* as a start.

Casual, unthinking racism infects Americans of all political persuasions as much as anyone else. ("25 Examples of Liberal Racism in Quotes." and "9 Racist Things that Big Democrats Have Said and the Media Has Forgotten") Many white males of the working class are perfectly unselfconscious using terms like "nigger" and "nigger-rigged" with other whites, assuming we will not be offended. Recently a PR exec sent a racist tweet about AIDS, Africa, and being white. ("IAC PR exec fired over offensive AIDS tweet"). She was unemployed when her plane landed. She was in Public Relations--she should have been fired for stupidity before they even got to the racism.

I have a friend, a woman of intellect and class. In the 40 plus years I've known her, I never heard her utter a racist remark--except once. Years ago, her elderly mother was robbed and savagely beaten by three young black males on the street in Worcester, MA. For about three days, all I heard from her was, 'Those Goddamned Niggers." I don't think that makes her a racist.

People who are wronged, hurt, and outraged often lash out in bitter, nasty ways at the perpetrator, though that individual isn't there to hear. If an obese person cheats you, you might refer to him as, "That fat prick," though holding an animus towards the overweight takes in a lot of folks in our society today---a fact Chris Christy exploited when Jon Corzine made the mistake of referencing Christy's weight.

If the wrongdoer is of Italian or Irish heritage, you are likely to hear ethnic slurs like "Whop" or "Mick" from the victim, though he has no real bias towards the whole ethnic group.

Another friend, a Marine buddy, is a tough, raw-spoken man who calls a spade a "Goddamn Shovel." He is likely to drop the N word into conversation with white males, without a second thought. Is he a racist? He has also built a very successful auto body business, where he hires black felons right out of prison to sweep the floor or wash cars. He gives them overtime and health benefits so they can make a living. They get to develop work skills, a work history, and perhaps learn and move into a better paying position. He doesn't let anyone use the N word in his shop.

Visiting his business, I met a young black employee who had been in jail and was a registered sex offender. When he was 18, some busybody saw him petting with his younger girlfriend, and had him charged with molesting a child. (There but for the grace of God...) I wondered if a white kid would not have walked in the same situation.

The guy was getting grief from the parole board. My buddy told him, "Look. You have six months to do. Go back to jail, and I'll hold your job for you." He went to jail and had a job when he was released. My buddy is now working with the guy to set up a chance to have the record expunged. So this "racist" has helped more down and out black guys than ten Ivy league professors speak to in a year.

Some cases are easy. Not being a basketball guy, I had never heard of Donald Sterling until his recent taped comments made him front page news. For all I know he rescues kittens, but reading of his past conduct and current life style, it's hard not to conclude he's an unrepentant racist and vile in many other ways; a rich jerk who has let his sense of entitlement go to his head.

I don't get conservatives saying, "He's bad, but what about..." No excuses. I had zero objection to the NBA's fine or the lifetime suspension of him. But a couple of notes. First, he was suspended for life, while athletes who have committed crimes, fathered children they don't parent, or engaged in domestic or other violence are still happily earning millions playing. I'm not sure if this is because racism is now considered worse than these crimes, or because suspending good players has an economic cost to the league that suspending an owner doesn't.

The second point is that, despite his clearly racist views, he has long employed black players, a black coach and a black general manager. (Not to mention employing a bi-racial mistress.) As Dr. Thomas Sowell has pointed out, discrimination often gives way to economic self-interest, but surfaces when it is cost free. Before the racist white unions pushed through minimum wage laws to disadvantage blacks who were under-bidding them, blacks had a higher employment rate than whites, because discriminating against them carried an economic cost. Once they couldn't compete on price, discrimination was cost free, and blacks have had a lower employment rate ever since. (*Race and Economics*)

The case on Cliven Bundy is harder to judge, because he became a focal flash point in the political divide, with excessive spin from both sides. ("Cliven Bundy Under Fire for 'Negro' Comments, Wondering Whether Blacks Would Be 'Better Off as Slaves, Picking Cotton,'" "Unedited Video Shows Bundy Making Pro-Black, Pro-Mexican Comments" and "CNN Talks To Black Bundy Bodyguard: 'He Is Not A Racist. He's Pretty Much Treating Me Just Like His Own Family'") Despite the fact that everybody admitted that Bundy was legally in the wrong, small government conservatives rallied to his defense before his comments came to light., especially because there was a whiff of green-crony profits and well-connected lobbyists wanting the land. Big government types came down hard on him and rejoiced when Bundy's comments discredited him and his supporters.

Then it turned out that the *NY Times,* to no conservative's surprise, had edited out some things he said that were pro-black and especially pro-Hispanic. His black bodyguard says he's not a racist. He may, of course, indeed be a racist. Or a confused, inarticulate old guy who has some politically-incorrect terms imbedded in his vocabulary. I think the jury's out--but we will never know for sure, as the big guns (big mouths?) on both sides have a self-interest in making Bundy fit their narrative.

Despite the ethnic biases embedded in our psyches, I don't think everyone is racist. Most people recognize it as wrong, and try to overcome it, letting the "better angels" of their nature guide them.

My definition: A racist is a person who embraces racism, sees nothing wrong with it, and often happily engages in the behavior I define as racist above. Yes, anyone can be a racist. David Duke and Al Sharpton both fit the bill. Jesse Jackson's racial blackmail of Budweiser to give his son, Jesse Jackson, Jr. (D-Prison) a lucrative beer distributorship may not be racist, just old fashioned extortion using race as the bludgeon

Is Affirmative Action racist? It fits my above definition. ("Beyond affirmative action to colorblindness."). And as Thomas Sowell points out, it disadvantages black students, who are pushed into schools where they cannot compete, but who would do well in lower ranked schools. ("Liberalism versus Blacks ") The end results for black students don't matter, of course, as long as the academics can feel good about achieving diversity.

There was a time—in my life time—when people saw black professionals (doctors, lawyers, accountants) and thought they must be very good to have overcome racism and other obstacles like poverty and poor schools. Now too many people wonder if they achieved their success from the liberal view that blacks cannot compete with Whites or Asian (who certainly suffered equally bad discrimination), and must be given lower college admission standards, grade standards, hiring standards, and promotion standards to achieve diversity, to overcome past racism or the effects of slavery, or, in my view, to buy votes from a large black population they have instilled with the victim, we-can't-compete mentality that would have outraged earlier generations of blacks with higher employment rates than whites. As one group of former slaves petitioned the Freedman's Bureau, "We are a working class of people." Successful professionals like Thomas Sowell, PhD and Walter Williams,

PhD, who became national prominent economists without affirmative action, are incensed, as they reject this condescending (and in my view, racist) view of black people .

From Paul Ryan to Bill Cosby (who earned instant "Uncle Tom" status for having the courage to address the issue--see "Dr Bill Cosby Speaks") much has been made of the pathologies in the poor (inner city!) black community: violence, the non-marital birth rate, lack of a work ethic in young males, drugs and crime. But these pathologies are present throughout our culture today, not just among blacks. (*Coming Apart*) They are advanced among blacks because of higher poverty, less education and the dependency culture that has been fobbed off on them by their "friends." ("'Friends' of blacks.") The damage is magnified by those who scream "Racist" or "Uncle Tom" at any attempt to address these issues.

While 70% of black babies are non-marital births, so are 50% of Hispanic babies and 30% of white babies. This is devastating for all those groups, because the poverty correlation is so high. ("Ignoring Single-Parent Families in the Inequality Debate," "To defeat poverty, look to marriage," " Benefits of Marriage," and " Paternal Involvement Increases College Graduation Rates.") Not honestly discussing this hurts blacks worst of all. That's racist!

Is this a legacy of slavery? No. Despite the forced breakup of families and higher mortality rates, most slaves lived in dual-headed households and many had long-term marriages. Most slave children grew up in two-parent families, far more than whites or blacks today. (*The Black Family in Freedom and Slavery*.) They would be ashamed of us, black or white.

I keep reading that the Trayvon Martin case demonstrates that it isn't safe for a black teen to be in a white neighborhood at night. But there was little outcry when the case was black on white violence. ("What if Trayvon Had Been White, and the Shooter Black?") And "stand your ground" laws, such as the one sponsored by then-state senator Barack Obama in Illinois played no part in either of these cases. In fact, blacks in Florida have used the "stand your ground" defense proportionally more often than whites. ("Blacks benefit from Florida 'Stand Your Ground' law at disproportionate rate")

The facts are contrary to the narrative. Blacks murder whites at twice the rate whites murder blacks. According to the FBI, blacks make up 13% of the population, but commit 53% of the murders. (Yet it's racist that blacks outnumber whites in prison?) But both white on black and black on white murder are small problems. Just as the vast majority of Islamist murders are of Muslims, the vast majority of black murders are of fellow blacks. It's just that Al Sharpton gets no benefit for splashing them in the media. That it's politically incorrect to discuss this genocide of black people is the worst kind of racism.

What can we do about racism?

First we need to recognize that everyone, black, white, yellow or brown, has ethnic biases imbedded in them. When it rears its ancient head in us, we need to recognizes it as unworthy, and fight to rise above it. Most of us do, but the internal battle will always be there.

Second, we need to realize that politicians screaming about racism on both sides are not really concerned about racism. Their agenda is getting power, and racism is just one more tool. The media has an agenda of driving readers/viewers to increase revenue.

Third, we need to understand that there are people of good will on all sides of this issue, however much they may be drowned out by the political and media whores, and we need to work with the good ones. There is no objective right or wrong on much of this, only individual perspectives.

Fourth, we need to understand that these biases will always be a part of every person, and deal with it. No one deserves to be self-righteous on these issues. It's not "Check your privilege," but "Check your humanity."

Lastly, we cannot be intimidated from trying to address the real problems that people of all ethnic groups have by shrill, agenda-driven folks trying to stop discussion with charges of racism.

Ethnic bias is a chronic disease of the human condition that will never be fully cured. But it can be ameliorated by people of good heart to make life better for everyone. All we can do is try.

For Further Reading on Racism

I have tried to include books and articles I have read that provide nuance and context into these issues beyond the shallow talking (shouting) points of conservatives who think racism is no longer an issue, and liberals who think any opposition to the policies of a black liberal (but not a black conservative!) is racist and who see every dictionary entry as a racial code word when used by someone who disagrees with them. These are not necessarily in any order. I realize this is a long list, but they are all worth reading, so you will have to skim and pick and choose. You should read everything on the list with a critical eye. I have indicated where comments are mine and not from the work. The books have links to Amazon so you can read the synopsis and the reviews, while the articles have links (I hope) to on-line versions.

Books

Race and Culture: A World View. By Thomas Sowell
http://www.amazon.com/Race-And-Culture-World-View/dp/0465067972/ref=sr_1_1?
ie=UTF8&qid=1398031526&sr=8-1&keywords=Race+and+Culture+Sowell
The challenges of race and culture that confront us are not unique to America. Again, Sowell's excellent research and pertinent examples put these problems into perspective. You will come away with a better understanding and new view of these issues. ~Bob

Ethnic America: A History. By Thomas Sowell
http://www.amazon.com/Ethnic-America-History-Thomas-Sowell/dp/0465020755/ref
=sr_1_1?ie=UTF8&qid=1398027365&sr=8-1&keywords=Ethnic+America+Sowell
Dr. Sowell looks at the history and integration in to American life of several
ethnic groups, such as Jews, Germans, Irish, Mexicans, blacks, etc., as well as the
intersection of the cultures they brought with them and the cultures they developed in
America. Published in 1981, much of the data has been outdated by demographic and
immigration changes, but his insights into these issues are timeless. Pertinent to this
essay is the chapter on the history and development of black Americans under slavery
and since. ~Bob

Black Rednecks and White Liberals. By Thomas Sowell.
http://www.amazon.com/Black-Rednecks-Liberals-Thomas-Sowell-ebook/dp/
B003XRDBYE/ref=sr_1_5?ie=UTF8&qid=1398031526&sr=8-5&keywords=Race+a
nd+Culture+Sowell
All of these essays, as usual with Dr. Sowell, are worth reading. Pertinent to this
discussion is the title essay, which postulates that black, inner-city culture, is based
on poor southern white "cracker culture" (which was violent, touchy about honor
or being "dissed," had a poor work ethic and was promiscuous) which freed slaves
adopted from poor whites they were in contact with. Also, "The Real History of
Slavery" (You can listen to it being read on YouTube: https://www.youtube.com/
watch?v=ao7FKReHYKY) puts that issue into a world historical context. Americans
tend to view slavery as an American phenomenon over a few centuries, when every
culture practiced slavery and people of every race, religion and ethnic group were
enslaved. Only western culture turned against slavery. ~Bob

Race & Economics: How Much Can Be Blamed on Discrimination? By Walter E.
Williams
http://www.amazon.com/Race-Economics-Discrimination-Institution-
Publication/dp/0817912452/ref=sr_1_1?ie=UTF8&qid=1390233354&sr=8-
1&keywords=Race+%26+Economics
Dr. Williams, a nationally known economist, provides excellent research into these
problems, and details how government programs have discriminated economically
against black citizens, usually at the behest of special interest, such as labor unions
that wanted to eliminate competition from blacks for their white members. Worth
reading. ~Bob

The Black Family in Slavery and Freedom, 1750-1925. By Herbert G. Gutman
http://www.amazon.com/Black-Family-Slavery-Freedom-1750-1925/dp/0394724518
This well researched and extensively documented history, published in 1976, presents
a far more positive and uplifting view of black people living under the evil of slavery
than the current standard, and in my view condescending and racist view of blacks,
then and now, and that today's pathologies in the black community are a result of
slavery, which destroyed the black family. Unfortunately, despite extensive, data-
driven research, it has failed to change the national understanding of slavery and
blacks. ~Bob

Coming Apart: The State of White America, 1960-2010 By Charles Murray
http://www.amazon.com/Coming-Apart-State-America-1960-2010/dp/0307453421/ref
=sr_1_1?s=books&ie=UTF8&qid=1349042135&sr=1-1&keywords=coming+apart
Excerpt: Despite the subtitle, this is a book about class, not race. The author is looking
at a lot of data that suggested the upper class that runs the country, which he calls
the Narrow Elite and the Broad Elite, is increasingly wealthy, increasingly takes in
both liberals and conservatives with high IQs and is increasingly isolated from the
experience of the rest of America. He focuses on whites because that Narrow Elite is
overwhelmingly white. He also focuses on the white lower class, so the comparison
will not be between a white upper class and a minority lower class. He looks at a lot of
data suggesting the white lower class is being destroyed by several trends: decreasing
industriousness and ability to hold jobs among males, decreasing participation in civic
organizations or churches, decreasing marriage rates, decreasing rates of trust and
neighborliness, and sharply escalating non-marital birth rates, all trends that suggest
the destruction of both happiness for these folks and what he calls the "American
Project."

The Known World by Edward P. Jones
http://www.amazon.com/The-Known-World-Edward-Jones/dp/0061159174/ref=sr_1_
1?ie=UTF8&qid=1396311308&sr=8-1&keywords=Known+World
This excellent novel is about a little-known facet of American history: Southern free
black slave owners before the Civil War and emancipation. See also "Black Slave
Owners" by Joseph Holloway
http://slaverebellion.org/index.php?page=the-black-slave-owners
According to this article, there were 3,000 free black slave owners in New Orleans in
1860 and over 400 in Charleston, SC in 1830. ~Bob

A Personal Odyssey by Thomas Sowell
http://www.amazon.com/A-Personal-Odyssey-Thomas-Sowell/dp/0684864657/ref=sr
_1_1?ie=UTF8&qid=1398363419&sr=8-1&keywords=personal+sowell
Autobiography

Bridging the Divide: My Life by Edward W. Brooke
http://www.amazon.com/Bridging-Divide-Professor-Edward-Brooke/dp/0813539056/
ref=sr_1_sc_1?ie=UTF8&qid=1399342685&sr=8-1-spell&keywords=Bridiging+Div
ide+Brooke
The autobiography of my mentor and friend, US Senator Edward Brooke. ~Bob

Up from the Projects: An Autobiography by Walter E. Williams
http://www.amazon.com/Up-Projects-Autobiography-Walter-Williams/
dp/081791255X/ref=sr_1_1?ie=UTF8&qid=1398363508&sr=8-1&keywords=up+fro
m+projects+williams

Maybe I'll Pitch Forever. By Leroy Satchel Page
http://www.amazon.com/Maybe-Pitch-Forever-Leroy-Satchel/dp/0803287321/ref=sr_
1_1?ie=UTF8&qid=1398613826&sr=8-1&keywords=Pitch+Forever+Paige
I'm not a sports guy, but I read Satchel's terrific autobiography in college. He was
perhaps the best pitcher ever, but due to racial discrimination, he had to pitch in the
Negro Leagues and didn't get into the American League until he was 42--and still
pitched for years. It's another lesson on the loss to the nation of racial discrimination.
Today Paige would be making $10M a year. ~Bob

Up from Slavery. By Booker T. Washington
http://www.amazon.com/Up-Slavery-Dover-Thrift-Editions/dp/0486287386/ref=sr_1_
2?ie=UTF8&qid=1398614283&sr=8-2&keywords=up+from+Slavery+Washington
I have read good books this year that I can't remember the titles of, but in 8th grade,
I was working my way through my grandmother's collection of *Reader's Digest
Condensed Books*, and came across Washington's autobiography. It stuck with me
and long influenced my views on race. Washington has fallen out of favor with the
grievance mongers, because he advocated self improvement for the freed slaves like
himself, over agitation for civil rights. He had a long conflict with W. E. B. Du Bois
over this, covered in *Ethnic America*, above. Well worth reading. ~Bob

All on Fire: William Lloyd Garrison and the Abolition of Slavery. By Henry Mayer
http://www.amazon.com/All-Fire-William-Garrison-Abolition/dp/0393332365/ref=sr_
1_1?ie=UTF8&qid=1398762348&sr=8-1&keywords=All+on+Fire
A wonderful biography of one of the leading American abolitionists. Garrison, like
Wilberforce in Britain, was the conscience of a nation at a time when even many
northerners who hated slavery thought that abolishing it and putting uneducated
blacks into the society would be bad for everyone. He deserves to be remembered and
honored. ~Bob

*'White Girl Bleed A Lot': The Return of Racial Violence to America and How the
Media Ignore It* by Colin Flaherty
http://www.amazon.com/White-Girl-Bleed-Lot-Violence/dp/1938067061/ref=sr_1_1?
s=books&ie=UTF8&qid=1399373750&sr=1-1&keywords=white+girl+bleed+a+lot
The author has been praised for having the courage to expose the issue and excoriated
as a racist for talking about black on white violence. It's worth reading to make up
your own mind. It is certainly true that the media goes to great length not to mention
the ethnicity of perpetrators of crime and violence unless it is a case of white (or
"white Hispanic") on black violence. (In Europe, Muslims screaming "Allah Akbar"
as they riot, or commit violence or other crimes against non-Muslims are routinely
described as "youth" or "Asians," to avoid any mention of Islam.) Not every case
of inter-racial violence is based on racism, but many of these cases fit the definition
I offer in the essay. Let me repeat here, that the vast majority of black violence
is directed at other black people, just as the vast majority of people murdered by
Muslims in the name of Allah are fellow Muslims who believe slightly differently, or
are not as committed as the murderers, or are not cooperating with them. ~Bob

Movies

Note that these movies are all based on true stories. That doesn't mean that Hollywood has not taken liberties with the historical facts to "improve" the stories--they always do. Worth seeing, but view critically. ~Bob

Amazing Grace
http://www.amazinggracemovie.com/
A must-see movie about William Wilberforce and the effort in Britain to abolish the slave trade. ~Bob

The Blind Side
http://www.amazon.com/Blind-Side-Sandra-Bullock/dp/B002VECM6S/
ref=sr_1_1?s=movies-tv&ie=UTF8&qid=1399415855&sr=1-
1&keywords=the+blind+side+movie
Great story about a white family who adopt a black teen who becomes a football star. ~Bob

Schindler's List
http://www.amazon.com/Schindlers-List-Liam-Neeson/dp/B00BP4X3W2/
ref=sr_1_1?s=movies-tv&ie=UTF8&qid=1399416044&sr=1-
1&keywords=schindlers+list+movie
The holocaust up close and personal. A must-see movie. ~Bob

Glory
http://www.amazon.com/Glory-Matthew-Broderick/dp/0800177967/
ref=sr_1_2?s=movies-tv&ie=UTF8&qid=1399416201&sr=1-2&keywords=glory
The story of the 54th Massachusetts Volunteer Infantry. a black Civil War regiment whose valor helped black troops be accepted by the Union armies. ~Bob

Articles and Columns

Politics Versus Education. By Thomas Sowell
http://townhall.com/columnists/thomassowell/2014/01/14/politics-versus-education-n1778405?utm_source=thdaily&utm_medium=email&utm_campaign=nl
Excerpt: Anyone who has still not yet understood the utter cynicism of the Obama administration in general, and Attorney General Eric Holder in particular, should look at the Justice Department's latest interventions in education. If there is one thing that people all across the ideological spectrum should be able to agree on, it is that better education is desperately needed by black youngsters, especially in the ghettoes.

Demonizing the Helpers. By Thomas Sowell
http://www.frontpagemag.com/2014/thomas-sowell/demonizing-the-helpers/?utm_source=FrontPage+Magazine&utm_medium=email&utm_campaign=ce8b987219-Mailchimp_FrontPageMag&utm_term=0_57e32c1dad-ce8b987219-156414477

Excerpt: It is not easy to demonize people who have spent hundreds of millions of dollars of their own money to help educate poor children. But some members of the education establishment are taking a shot at it. The Walton Family Foundation — created by the people who created Walmart — has given more than $300 million to charter schools, voucher programs and other educational enterprises concerned with the education of poor and minority students across the country. The Walton Family Foundation gave more than $58 million to the KIPP schools, which have had spectacular success in raising the test scores of children in ghettoes

The Left Versus Minorities. Thomas Sowell
http://townhall.com/columnists/thomassowell/2014/03/11/the-left-versus-minorities-n1806660?utm_source=thdaily&utm_medium=email&utm_campaign=nl
Excerpt: If anyone wanted to pick a time and place where the political left's avowed concern for minorities was definitively exposed as a fraud, it would be now -- and the place would be New York City, where far left Mayor Bill de Blasio has launched an attack on charter schools, cutting their funding, among other things. These schools have given thousands of low income minority children their only shot at a decent education, which often means their only shot at a decent life. Last year 82 percent of the students at a charter school called Success Academy passed city-wide mathematics exams, compared to 30 percent of the students in the city as a whole.

Republicans and Blacks. By Thomas Sowell
http://townhall.com/columnists/thomassowell/2014/03/25/republicans-and-blacks-n1813881?utm_source=thdaily&utm_medium=email&utm_campaign=nl
Excerpt: The issue on which Democrats are most vulnerable, and have the least room to maneuver, is school choice. Democrats are heavily in hock to the teachers' unions, who see public schools as places to guarantee jobs for teachers, regardless of what that means for the education of students. There are some charter schools and private schools that have low-income minority youngsters equaling or exceeding national norms, despite the many ghetto public schools where most students are nowhere close to meeting those norms. Because teachers' unions oppose charter schools, most Democrats oppose them, including black Democrats up to and including President Barack Obama.

A Challenge to Our Beliefs. By Thomas Sowell
http://townhall.com/columnists/thomassowell/2013/12/03/a-challenge-to-our-beliefs-n1756023?utm_source=thdaily&utm_medium=email&utm_campaign=nl
Excerpt: What do low-income whites in England and ghetto blacks in the United States have in common? It cannot be simply low incomes, because children from other groups in the same low-income brackets outperform whites in England and outperform blacks in America. What low-income whites in England and ghetto blacks in the United States have in common is a generations-long indoctrination in victimhood. The political left in both countries has, for more than half a century, maintained a steady and loud drumbeat of claims that the deck is stacked against those at the bottom.

Rosa Parks and history. By Thomas Sowell
http://townhall.com/columnists/thomassowell/2005/10/27/rosa_parks_and_history/page/full
Excerpt: Why was there racially segregated seating on public transportation in the first place? "Racism" some will say -- and there was certainly plenty of racism in the South, going back for centuries. But racially segregated seating on streetcars and buses in the South did not go back for centuries. Far from existing from time immemorial, as many have assumed, racially segregated seating in public transportation began in the South in the late 19th and early 20th centuries. Those who see government as the solution to social problems may be surprised to learn that it was government which created this problem. Many, if not most, municipal transit systems were privately owned in the 19th century and the private owners of these systems had no incentive to segregate the races.

'Friends' of blacks. By Thomas Sowell
http://townhall.com/columnists/thomassowell/2002/09/04/friends_of_blacks/page/full
Excerpt: Who was it who said, "if the Negro cannot stand on his own legs, let him fall"? Ronald Reagan? Newt Gingrich? Charles Murray? Not even close. It was Frederick Douglass! This was part of a speech in which Douglass also said: "Everybody has asked the question … 'What shall we do with the Negro?' I have had but one answer from the beginning. Do nothing with us! Your doing with us has already played the mischief with us. Do nothing with us!" Frederick Douglass had achieved a deeper understanding in the 19th century than any of the black "leaders" of today. Those whites who feel a need to do something with blacks and for blacks have been some of the most dangerous "friends" of blacks.

Liberalism versus Blacks. By Thomas Sowell
http://www.creators.com/opinion/thomas-sowell/liberalism-versus-blacks.html
Excerpt: Liberals have pushed affirmative action, supposedly for the benefit of blacks and other minorities. But two recent factual studies show that affirmative action in college admissions has led to black students with every qualification for success being artificially turned into failures by being mismatched with colleges for the sake of racial body count.

Will Dunbar Rise Again? By Thomas Sowell
http://townhall.com/columnists/thomassowell/2014/05/01/will-dunbar-rise-again-n1830522?utm_source=thdaily&utm_medium=email&utm_campaign=nl
Excerpt: What is different about the history of Dunbar is that, from its founding in 1870 as the first public high school in the country for black students, until the mid 1950s, it was an outstanding academic success. As far back as 1899, when tests were given in Washington's four academic high schools at that time, the black high school scored higher than two of the three white high schools. That was the M Street School that was renamed Dunbar High School in 1916.

Recycled 'racism.' By Thomas Sowell
http://townhall.com/columnists/thomassowell/2005/09/21/recycled_racism/page/full
Excerpt: For example, neither study took credit histories into account. People with lower credit ratings tend to get turned down for loans more often than people with higher credit ratings, or else they have to go where loans have higher interest rates. This is not rocket science. It is Economics 1. Blacks in the earlier study turned out to have poor credit histories more often than whites. But the more recent news story did not even look into that.

Rattling the chains. By Thomas Sowell
http://townhall.com/columnists/thomassowell/2004/03/24/rattling_the_chains/page/full
Excerpt: Slavery was an ugly, dirty business but people of virtually every race, color, and creed engaged in it on every inhabited continent. And the people they enslaved were also of virtually every race, color, and creed. A recently published book titled "Christian Slaves, Muslim Masters" by Robert Davis shows that a million Europeans were enslaved by North Africans between 1500 and 1800. Nor were they the only Europeans enslaved.

Race and IQ. By Thomas Sowell
http://townhall.com/columnists/thomassowell/2002/10/01/race_and_iq/page/full
Excerpt: This is just one of many unsolved mysteries that is likely to remain unsolved, because doing research on race and IQ has become taboo in many places. ... In other words, black Americans' test score results in 1995 would have given them an average IQ just over 100 in 1945. Only the repeated renorming of IQ tests upward created the illusion that blacks had made no progress, but were stuck at an IQ of 85. But we would never have known this if some researchers had not defied the taboo on studying race and IQ imposed by black "leaders" and white "friends."

Race and IQ: Part II. By Thomas Sowell
http://townhall.com/columnists/thomassowell/2002/10/02/race_and_iq_part_ii/page/full
Excerpt: Professor John McWhorter, a black faculty member at the University of California at Berkeley, has made a suggestion that is explosive in itself and directly the opposite of what is being said by those who are seeking to promote lower college admissions standards for blacks through affirmative action. One of the reasons given for wanting more black students on a given campus, even if that means lowering admissions standards, is the claim that a certain number of blacks -- a "critical mass" -- on campus is necessary, in order for these students to feel comfortable enough to relax and do their best work. It sounds plausible, but lots of things have sounded plausible. Professor McWhorter says just the opposite in his book *Losing the Race*. According to McWhorter, anti-intellectualism in the black culture keeps many black youngsters from doing their best.

Race and IQ: Part III. By Thomas Sowell
http://townhall.com/columnists/thomassowell/2002/10/03/race_and_iq_part_iii/page/full
Excerpt: Back in the days of the Roman Empire, Cicero warned his fellow Romans not to buy British slaves, because he found them hard to teach anything. A 10th-century Moslem scholar noted that Europeans grew more pale the farther north they were and that the "farther they are to the north the more stupid, gross, and brutish they are." With our love of labels today, we might dismiss both these statements as "racism." In reality, both statements were probably true, as of the time they were made. At the very least, the people who said these things were eyewitnesses, which we cannot possibly be.

Black History Month. By Thomas Sowell
http://townhall.com/columnists/thomassowell/2002/02/26/black_history_month/page/full
Excerpt: Obviously, there is current political mileage to be gotten from historic grievances. At a minimum, politicians and activists get the media attention that is the lifeblood of their careers. Then there are racial quotas, money for special minority programs and hopes for reparations for slavery. If nothing else, some people get excuses for their own shortcomings -- and excuses are very important. One of the many penetrating insights of the late Eric Hoffer was that, for many people, an excuse is better than an achievement

Bravo for Bill Cosby. By Thomas Sowell
http://townhall.com/columnists/thomassowell/2004/05/25/bravo_for_bill_cosby/page/full
Excerpt: He also denounced both those children and those adults in the black community who refuse to speak the king's English. "Everybody knows it's important to speak English except these knuckleheads," Cosby said. "You can't be a doctor with that kind of crap coming out of your mouth." He also mocked those who referred to "the incarcerated" as "political prisoners."

Dr Bill Cosby Speaks
http://www.eightcitiesmap.com/transcript_bc.htm

Quota 'logic.' By Thomas Sowell
http://townhall.com/columnists/thomassowell/2003/04/22/quota_logic/page/full
Excerpt: In short, older white males of Professor McPherson's generation benefitted unfairly, so reparations are owed to minorities and women -- not from those who benefitted, but from white males of this generation, including those too young to have had anything to do with the advantages and disadvantages he describes. And we thought The Shadow could cloud men's minds! This is classic academic self-indulgence in the name of noblesse oblige. Professor McPherson can get credit for noblesse and force someone else to pay the cost of oblige.

Quota 'logic' part II. By Thomas Sowell
http://townhall.com/columnists/thomassowell/2003/04/23/quota_logic_part_ii/page/full
Excerpt: First of all, he mentions that his academic career began in 1962 at Princeton, as a result of what he now calls "the infamous 'old boy network,' " which he characterizes as affirmative action for white males. Despite being black, my own academic career also began that very same year, 1962, just a few miles up the road from where McPherson's career began, at Douglass College, Rutgers University. I too received my appointment via the old boys' network, being recommended by my mentors at the University of Chicago, just as McPherson was recommended by his mentor at Johns Hopkins. Women were hired the same way, out of the same "old boys' network," which was also an old girls' network.

Gary Becker (1930-2014). By Thomas Sowell
http://townhall.com/columnists/thomassowell/2014/05/06/gary-becker-19302014-n1833852?utm_source=thdaily&utm_medium=email&utm_campaign=nl
Excerpt: More than half a century after Professor Becker's landmark work on the economics of discrimination, most controversies on that subject, both in the media and in politics, go on in utter ignorance of his penetrating insights. So do laws and policies that make discrimination worse. As someone who has written about racial discrimination within the framework of analysis that Becker created, I am especially indebted to him, and wish only that more people were aware of that framework, which could spare us much rhetoric and offer some useful understanding instead. (I have not read Becker's book, *The Economics of Discrimination* (Economic Research Studies). It is linked here: http://www.amazon.com/Economics-Discrimination-Economic-Research-Studies/dp/0226041166/ref=sr_1_1?ie=UTF8&qid=1399378396&sr=8-1&keywords=Economics+of+Discrimination+Becker ~Bob)

Black People Duped. By Walter Williams
http://www.frontpagemag.com/2014/walter-williams/black-people-duped/
Excerpt: For several decades, blacks have held significant political power, in the form of being mayors and dominant forces on city councils in major cities such as Philadelphia, Detroit, Washington, Memphis, Tenn., Atlanta, Baltimore, New Orleans, Oakland, Calif., Newark, N.J., and Cincinnati. In these cities, blacks have held administrative offices such as school superintendent, school principal and chief of police. Plus, there's the precedent-setting fact of there being 44 black members of Congress and a black president. What has this political power meant for the significant socio-economic problems faced by a large segment of the black community? Clearly, it has done little or nothing for academic achievement; the number of black students scoring proficient is far below the national average.

Sex and Race Equality. By Walter E. Williams
http://patriotpost.us/opinion/24474
Excerpt: There are several race and sex issues that need addressing. Let's look at a few of them with an ear to these questions: Should we insist upon equal treatment

of people by race and sex or tolerate differences in treatment? And just how equal are people by race and sex in the first place? According to the National Institutes of Health, male infants 1 to 3 months old should be fed 472 to 572 calories per day, whereas their female counterparts should receive 438 to 521 calories per day. That's an official sex-based caloric 10 percent rip-off of baby females. In addition to this government-sanctioned war on women, one wonders whether the NIH has a race-based caloric rip-off where they recommend that black newborns receive fewer calories than white newborns.

Coming End to Racial Preferences. By Walter E. Williams
http://townhall.com/columnists/walterewilliams/2014/05/07/coming-end-to-racial-preferences-n1833640?utm_source=thdailypm&utm_medium=email&utm_campaign=nl_pm
Excerpt: She went on to make the incredible argument that the amendment, which explicitly forbids racial discrimination, itself amounts to racial discrimination. Her argument was that permissible "race-sensitive admissions policies," the new name for racial preferences, both serve the compelling interest of obtaining the educational benefits that flow from a diverse student body and inure people to the benefit of racial minorities. By the way, no one has come up with hard evidence of the supposed "educational benefits" that come from a racially mixed student body, and there's mounting evidence of harm done to minorities through academic mismatching.

Equality in Discipline. By Walter E. Williams
http://townhall.com/columnists/walterewilliams/2014/04/16/equality-in-discipline-n1824229?utm_source=thdaily&utm_medium=email&utm_campaign=nl
Excerpt: George Leef, director of research for the North Carolina-based John William Pope Center for Higher Education Policy, authored a Forbes op-ed article titled "Obama Administration Takes Groupthink To Absurd Lengths." The subtitle is "School Discipline Rates Must Be 'Proportionate.'" (http://tinyurl.com/mxnlg9h). Let's examine some of the absurdity of the Obama administration's take on student discipline.

OK to Feel Sorry. By Walter E. Williams
http://patriotpost.us/opinion/22838
Excerpt: The widespread and open criticism of Rodman shows that there's been considerable progress and that I don't have to feel as sorry for white people. But what about the weak media response to Rep. Henry C. Johnson, D-Ga., who, during a 2010 House Armed Services Committee hearing concerning U.S. military buildup on Guam, told Adm. Robert F. Willard, the then commander of U.S. Pacific Command, "My fear is that the whole island will become so overly populated that it will tip over and capsize"? Adm. Willard replied, with all sincerity, "We don't anticipate that." I'd pay serious money to know what the admiral and his white staff said about Johnson after they left the hearing room. Then there's Rep. Sheila Jackson Lee, D-Texas, who asked NASA scientists whether they could drive the Mars rover to where Neil Armstrong placed the American flag.

Beyond affirmative action to colorblindness. By Ben S. Carson
http://americancurrentsee.com/ac/article/news/2014/feb/18/carson-beyond-affirmative-action/
Excerpt: As a child growing up in Detroit and Boston, I had many opportunities to experience the ugly face of racism and witnessed the devastating toll exacted by its mean-spirited nature. I was a victim of the racism of low expectations for black children, but in retrospect, I can see that many of those attitudes were based on ignorance. Large numbers of white people actually believed that blacks were intellectually inferior, and there were a host of other inaccurate beliefs that whites held about blacks and that blacks held about whites.

Neurosurgeon, opinion maker Dr. Ben Carson visits Mississippi College
http://www.clarionledger.com/story/news/2014/04/23/neurosurgeon-opinion-maker-dr-ben-carson-visits-mississippi-college/8047045/
Excerpt: "It starts with the people. The people must understand that they are being manipulated. We have to start talking to each other, and not allow our talking points to be taken from the media, and from the political class, and particularly from the purveyors of political correctness," Carson said.

NAACP requires marchers protesting North Carolina voter ID law TO SHOW PHOTO ID
http://dailycaller.com/2014/02/08/naacp-requires-marchers-protesting-north-carolina-voter-id-law-to-show-photo-id/#ixzz2zYQa92lu
Excerpt: North Carolinians marching to protest voter-ID laws must present a valid photo ID to participate in an NAACP-hosted protest against voter-ID laws in Raleigh on Saturday.

A Black Conservative Takes on the 'Poverty Pentagon'
http://patriotpost.us/articles/25063
Excerpt: Woodson says the flap over Ryan's comments may end up being beneficial if it sparks the "right conversation" about helping the poor. "Low-income people haven't been on President Obama's agenda for five years," he says. We'd only add that while low-income people have indeed been left behind in Obama's "recovery," they have occasionally shown up on his teleprompter.

Black Slave Owners by Joseph Holloway
http://slaverebellion.org/index.php?page=the-black-slave-owners
According to this article, there were 3,000 free black slave owners in New Orleans in 1860 and over 400 in Charleston, SC in 1830. ~Bob

In a tangle over euphemisms for affirmative action. By George F. Will
http://www.washingtonpost.com/opinions/george-f-will-the-supreme-court-tangles-over-euphemisms-for-affirmative-action/2014/04/25/9bed399c-cbd1-11e3-95f7-7ecdde72d2ea_story.html?wpisrc=nl_opnsat
Excerpt: Anodyne euphemisms often indicate an uneasy conscience or a political

anxiety. Or both, as when the 1976 Democratic platform chose "compensatory opportunity" as a way of blurring the fact that the party favored racial discrimination in the form of preferences and quotas for certain government-favored minorities in such matters as government hiring, contracting and college admissions. Since then, "affirmative action" has become the ubiquitous semantic evasion.

Ignoring Single-Parent Families in the Inequality Debate
http://www.ncpa.org/sub/dpd/index.php?Article_ID=24344&utm_
source=newsletter&utm_medium=email&utm_campaign=DPD
Excerpt: The rise of single-parent families over the last 50 years is the strongest correlate of inequality in the United States, yet few politicians and researchers will even address the issue when they talk about inequality, say Robert Maranto, a professor in the Department of Education Reform at the University of Arkansas, and researcher Michael Crouch. The United States has seen a rapid decline in the traditional two-parent family: In 1960, more than 76 percent of African-Americans and almost 97 percent of whites were born to married couples. Today, only 30 percent of black children are born to married couples. For white children, that figure is 70 percent. Hispanics had an out-of-wedlock birthrate of more than 50 percent in 2006. With out-of-wedlock births and high divorce rates, one quarter of American children live in single-parent homes. This is twice the rate in Europe. ... Just 2 percent of children raised in two-parent families experience poverty long-term, while more than 20 percent of children in single-parent families live in long-term poverty. Penn State sociologist Molly Martin estimated in 2006 that 41 percent of economic inequality generated between 1976 and 2000 was the result of changed family structure. According to researchers at the Brookings Institution, the U.S. poverty rate would be a full 25 percent lower today if the U.S. family structure resembled that of 1970.

What if Trayvon Had Been White, and the Shooter Black? By Michael Filozof
http://www.americanthinker.com/2012/03/what_if_trayvon_had_been_white_and_
the_shooter_black.html#ixzz1qBLNnX9L
Excerpt: We know what would happen in such a case. There would be no white mobs in the street chanting "No justice, no peace!" There would be no whites holding a "million hoodie march" in New York City. ... We know this because in fact, such an event occurred in 2009 in Greece, N.Y., a suburb of Rochester. Roderick Scott, a black man, shot and killed an unarmed white teen, Christopher Cervini, whom he believed was burglarizing a neighbor's car, with a licensed .40 cal. handgun.

Blacks benefit from Florida 'Stand Your Ground' law at disproportionate rate. By Patrick Howley
http://dailycaller.com/2013/07/16/blacks-benefit-from-florida-stand-your-ground-law-at-disproportionate-rate/
Excerpt: African Americans benefit from Florida's "Stand Your Ground" self-defense law at a rate far out of proportion to their presence in the state's population, despite an assertion by Attorney General Eric Holder that repealing "Stand Your Ground" would help African Americans. Black Floridians have made about a third of the state's

total "Stand Your Ground" claims in homicide cases, a rate nearly double the black percentage of Florida's population. The majority of those claims have been successful, a success rate that exceeds that for Florida whites.

Civil Rights Act of 1964, Voting by party
https://www.govtrack.us/congress/votes/88-1964/h182
Over 80% of Republicans in the House and Senate voted for the bill. Fewer than 70% of Democrats did. But a great many of the Democrats that voted no were from the south.

The 'Racism' Wrecking Ball: Indiscriminate charges of racism do more harm than good, as Martin Luther King well knew. By John Fund
http://www.nationalreview.com/article/367176/racism-wrecking-ball-john-fund
Excerpt: Shouting "racism" in a crowded media and political theater has become a substitute for thought and debate in America.

IAC PR exec fired over offensive AIDS tweet
http://www.politico.com/blogs/media/2013/12/iac-pr-executive-fired-over-offensive-aids-tweet-180121.html
In case you think casual, thoughtless racism doesn't exist today. ~Bob

Cliven Bundy Under Fire for 'Negro' Comments, Wondering Whether Blacks Would Be 'Better Off as Slaves, Picking Cotton'
http://www.theblaze.com/stories/2014/04/24/cliven-bundy-under-fire-for-negro-comments-wondering-whether-blacks-would-be-better-off-as-slaves-picking-cotton/
Excerpt: "And because they were basically on government subsidy, so now what do they do?" he continued. "They abort their young children, they put their young men in jail, because they never learned how to pick cotton. And I've often wondered, are they better off as slaves, picking cotton and having a family life and doing things, or are they better off under government subsidy? They didn't get no more freedom. They got less freedom."

Unedited Video Shows Bundy Making Pro-Black, Pro-Mexican Comments
http://www.infowars.com/unedited-video-shows-bundy-making-pro-black-pro-mexican-comments/
Excerpt: The controversy over Cliven Bundy's "racist" remarks has taken a new turn after longer unedited footage emerged showing the Nevada cattle rancher making pro-black and pro-Mexican comments that were excised out of media reports. ... We've progressed quite a bit from that day until now, and sure don't want to go back; we sure don't want the colored people to go back to that point; we sure don't want the Mexican people to go back to that point; and we can make a difference right now by taking care of some of these bureaucracies, and do it in a peaceful way. ... Now, let me talk about the Spanish people. You know I understand that they come over here against our constitution and cross our borders. But they're here and they're people – and I've worked side-by-side a lot of them. Don't tell me they don't work, and don't

tell me they don't pay taxes. And don't tell me they don't have better family structure than most of us white people. When you see those Mexican families, they're together, they picnic together, they're spending their time together, and I'll tell you in my way of thinking they're awful nice people.

CNN Talks To Black Bundy Bodyguard: 'He Is Not A Racist. He's Pretty Much Treating Me Just Like His Own Family'
http://patdollard.com/2014/04/cnn-talks-to-black-bundy-bodyguard-he-is-not-a-racist-hes-pretty-much-treating-me-just-like-his-own-family/

President Obama: Alleged Donald Sterling remarks 'incredibly offensive'
http://www.politico.com/story/2014/04/president-obama-donald-sterling-remarks-106062.html#ixzz30Gfnfk3V
Excerpt: TMZ first posted an audio recording Friday of a conversation reportedly between Sterling and his girlfriend, V. Stiviano, where the owner told her not to bring black players to team games or post pictures with African-Americans on Instagram. "It bothers me a lot that you want to broadcast that you're associating with black people. Do you have to?" the voice in the recording says.

Clippers owner Donald Sterling banned for life from NBA, fined $2.5 million by NBA
http://www.foxnews.com/sports/2014/04/29/clippers-owner-donald-sterling-banned-for-life-from-nba-fined-25-million-by-nba/
Excerpt: The NBA threw the book at LA Clippers owner Donald Sterling, banning him for life, fining him $2.5 million and raising the possibility of a forced sale of the team over racist remarks he made to an ex-girlfriend that surfaced on a tape recording.

Authorities investigate alleged racial threat in Stoughton
http://www.jsonline.com/news/wisconsin/authorities-investigate-alleged-racial-threat-in-stoughton-b99251411z1-255845831.html
Excerpt: The family of the 18-year-old man told police a letter sent to their home in Stoughton included a photo showing two men hanging from a tree, with his picture superimposed onto one of the men, according to a posting on the newspaper's website.

More Tea Party Racists?
http://tartanmarine.blogspot.com/2014/04/more-tea-party-racists.html
Photo of black Tea Party members. I have not verified the picture. ~Bob

Thug Life: Who's your daddy? Apparently, no one. By Crystal Wright (Black Writer)
http://communities.washingtontimes.com/neighborhood/crystal-wright-conservative-black-chick/2014/jan/9/thug-life-whos-your-daddy-apparently-no-one/#ixzz2pwBKK1rw
Excerpt: Liberals and some liberal blacks have expressed disdain for the Omaha police in posting the video, claiming it stereotypes blacks and the man's behavior is an anomaly. But the opposite is true. In DC where I currently live and witness frequently uneducated blacks calling each other and their children the same sorts of heinous

names. I have never seen white people talk to each other this way, much less their children.

'Racist' Storm Over Black Toddler Being Taught Obscenities
http://patdollard.com/2014/01/racist-storm-over-black-toddler-spouting-obscenities/
Excerpt: After the Omaha Police Officers' Association highlighted a shock video of a black toddler being encouraged by his family to spout obscenities as a warning against the "cycle of violence and thuggery," subsequent outrage was not directed against the family but against the police association for being racist.

Why People Fail. By Daniel Greenfield
http://www.frontpagemag.com/2014/dgreenfield/why-people-fail/?utm_source=FrontPage+Magazine&utm_medium=email&utm_campaign=6e6a2f5dc6-Mailchimp_FrontPageMag&utm_term=0_57e32c1dad-6e6a2f5dc6-156414477
Excerpt: And yet it's undeniable that some cultures succeed where others fail. The left refuses to distinguish between culture and race; denouncing everything from criticism of Islam to complaints about gang culture as racist. It treats culture as equivalent to race because it doesn't believe that people are capable of change.

To defeat poverty, look to marriage. By Kathleen Parker
http://www.washingtonpost.com/opinions/kathleen-parker-to-defeat-poverty-look-to-marriage/2014/01/14/33e274ae-7d5f-11e3-95c6-0a7aa80874bc_story.html?wpisrc=nl_opinions
Excerpt: The really lucky ones are also born into stable, educated families with financial security and grown-up parents. Then there are the unlucky, who, whatever their relative talents, are born into broken families, often to single mothers, in neighborhoods where systemic poverty, inferior educational opportunities and perhaps even crime constitute the culture in which they marinate.

Benefits of Marriage
http://www.familyfacts.org/briefs/1/the-benefits-of-marriage

Paternal Involvement Increases College Graduation Rates
http://www.ncpa.org/sub/dpd/index.php?Article_ID=24369&utm_source=newsletter&utm_medium=email&utm_campaign=DPD
Excerpt: Teenagers with involved fathers are significantly more likely to graduate from college, says Bradford Wilcox, associate professor in the department of sociology at the University of Virginia and visiting scholar at the American Enterprise Institute. ... Teenagers with involved fathers were 98 percent more likely to graduate from college than teens who reported that their fathers were not involved. Those with very involved fathers were 105 percent more likely to graduate from college.

Black Unemployment: Not Just a Disgrace, a Sin. By John Ransom
http://finance.townhall.com/columnists/johnransom/2014/01/14/obama-the-mancaused-disaster-for-black-men-in-america-n1778564?utm_source=thdaily&utm_medium=email&utm_campaign=nl
Excerpt: "Blacks disproportionately left the labor market," said Dean Baker, co-director of the Center for Economic and Policy Research, a liberal economic outfit, "with the labor force participation rate for African Americans dropping by 0.3 percentage points to 60.2 percent, it's lowest rate since December of 1977. The rate for African American men fell 0.7 percent to 65.6 percent, the lowest on record."

The Left Versus the Realities of Race. By Jack Kerwick
http://www.frontpagemag.com/2014/jack-kerwick/the-left-versus-the-realities-of-race/?utm_source=FrontPage+Magazine&utm_medium=email&utm_campaign=155958ee10-Mailchimp_FrontPageMag&utm_term=0_57e32c1dad-155958ee10-156414477
Excerpt: In almost every instance of the so-called "knock out game," perpetrators have been black and their victims mostly white and/or Asian. There is one—and only one—case in which the racial dynamics of this violence reversed course, an incident from Texas involving a white predator and a black prey. Not unsurprisingly, this is the only instance of "the game" that Barack Obama's Department of Justice is choosing to pursue as a "hate crime."

Black residents oppose Trader Joes in Portland neighborhood, claim it would attract too many white people
http://topconservativenews.com/2014/02/black-residents-oppose-trader-joes-in-portland-neighborhood-claim-it-would-attract-to-many-white-people/

Trader Joe's pulls plug on Northeast Portland development after 'negative reactions' from community
http://www.oregonlive.com/portland/index.ssf/2014/02/trader_joes_pulls_plug_on_nort.html
Black "leaders" often complain that black neighborhoods have higher food prices and fewer jobs due to racism. Imagine if white folks opposed a business because it would bring in too many blacks! Not to mention that this type of racist statement from blacks encourages white racism in response. ~Bob.

Mob of teens film themselves attacking and robbing disabled vet while shouting 'Knock that white boy out!'
http://www.dailymail.co.uk/news/article-2559894/Mob-teens-film-attacking-robbing-disabled-vet-shouting-Knock-white-boy-out.html
Excerpt: Three teenagers accused of beating and robbing a disabled Army veteran on an Ohio bus while shouting racial slurs have been arrested. (While this hurts the victim, it also hurts decent black folks who will suffer from the stereotype of black violence. ~Bob)

Obama Kicking a Door: Racist
http://conservativebyte.com/2014/02/student-forced-apologize-emailing-pic-obama-kicking-door-racism/
Excerpt: Anything critical of Obama is racist anymore. Check it out: A student at McGill University in Montreal, Canada was forced to issue a formal apology for emailing a picture of President Obama kicking open a door–all because some students thought the image was somehow racist. (When everything is racist, nothing is racist. This hurts black folks most of all, as it disguises real racism which still exists and makes folks not believe in it. ~Bob)

Medal Of Honor Awarded To Veterans Possibly Passed Over Due To Racism
http://www.huffingtonpost.com/2014/02/22/medal-of-honor-racism_n_4837454.html?utm_hp_ref=email_share
I think this rights a wrong, as it is very likely in my view they were downgraded due to race. Impossible to know what was in the reviewers' heads, of course. ~Bob

NYC: More Black Babies Killed by Abortion Than Born
http://www.cnsnews.com/news/article/michael-w-chapman/nyc-more-black-babies-killed-abortion-born
Excerpt: In 2012, there were more black babies killed by abortion (31,328) in New York City than were born there (24,758), and the black children killed comprised 42.4% of the total number of abortions in the Big Apple, according to a report by the New York City Department of Health and Mental Hygiene. (Somewhere, eugenicist Margaret Sanger -- founder of Planned Parenthood Federation of America and a staunch proponent of the forced sterilization and abortions of black and minority children -- is smiling. --The Patriot Post.)

Saudi Arabia: The Middle East's Real Apartheid State. By Daniel Greenfield
http://www.frontpagemag.com/2014/dgreenfield/saudi-arabia-the-middle-easts-real-apartheid-state/?utm_source=FrontPage+Magazine&utm_medium=email&utm_campaign=cace5002a4-Mailchimp_FrontPageMag&utm_term=0_57e32c1dad-cace5002a4-156414477
Excerpt: There is a country in the Middle East where 10 percent of the population is denied equal rights because of their race, where black men are not allowed to hold many government positions, where black women are put on trial for witchcraft and where the custody of children is granted to the parent with the most "racially superior" bloodline. This Apartheid State is so enormously powerful that it controls American foreign policy in the Middle East even as its princes and princesses bring their slaves to the United Kingdom and the United States.

Why Does Hollywood Ignore White Slavery? By Jim Goad
http://takimag.com/article/why_does_hollywood_ignore_white_slavery_jim_goad#axzz2w41N67MI
Excerpt: Yet I can't recall ever seeing a film that deals with the fact that in 1775, George Washington offered a reward for the capture and return of eight runaway white servants who'd escaped his clutches.

Supreme Court upholds Michigan affirmative action ban
http://www.foxnews.com/politics/2014/04/22/supreme-court-upholds-michigan-affirmative-action-ban/
Excerpt: The Supreme Court on Tuesday upheld Michigan's ban on using race as a factor in college admissions. The justices said in a 6-2 ruling that Michigan voters had the right to change their state constitution to prohibit public colleges and universities from taking account of race in admissions decisions. The justices said that a lower federal court was wrong to set aside the change as discriminatory.

Political Competition, Not Racism, Changes Voter Alignments. By Michael Barone
http://jewishworldreview.com/michael/barone042314.php3#.U1feUPldXqQ
Excerpt: You can find a more nuanced and thoughtful analysis in Jonathan Chait's recent New York magazine article, "The Color of His Presidency." Chait, a liberal, starts off by noting that the post-racial America that Obama seemed to promise in his 2004 national convention speech and his 2008 campaign has not come into being. On the contrary, "Race, always the deepest and most volatile fault line in American history," he writes, "has now become the primal grievance in our politics, the source of a narrative of persecution each side uses to make sense of the world." Many liberals see racism in every criticism of the Obama presidency, even though, as Chait points out, Bill Clinton met with similar and in some cases more strident opposition.

The Color of His Presidency. By Jonathon Chait
http://nymag.com/news/features/obama-presidency-race-2014-4/
Excerpt: A different, unexpected racial argument has taken shape. Race, always the deepest and most volatile fault line in American history, has now become the primal grievance in our politics, the source of a narrative of persecution each side uses to make sense of the world. Liberals dwell in a world of paranoia of a white racism that has seeped out of American history in the Obama years and lurks everywhere, mostly undetectable. Conservatives dwell in a paranoia of their own, in which racism is used as a cudgel to delegitimize their core beliefs. And the horrible thing is that both of these forms of paranoia are right. (It's hard to get to the full article, but what you can read is interesting. ~Bob)

It's Hard to See Racism When You're a Collectivist. By Daniel Greenfield
http://www.frontpagemag.com/2014/dgreenfield/its-hard-to-see-racism-when-youre-a-collectivist/?utm_source=FrontPage+Magazine&utm_medium=email&utm_campaign=f1f03855c1-Mailchimp_FrontPageMag&utm_term=0_57e32c1dad-f1f03855c1-156414477
Excerpt: It's not that the left believes that affirmative action isn't racist. It's that it believes that there is no such thing as racism against white people. Like the Knockout Game or white students who qualify on merit but can't get into college because of racial diversity quotas; it's an invalid category. A myth. And if it's a myth, then there's nothing wrong with a little racial violence or a few racial preferences.

Some Of The Lost History In The Civil Rights Movement. By Robert Rohlfing
http://canadafreepress.com/index.php/article/some-of-the-lost-history-in-the-civil-rights-movement
Excerpt: It should also be noted that LBJ was not the great Crusader of Civil Rights. President Johnson made a 360— turn in his civil rights position when he became President, from 1940 to 1960 Johnson voted with the South 78% on civil rights issues. Prior to 1957, Johnson voted with the South 100% on civil rights issues. He also voted against the C.R.A. of 1957 and 1960. Were you aware that in order to break the racist ways of Southern Democrats, it was Republican President Eisenhower who sponsored both Civil Rights Act and Voting Rights Act and it was a LBJ lead Senate who fought tooth and nail against them? Ike finally signed a watered down Civil Rights Bill. Yes, let me repeat that, Republican President Dwight Eisenhower sponsored and signed the first Civil Rights Bill. (Interesting "facts," but note the writer is a conservative so is spinning them his way. Take for what it is worth. ~Bob)

What My Father Told Me About LBJ and "Niggers." By Robert Morrow
http://www.economicpolicyjournal.com/2013/08/what-my-father-told-me-about-lbj-and.html
Excerpt: They were sitting on either side of a narrow coffee table in the Oval office and big Lyndon with his long strong arms and big powerful Texas rough hands reached over and slapped both Seymore and George hard on their knees and held their legs a moment and said "Now you boys, you gotta get your G--damned asses back down to Alabama and make those G--damned niggers act right and calm the hell down! I am G--damned tired of hearing 'bout those G--damned niggers on the G--damned news every night! ... From Ronald Kessler, Inside the Whitehouse, pp. 33-34: During one trip, Johnson was discussing his proposed civil rights bill with two governors. Explaining why it was so important to him, he said it was simple: "I'll have them niggers voting Democratic for two hundred years." That was the reason he was pushing the bill," said [Robert M. MacMillan, an Air Force One steward], who was present during the conversation. "Not because he wanted equality for everyone. It was strictly a political ploy for the Democratic party. (The reported LBJ "Niggers voting Democrat" remarks are widely quoted on conservative websites, including by black conservatives, but ignored or dismissed by liberals. I'd rate it as second hand hearsay, but it may still be true. Certainly other sources confirm that LBJ had a foul mouth, and we know about his integrity from his first senate primary and his undeserved Silver Star from one flight in the Pacific during WWII. The quote is disputed on the liberal site below. ~Bob)

Highly Dubious LBJ Quote & What It Says About Those Who Eagerly Believe It
http://w-dervish.blogspot.com/2014/01/highly-dubious-lbj-quote-what-it-says.html
Excerpt: For instance, DeMaio has been the target of homophobic attacks. But where are those attacks coming from? It's not always from the far right social conservatives you'd expect; rather, it's been from DeMaio's left – the liberal and Democrat-affiliated groups that you'd think would be proud that an openly gay successful businessman has decided to run for office. One false attack drew the attention of the San Diego

Ethics Commission. An anonymous left-wing group funded a SuperPac and sent mailers of DeMaio Photoshopped next to a drag queen to neighborhoods with a majority of elderly and African-American voters, knowing that such a photo would depress support for DeMaio. That was so egregious and false that the group was fined by the city's Ethics Commission, but even after that, and with his 100 percent voting record with the LGBT community, the Left still didn't speak up to defend him. They told DeMaio, "It's complicated."

25 Examples of Liberal Racism in Quotes. By John Hawkins
http://townhall.com/columnists/johnhawkins/2013/03/26/25-examples-of-liberal-racism-in-quotes-n1549044/page/full

9 Racist Things that Big Democrats Have Said and the Media Has Forgotten
http://clashdaily.com/2014/04/9-racist-things-big-democrats-said-media-forgotten/
Some different from above. ~Bob

10-Eye-Opening Quotes From Planned Parenthood Founder Margaret Sanger
http://www.lifenews.com/2013/03/11/10-eye-opening-quotes-from-planned-parenthood-founder-margaret-sanger/
Excerpt: Margaret Sanger has been lauded by some as a woman of valor, but a closer look reveals that Planned Parenthood's audacious founder had some unsavory things to say about matters of race, birth control, and abortion. An outspoken eugenicist herself, Sanger consistently promoted racist ideals with a contemptuous attitude.

8 Things That Won't Get You Banned by the NBA
http://www.breitbart.com/Breitbart-Sports/2014/04/29/8-Things-That-Wont-Get-You-Banned-by-the-NBA?utm_source=e_breitbart_com&utm_medium=email&utm_conte
nt=Breitbart+News+Roundup%2C+April+30%2C+2014&utm_campaign=20140430_
m120218059_Breitbart+News+Roundup%2C+April+30%2C+2014&utm_term=More
Excerpt: 3. Being a publicly vicious racist while black. Spike Lee has stated that white gentrification of Harlem has been horrible, has posted the address of George Zimmerman's parents online to spur violence, has explained after visiting South Africa in the early 1990s, "I seriously wanted to pick up a gun and shoot whites. The only way to resolve matters is by bloodshed." He, like Donald Sterling, is no fan of interracial dating: "I give interracial couples a look. Daggers. They get uncomfortable when they see me on the street."

Stephen Colbert's Politically Incorrect Joke on Twitter Has People Calling for His Show to Be Cancelled. By Jason Howerton
http://www.theblaze.com/stories/2014/03/27/stephen-colberts-politically-incorrect-joke-on-twitter-has-people-calling-for-his-show-to-be-cancelled/
Excerpt: Apparently channeling the "ignorant" character that he plays on his TV show, comedian Stephen Colbert tweeted on Thursday, "I am willing to show #Asian community I care by introducing the Ching-Chong Ding-Dong Foundation for Sensitivity to Orientals or Whatever."

Michelle Obama at Bowie State: Too many young people "fantasize about being a baller or a rapper"
http://www.blackyouthproject.com/2013/05/michelle-obama-at-bowie-state-too-many-young-people-fantasize-about-being-a-baller-or-a-rapper/

"What shall we do with the Negro?" By Frederick Douglass
http://www.lexrex.com/enlightened/writings/douglas.htm
"What shall we do with the Negro?" I have had but one answer from the beginning. Do nothing with us! Your doing with us has already played the mischief with us. Do nothing with us! If the apples will not remain on the tree of their own strength, if they are worm eaten at the core, if they are early ripe and disposed to fall, let them fall! I am not for tying or fastening them on the tree in any way, except by nature's plan, and if they will not stay there, let them fall. And if the Negro cannot stand on his own legs, let him fall also. All I ask is, give him a chance to stand on his own legs! Let him alone!

Paul Ryan Laments Inner-City Culture Of Not Working
http://www.huffingtonpost.com/2014/03/12/paul-ryan-inner-cities_n_4949165.html
Excerpt: "We have got this tailspin of culture, in our inner cities in particular, of men not working and just generations of men not even thinking about working or learning the value and the culture of work," the Wisconsin Republican said on Bill Bennett's "Morning in America" radio show. "There is a real culture problem here that has to be dealt with." Rep. Barbara Lee (D-Calif.) called Ryan's remark "deeply offensive." "My colleague Congressman Ryan's comments about 'inner city' poverty are a thinly veiled racial attack and cannot be tolerated," Lee said in an email to reporters. "Let's be clear, when Mr. Ryan says 'inner city,' when he says 'culture,' these are simply code words for what he really means: 'black.'"

The Good News about Racism in America. By Bernard Goldberg
http://www.bernardgoldberg.com/good-news-racism-america/?utm_source=BernardGoldberg.com+Newsletter&utm_campaign=4dfd0698dd-NEWSLETTER&utm_medium=email&utm_term=0_c1903183b6-4dfd0698dd-284965241
Excerpt: And that so many Americans – of all races — have turned against him and his bigotry is a good thing. That's what's missing from coverage of the Donald Sterling story. And if you want to know how seriously we take Sterling's racist remarks, consider this: CNN has finally ended its non-stop coverage of the missing Malaysian jetliner and now is going all out on Sterling. In a country of more than 300 million people there are always going to be some bigots. But they've become outliers in our culture – outcasts, actually.

Meet The Poster Child For 'White Privilege' – Then Have Your Mind Blown. By Jennifer Kabbany
http://www.thecollegefix.com/post/17230/
Excerpt: His name is Tal Fortgang, and just eight months into his Ivy League

experience, he's been told on numerous occasions to "check his privilege" – a phrase that has taken social media social justice campaigning by storm. It is meant to remind white, heterosexual males that they have it so good because they're white, heterosexual males. They haven't faced tough times, they don't know what it's like to be judged by the color of their skin. Oh, but they do. Those sick of being labeled are the very same ones doing it to others, and Tal Fortgang has a powerful message for them:

The Dividends of Racial Politics. By Star Parker
http://townhall.com/columnists/starparker/2014/05/02/the-dividends-of-racial-politics-n1832913?utm_source=thdaily&utm_medium=email&utm_campaign=nl
Excerpt: Isn't race supposed to be behind us? Hasn't America elected, twice, a black man as its president? But these days our president is far less popular than he was when, with much fanfare, he was first elected. ... Race is not going to go away because it is too useful to the party of the left. In fact, it has never been so important. (Star Parker [a black writer] is founder and president of CURE, the Center for Urban Renewal and Education, a 501c3 think tank which explores and promotes market based public policy to fight poverty, as well as author of the newly revised Uncle Sam's Plantation: How Big Government Enslaves America's Poor and What We Can do About It.)

Ala. Dem Offers $100K for Proof of White Families Adopting Black Kids; Families Show Up. Lawmaker previously lashed out against Clarence Thomas by referencing his interracial marriage. By Andrew Johnson
http://m.nationalreview.com/article/376480/ala-dem-offers-100k-proof-white-families-adopting-black-kids-families-show-andrew
Excerpt: Mixed-race families from across Alabama rallied outside the state capitol recently to demand $100,000 in cash — or at least an apology — from a state representative. Earlier this month, Alvin Holmes, who has represented the Montgomery-area 78th District for 39 years, bet a substantial purse on his claim that Alabama whites were incapable of tolerating black children. "I will bring you $100,000 cash tomorrow if you show me a whole bunch of whites that adopted blacks in Alabama," Holmes said. "I will go down there and mortgage my house and get it in cash in $20 bills and bring it to you in a little briefcase."

From a woman of faith who loves America: 'Black people have been deceived'
http://dailycaller.com/2013/12/01/from-a-woman-of-faith-who-loves-america-blacks-have-been-deceived-video/#ixzz30xH17cFt
Excerpt: Dr. Carol Swain, professor of law and political science at Vanderbilt Law School, is a woman of faith who loves this country and the Constitution. ... As a black person, it bothers me that the America I know and love I feel like is being destroyed by a black man. I don't understand why," she said, discussing her serious concerns about President Obama's legacy in an interview with The Daily Caller.

Islamic Antisemitism
http://wikiislam.net/wiki/Islamic_Antisemitism

Slavery still exists

'I Abducted Your Girls,' Nigerian Extremist Leader Admits
http://time.com/87658/boko-haram-nigeria-kidnapped-girls/
Excerpt: Extremist group Boko Haram's leader owned up to the April kidnapping of 276 schoolgirls in Nigeria and vowed to "sell them on the market." He also warned that his group plans to attack more schools and abduct more girls.

Muslim Cleric Urges Homeless Women to Become Sex-Slaves. By Raymond Ibrahim
http://www.frontpagemag.com/2014/raymond-ibrahim/muslim-cleric-urges-homeless-women-to-become-sex-slaves/?utm_source=FrontPage+Magazine&utm_medium=email&utm_campaign=b007345ea3-Mailchimp_FrontPageMag&utm_term=0_57e32c1dad-b007345ea3-156414477
Excerpt: Now, the same Islamic cleric who issued this last "rape fatwa" has issued another fatwa urging destitute women in war torn Syria to become the "right hand possessions" of any man willing to support them—basically, to sell themselves into sex-slavery.

The Islamic Republic of) Mauritania agrees to adopt roadmap to eradicate slavery
http://www.middle-east-online.com/english/?id=64541
Excerpt: The United Nations envoy on modern-day slavery said on Thursday Mauritania had agreed to adopt a roadmap for eradicating the trade, which campaigners say remains widespread in the west African nation. The country was the last in the world to abolish slavery, in 1981, and since 2012 its practice has been officially designated a crime, but campaigners say the government has failed in the past to acknowledge the extent of the trade, with no official data available.

It doesn't matter who you vote for in November

If you look at the fiscal situation of the country, it probably makes no difference who you vote for, either in 2016 as I write or in the future. And this is the issue that will destroy the Republic, though the Jihadists, China, and illegal immigration will heavily contribute to our fiscal woes. Who uses what bathroom, though emotional, will make no difference in the long run. Big government types like Clinton and her long-time supporter and contributor, Trump, always have an advantage, as the public may hate taxes, but they love benefits if paid for by someone else, preferably future generations through borrowing.

The acknowledged Federal Debt, now I think north of $19T, is the small part of the fiscal problem. The big part is the unfunded liability, money the government has promised to spend for things like Social Security, Medicare, Medicaid, SS Disability, and now Obamacare, that it does not have in the bank. This is not considered debt because, though promised, it is not owed by contract and the government can legally default on these items. Thus creating chaos and social upheaval. (The Social Security Trust Fund is not cash, but special government bonds, which cannot be sold on the open market. The government borrowed the cash.) Social Security, now as always, is paid out from the FICA taxes taken in. When the income doesn't cover the outgo, the money to redeem the "bonds" must come from the general fund. When SS started, and folks didn't live as long; 38 workers supported one retiree. Now, with increased longevity and the expansion of benefits, 2.5 workers support one retiree. The average retiree now gets back much more than he or she paid in. You can graph the day not far in the future when it will be one worker supporting one retiree. I have seen estimates of the unfunded liability that run from $87T to $240T, depending on who counts, what is counted and how far out you project. Add to that the debt and unfunded liability of the states and cities, and there are not enough trees to print that much money. It is difficult for me to see how a fiscal and economic collapse, followed by social and political collapse, can be avoided. When governments can't meet their obligations, they always turn to printing fiat money, destroying the value of savings and retirement funds through hyper-inflation. Which is why I recently bought a billion dollars in Zimbabwe currency for about $8 bucks on eBay. And why it doesn't matter at all which corrupt, big-government, liberal you vote for in November. And why electing a true fiscal conservative could only slow the drive towards the cliff, not reverse it.

I suggest everyone read this Newsweek article, "**The West and the Tyranny of Public Debt**" http://www.newsweek.com/2010/12/27/the-west-and-the-tyranny-of-public-debt.html

I addressed this problem in my short book a few years back: *The Coming Collapse of the American Republic: And what you can do to prevent it.* http://www.amazon.com/Coming-Collapse-American-Republic-prevent/dp/1461122538/ref=sr_1_5?s=books&ie=UTF8&qid=1304815980&sr=1-5

All royalties go to a charity to help wounded veterans. For a free PDF of this 80-page book you can read on your computer, write me at: tartanmarine@gmail.com. Forget gold--invest in canned goods and ammo.

Fifteen Habits of Highly Effective Marines

By Anthony F. "Andy" Weddington and Robert A. Hall

Steven Covey's excellent bestseller, *The Seven Habits of Highly Effective People*, has become a cottage industry and rightly a must-read for people-managing. Marines also have habits, and a few more than seven (captured in principles and traits of leadership), that make them effective. Management Guru Peter Drucker said, "Efficiency is doing things right; effectiveness is doing the right things." Marines, as our illustrious history on and off battlefields about the globe shows, are both efficient and effective.

Following are fifteen habits (we have identified) that make Marines, well, Marines. As you read and ponder, what habits would you add that make Marines the most effective (and efficient) fighters in the world?

Highly Effective Marines do the "Must Dos" first: Marines know that in life there are "must-dos," "should-dos," and "like-to-dos." Marines do them in that order. People who procrastinate on the things that must be done, preferring the fun like-to-dos, rarely get around to them in a timely manner. Thus they are never effective.

Highly Effective Marines look out for the welfare of subordinates: Two time-tested Marine Principles of Leadership are "Know your subordinates and look after their welfare" and "Develop your subordinates." They are among the most violated principles in the civilian worlds of politics and business, and why Marine veterans are effective in those arenas as well – because they build strong, productive, and committed teams. Too often the civilian leader is the "big hog at the trough," first in line for pay raises, bonuses, perks and other benefits. This leaves the followers, who do the work, feeling resentful and of marginal value hence they offer a low commitment to the organization's mission which suffers as a result.

Highly Effective Marines take care of their gear: It starts with the rifle, of course, but effective Marines take care – through preventative maintenance and continuous care – of everything from personal 782 gear to tanks and planes. All else being equal, the unit with gear in good shape is going to out-perform one that is negligent or sloppy in this area. And this translates to winning and losing on the battlefield; to survival. The same is true in civilian life. Employees who take the, "Hey, it's not MY stuff" attitude quickly find their organization is out-performed by organizations where the employees treat their equipment as if they had paid for it themselves. The former can't figure out why they are unemployed. Ownership is pride and a workforce multiplier.

Highly Effective Marines stay calm under pressure: Calmness under pressure, even in the face of life-threatening danger, is a learned behavior and a vital survival tool. Nothing makes a leader more effective than staying calm, responding appropriately to the situation, and doing what needs to be done amidst chaos. This habit makes Marines – in the military and civilian world – the go-to guys.

Highly Effective Marines stay organized: Being organized is key to being effective. A couple of decades back, the Edinburgh Military Tattoo featured a Scots Territorial (reserve) Army engineering team versus a US Army team from Germany building a bridge. Every move of the Scots was precise, every man knew his role and where every part he was responsible for was, where it went--and when. The American team scurried about as if scrambling to pick up change from a spilled collection plate at church, hardly knowing who was doing what or with what. Embarrassing it was that the Scots beat the Americans night after night. But they were organized, thus far more effective.

Highly Effective Marines keep themselves in fighting trim: Yes, our society being what it is, even some Marine veterans carry too many pounds. Though an obese Marine is not as frequent a sight, we think, as seen in the rest of the population. Regardless of status (Active; Reserve; Retired; Not in a duty status; Dead – there are no "ex" nor "former" Marines) Marines know fitness – physiological and psychological – go hand-in-hand. Discipline is a critical habit to effective fitness.

Highly Effective Marines help fellow Marines every chance they get: It's part of teamwork and team building – Marines taking care of their own. As the saying goes, "Once a Marine, always a Marine," so it carries on after the Marine hangs up the uniform, and extends to helping non-Marines, too. Hardly a week goes by that we don't read of Marines going out of their way to help – from roadside aid to stopping a crime – someone. This habit, a trait called initiative, makes the team much stronger than whatever it faces.

Highly Effective Marines lead from the front (except in the chow line and akin times) and by example: This doesn't mean the OIC or NCOIC is first through the door clearing a building instead of providing overall control and command. It does mean leaders are with the troops, setting the example, sharing the hardships and dangers – not micro-managing from far away in relative safety. Again, it carries over to the civilian world where Marines never say, "Not my job," but pitch in with everybody to accomplish the mission.

Highly Effective Marines always exercise the moral courage to do what is right for the right reasons: Mark Twain wrote, "It is curious that physical courage should be so common in the world and moral courage so rare." An astute observer of human nature, it's no surprise that Twain's insight is just as true today, and it is sadly often true among the top leaders, who too often think of careers and benefits over the good of the nation or the organization. There may not be a decoration, per se, for moral courage but moral courage is represented by every decoration a Marine wears. Moral courage is as essential to military (and civilian) success as physical courage – or administration or logistics. Any organization where moral courage is not demonstrated, encouraged, and recognized rots from the inside out and is always ineffective.

Highly Effective Marines are not spectators, but make things happen: Several people are credited with versions of the proverb, "Some people make things happen. Some people watch things happen. And then there are those who wonder, 'What the hell just happened?'" Effective Marines always fall into the first category – they don't sit around grumbling, "Someone should do something!" Marines know another proverb is also true, "Not taking action is also a decision, often the worst decision." You cannot be effective if you don't get things done. And you don't get things done unless you make things happen. And, more often than not, forgiveness is easier than permission; especially if acting for the right reason(s) to do the right thing(s).

Highly Effective Marines keep themselves physically and morally squared away: Marines keep their gear, uniforms and consciences uncluttered and in serviceable condition. This makes them good-to-go in any situation, and able to command respect from other Marines, allies, onlookers and even the opposition.

Highly Effective Marines constantly seek self-improvement: Marines, through training and formal as well as off-duty education, strive for perfection. They know self-improvement makes for a more effective individual and, in turn, a more effective organization. Fail to improve then expect to fail.

Highly Effective Marines always have a plan, a backup plan, and a communications plan – then attack: Marines, by ethos and nature, take charge and always have a plan. They have already formulated that plan and in the back of their minds are shaping Plan B in case Plan A doesn't work – and it often doesn't. Marines adapt and keep moving forward. Meanwhile, they want to, must, communicate the plan to everyone who needs to know it. Yes there's the old joke, but reality, about the "10% who don't get the word," but if people don't know the plan or why it is, effectiveness suffers.

Highly Effective Marines never accept mediocrity: Recruits and officer candidates have the acceptance of mediocrity knocked out of them at Parris Island, San Diego and Quantico. "Mediocrity" is a synonym for "ineffective" and is neither in the Marine lexicon nor psyche. The mediocre military organization, business or sports team will always lose to the superior one--the more effective one.

Highly Effective Marines leave no doubt in the minds of others that they are Marines: Time after time, we have heard superior performance – in war, in politics, in sports or in business explained with, "Well, they're a Marine, you know." Co-author Bob Hall was at Fort Drum in 1978 for two weeks of active duty, his unit engaging an Army one for training. In the PX, a Marine he didn't know came up to him and said, "Hey, Marine, where'd you get that tee shirt?" Since it wasn't a USMC shirt, Hall asked, "How'd you know I was a Marine?" "By your bearing," the other Marine replied. Effective Marines project, through appearance and bearing and pride and confidence, they are Marines.

We know Marines, duty status notwithstanding, reading this article already practice most, if not all, of these habits. But thinking about them may help (you and other Marines) strengthen the habits of highly effective Marines. And, it may also help you think of other effective habits we've not cited.

Co-Author Colonel Andy Weddington, U.S. Marines (Retired) served as an infantry officer, 0302. He earned a BA in Psychology and an MA in Business Administration and Management. An accomplished well-known artist, he paints, teaches "seeing" and painting, writes, and occasionally stalks trout with his fly rod. In 2007 he published two books: *On 'Seeing' & Painting--An Interdisciplinary Perspective* (a primer for artists and non-artists alike) and *Making Marines* (a sketchbook – line and word – about recruit training). Gallery (art and books): http://weddingtonartgallery.com He blogs at http://acoloneloftruth.blogspot.com. This joint article is reprinted with his permission.

Thirteen Things Obama Cannot Change by Executive Order

The law of supply and demand.

The truth that nothing is free. When something is described as "free," it only means that the cost was born by someone else.

The law of unintended consequences.

The fact that even the pro-AGW scientists admit there has been no significant global warming since about 1995.

The truth that government cannot give anything to a person without taking it from someone else, because government does not produce wealth.

The law of diminishing returns.

The tendency of all people to make economic choices they believe are in their own or their family's best interests.

The tendency of people to stop trusting someone who has repeatedly lied to them, or made promises he knew he couldn't keep.

The conflict between his green base and creating jobs.

The fact that his many lies and broken promises are caught on video tape and cannot vanish like the IRS emails to him about targeting conservative groups.

The fact that tens of millions of Muslims believe in using violence to subjugated all Infidels to Muslim rule and Shari'a Law, to convert them or to exterminate them.

Give people back the health insurance plans he promised they could keep.

Make his government as transparent as he promised without putting his poll numbers in the teens and perhaps facing impeachment.

The Old Jarhead's Seabag

The Progressive Legacy

The term "progressive" is steadily replacing "liberal," because the pernicious effects of liberal policies became associated in the public mind with the name, much as "liberal" replaced "progressive" in an earlier age for the same reason. They might better, though more awkwardly, be called "transnational progressives," because of their general commitment to one-world government, the absurd principle that all cultures are equally valid, and opposition to "outmoded" concepts like American Exceptionalism and national sovereignty in the face of UN encroachments. Their ideal is the collapsing European Union, which they think we should beg to join.

"Liberal" is, in any case, confusing to scholars, because the classic liberalism of an earlier period was associated with limited government controlled by the popular will, respect for individual rights and responsibilities, freedom, property rights, free markets, self-reliance, and many values called conservative today. Thus the term "liberal democracy" refers to the kind of democracy envision by Thomas Jefferson, whose memory progressives revere as much as they despise his principles. Classical liberalism is anathema to progressives, and always has been. It does not fit well with the collectivist mind.

Progressives are not much on limited government. The checks and balances between the federal government and the states and between the three branches have been pretty well destroyed because they prevented them from forcing people to do what they *knew* was best for them. They aren't much on the "popular will" either, so the public's opposition to Obamacare, or big government, or late term abortion, or support of the Keystone pipeline, means nothing.

Nor are they much on free speech, pious claims to the contrary notwithstanding. People who say things they don't like must be stopped through hate speech codes and restricting criticism of Islamic terror by outlawing blasphemy. They would have you forget the Alien and Sedition type laws pushed by Progressive Saint Woodrow Wilson, as well as his support for segregation and opposition to women's suffrage, which passed with more GOP votes than Democrat ones.

The essence of progressivism is coercion, as people must be coerced to do things they don't want to do or don't think are in their interests, to serve "the greater good," as defined by the progressive elites.

Haters on both sides of the political divide fall into the trap of believing their opponents evil, stupid, or both. I have a very frustrated progressive relative who, since on the evidence he cannot easily put me in either category, apparently thinks I'm just being, in the lovely British phrase, "bloody minded." Thus his communications even on jokes take on a vicious political tone. Conservatives calling progressives names, such as "libtard," are, in my view, offensive, ethically wrong and counter productive, because insults are hardly the way to get either the opposition or the uncommitted to consider your viewpoint with an open mind. Thankfully, the left has at least as many unreasonably and vicious haters as the right. My bias tells me they have many more.

I believe that Dr. Jon Haidt is correct in his excellent book *The Righteous Mind: Why Good People are Divided by Politics and Religion* that progressives and conservatives think differently about issues because they hold different values, not because one side or the other is evil. Haidt, it should be noted, is an intellectually-honest leftwing academic who strongly supported both John Kerry and Barack Obama. But his book is based on solid research, and should be well received by anyone with an open mind. He has, by the way, ongoing research into values which you can participate in by responding to surveys on line.

I think, however, that it is even more important to look at the results of policies than the values that led to them. The ends can only justify the means if you take into account *all* of the ends, or results, and the balance and trade offs inherent in those outcomes. And the results of progressive policies have been brutal to societies and the majority of people—and they are shortly going to be far worse.

But this begs the question, why are progressives and their policies flourishing, indeed, seemingly in control of the destiny of a collapsing western civilization? Why do so many people go along with them as they push us towards the cliff? Why cannot they even consider, never mind take responsibility for, all the results of their policies?

I believe that progressives are so wrapped up in their good intentions, so busy trying to think well of themselves for fighting for the right things, that they cannot notice the unintended consequences. It's like a squirrel runs in front of their car, and they jerk the wheel over, swerving onto the sidewalk and killing a small girl. They are so busy congratulating themselves over saving the squirrel, and imaging the award they will get from PETA, that the dead child never registers. And as Dr. Thomas Sowell says in his fine book *Applied Economics: Thinking Beyond Stage One*, too many people cannot think to the next step that will result from a decision or course of action. And not just progressives. But progressive intentions are good and their policies sound good to the majority who cannot think beyond stage one.

Progressive literally cannot look at the results of their policies, lest that be an act of un-faith, just as the divines reportedly (but perhaps apocryphally) refused to look into Galileo's telescope. So progressives cannot even note that the 2009 $1.2 trillion stimulus failed to fulfill Obama's promise that it would bring unemployment under 5%, just as conservative economists had predicted. Noticing that inconvenient fact would be an act of apostasy.

But the more people who can see what progressive policies have done, not just to our country but to the world, and far worse, what they will shortly do to all of us, the better are our admittedly-slim chances of turning things around, thus preserving the country we love and civilization itself.

Therefore, this detailing of the Progressive Legacy:

<u>Progressives have virtually destroyed higher education</u>. Our universities, once bastions of independent thought, have become centers of politically correct group think, where students are not taught how to think, but what to think. The prevailing ideology is rigidly enforced, and every diversity is celebrated execet the one that really matters—diversity of thought. A conservative has little chance of being hired, and if so can only hope for tenure or promotion by hiding his or her opinions.

John Leo, in "Professors: Just As Liberal, Or More Moderate?" reports that a study "by *The Chronicle of Higher Education*, the voice of liberal academia, found that Liberals outnumber conservatives by 11-1 among social scientists and 13-1 among humanities professors. 25.5 percent of those who teach sociology identify themselves as Marxist. Self-identified radicals accounted for 19 percent of humanities professors and 24 percent of social scientists."

Worse, they are educating generations of high school and elementary teachers that indoctrination of students in progressive principles is the right way to teach. You only have to read the weekly stories of outrages on common sense by public school teachers to know their efforts have born fruit.

Progressives created the drug epidemic. When I was in high school, we might (and when I could, I did) indulge in alcohol, but drugs were something only the street bums over in Philadelphia did. I couldn't have told you the difference between a reefer and heroin. Then came the sixties and the leftwing glorifying of drugs; See Timothy Leary and *Turn on, Tune in, Drop out.* Hundreds of thousands did, tens of thousands died, thousands of families were ripped apart and lives ruined, crime soared, and prostitution and crime to support drug habits flourished. And the spiking market for drugs created in the US and other western counties by the new, progressive culture has destroyed Mexico as well, with 80,000 drug murders and rampant corruption, while also funding global terrorism. I want my culture back.

Progressives destroyed the family. If it feels good, do it: sex without responsibility and children without marriage were the result. Thanks to this cultural change, 70% of black babies today are non-marital births, with whites and Hispanics not that far behind. This increases poverty, traps generations, increases dysfunctional children, and sets them on the path to crime, government dependency and single parenthood for themselves.

Progressives supported abortion. With the US birthrate having fallen well below the replacement rate of 2.1 live births per woman, we are likely going to miss those 50 to 100 million aborted children, especially as progressives try to redeem their entitlement promised with a shrinking younger working population supporting a growing population of us geezers. Blacks make up 13% of the population, but have 40% of the abortions, so Planned Parenthood Founder and progressive saint Margaret Sanger's goal of preventing more of what she called "the unfit" from being born is "mission accomplished." If conservatives had killed this many black babies, they'd be shooting us in the street for racial genocide.

Progressives are grinding the poor. In order to feel good about their good intentions for saving the environment, progressives support energy policies that are and will continue to drive energy costs much higher for the poorest segments of society. They claim to care about the poor, but when it comes to spending billions of dollars in money extracted from the poor so they can feel good about lowering the Earth's temperature less than a degree in a hundred years, the poor will just have to suffer or starve so the progressives can enjoy feeling all green and fuzzy, like bad meat. So the war on coal, the war on fracking, the war on drilling, the war on the Keystone Pipeline goes forward, and the poor and working classes pay for them. Progressives get to feel good and the poor can, well, eat cake.

Progressives destroyed our cities. Detroit is not an accident. They have encouraged black thug culture in the cities that drove out the white and black middleclass, the taxpayers and job creators. In his great essay, "Black Rednecks and White Liberals," Dr. Thomas Sowell postulates that inner city black culture, with its touchy honor, violence, promiscuity and limited work ethic, is an inheritance they picked up from poor southern white rednecks after the civil war and brought north. Now, ironically it's defended as black culture, not subject to criticism.

But progressive policies have abetted the destruction. Vote buying from public employee unions has created debt and unfunded liabilities that can never be redeemed. They cannot now ask their union allies and welfare dependent voter base to taker a haircut—that would create riots. So they will continue to turn the screws on the productive, who will continue to flee the cities, feeding the death spiral. Welfare giveaway programs and political corruption have only fed the flames of what is now an unavoidable approaching fiscal disaster. And the more they disarm decent citizens, the more murder they get in their "gun free zones." In ten years, Chicago will be Detroit. Soon whole states like Illinois and California will follow the cities into the abyss.

Progressives are destroying the country through fiscal fecklessness. Vote buying by progressives in both parties has created an unfunded liability and debt that, like the cities, though far vaster, can never be paid. As I say in *The Coming Collapse of the American Republic*, I do not see how we can avoid fiscal collapse, followed by economic, social and political collapse, hyper-inflation, chaos, starvation, riots, violence and widespread death. But you cannot touch one of the entitlement programs in even a minor way, (Social Security, Disability Insurance, Food Stamps, Medicare, Public Employee Pensions, Medicaid and now Obamacare) without howls of outrage. Google "The West and the Tyranny of Public Debt," an excellent *Newsweek* article from 2010 that details the impact uncontrolled debt has had on other societies. With an acknowledged debt of $16T (now $19T) and unfunded liabilities estimated from $87T to triple that, your grandkids will not live in the United States, though perhaps in a rump dictatorship incorporating that name.

It's not just our country. Progressives have had a worldwide pernicious impact through their policies.

Vietnam: Progressives foamed at the mouth over US support for the Republic of Vietnam, the government in the south. They worked hard, often secretly guided by the communists we now know, and finally elected a post-Watergate congress that reneged on our treaty obligations to the South. Without supplies, spare parts and ammo, the South was soon overwhelmed by a communist North that was well supplied by China and the USSR—they invaded South Vietnam with more tanks than the Germans invaded France with in 1940.

While the Republic of Vietnam was admittedly no Jeffersonian democracy, it did allow multiple political parties, some press freedom and religious freedom. None of these are available to the people of Vietnam today under the communists. Christians are suppressed. The Cambodian reds murdered a quarter of the population. Tens of thousands of Vietnamese died in re-education camps or trying to escape as "boat people." The Montagnards, a racial minority who supported us, are steadily being exterminated. Reports claim that twice as many people were murdered by the communists in the first two years after they won as died in the entire war. It's hard to verify, because today's Vietnam is a completely closed society.

And the response from the left? With the notable exception of Joan Baez, crickets.

One leftist, asked about the mass murders, said he didn't believe in criticizing socialist states. You see, to acknowledge the oppression and death brought on the Vietnamese people by the communist victory would mean they owned it. It might jeopardize their ability to feel good about themselves for opposing the evil Republic of Vietnam. Far more comfortable not to notice the suffering they created, because, after all, their intentions were good.

DDT: Progressives all read *Silent Spring* by Rachel Carson and sprang into action to ban DDT, to "save the birds." They never thought about what other results might follow. The major result was that Malaria, which had been in a world wide decline, spiked back up. Millions died, many of them black, brown and yellow kids in the third world. And they go on dying today. I consider Carson the fourth most successful mass murderer of the twentieth century, behind, in order, Mao, Stalin and Hitler. But she's gaining. (A minor result is the bedbug, West Nile Virus and now Zika Virus epidemics in the US.)

Leftists can't bear to notice these deaths from Malaria, because to do so would hurt their entitlement to feel good about themselves for saving the birds. Ironically, they now support eagle-chopper wind farms that slaughter thousands of these same birds, so they can feel good about fighting global warming.

Iran: Progressives looked at the repressive Shah of Iran, and mounted a campaign to force him out. They take no responsibility that the success of their campaign put in place a far more repressive theocracy that hangs gays, stones women for adultery, oppresses women, started a war with Iraq in which a million died, including young boys the mullahs used as human mine-clearing devices, supports terrorism around the world, and is developing atomic weapons. If we lose New York City in an atomic blast, they will still be so busy feeling good about opposing the Shah they won't notice. Except for those living close enough to die of radiation sickness or starvation, but not incinerated instantly in the blast.

Zimbabwe: Progressives hated the oppressive white rule in then-Rhodesia. So they launched a campaign for black rule. They are too busy celebrating to notice that Zimbabwe, which once exported food, is now starving, as the appropriation of white-owned farms for black supporters of the thugocracy failed to expropriate their work ethic or knowledge of farming. That the result of black rule was to drop *black* life expectancy from about 63 to about 36 didn't bother them at all. (It has recovered a bit into the 40s, I've read.) Nor did the destruction of Zimbabwe's economy by the rule of greedy and incompetent thugs, with hyper-inflation destroying everyone's hope of prosperity—except those with the guns—bother them. You can buy billions of dollars in Zimbabwean currency on eBay for a few bucks, getting in on the progressive utopia.

South Africa: All right-thinking progressives opposed apartheid and white rule, and black rule leaves South Africa not far behind Zimbabwe. A 2009 article in *Newsweek* expressed surprise to find that "… 800,000 out of a total white population of 4 million have left since 1995, by one count. But they're hardly alone. Blacks, coloreds (as people of mixed race are known in South Africa) and Indians are also expressing the desire to leave. In the last 12 years, the number of blacks graduating in South Africa with advanced degrees has grown from 361,000 to 1.4 million a year. But in that time the number of those expressing high hopes to emigrate has doubled." It's really no surprise, as crime and corruption under black rule has soared, and regardless of color, those with the education or finances to thrive elsewhere are fleeing, leaving the country without the knowledge and skills to operate government, business or industry, creating an eventual death spiral.

A 2010 article in the *Times Live* of Johannesburg, "South Africa's Black Brain Drain" by Subashni Naidoo notes that "Almost half of South Africa's middle-class black teenagers plan to flee the country for greener pastures. ... Reflecting views similar to their white and Indian counterparts, 71% of black youth felt it was impossible to get employment in South Africa; 58% said crime made them want to live in another country, and 73% felt government was not living up to its promises."

According to the Genocide Watch website, "... there is a coordinated campaign of genocide being conducted against white farmers, known as Boers." I have read that many countries won't take immigrants from South Africa because it's better they stay there and die than flee and contribute to the destruction through the brain drain. But with this flight, South Africa cannot be far behind Zimbabwe as the next progressive paradise.

Why all this unnoticed suffering and death following progressive policies?

It is not because progressives are evil, but that they are so wrapped up in feeling good about their good intentions that they cannot allow the unintended evil results to intrude on their euphoria. They perfectly fit my favorite quote from T. S. Eliot: "Half the harm that is done in this world is due to people who want to feel important. They don't mean to do harm—but the harm does not interest them. Or they do not see it, or they justify it because they are absorbed in the endless struggle to think well of themselves."

So you would be wrong to hate progressives. But if you care about the results for real people and the lives of the non-elite struggling in this world, or about future generations whose hope of freedom and prosperity is being destroyed, you have a moral obligation to oppose progressive policies with every fiber of your being. You must notice the suffering progressives ignore—and do what you can to stop them from making it worse.

Turning the economy around

As the economy grows ever more stagnant and people abandon the workforce, everyone seems to have a plan to turn the economy around. So, why not me?

Sure, I don't have a lot of training in economics, but neither does Obama, Clinton, Trump or most members of Congress, though I'm probably better read in the subject then they are. And there are economists supporting and opposing every idea that's floating around.

So here goes:

My plan is built on some basic assumptions:

1. Investment drives job creation. Large companies or small businesses, all need money to operate, expand and create jobs.

2. People take the risk of investing money because they hope for a Return on Investment (ROI). Why put your money in a CD, instead of your safe deposit box? You want to get paid interest. Why take the risk of buying stocks or starting a business, when your money would be safer under the mattress? You want to make more money. No return—no investment. It's promises of great returns (and low risk) that suck people into Ponzi schemes, like the Madoff Hedge Fund or Social Security.

3. Investors like the security of knowing what the rules are, of stability, and of a level playing field, reasonably free of corruption. One of the reasons many third world countries are so poor is that individuals and companies won't invest there. There's no guarantee your profits won't be siphoned off by corrupt officials, or your factory "nationalized" or taxed out of existence.

Companies want to invest in new facilities in areas that have stable rules, with the opportunity to make good profits.

4. There's a lot of scared money hiding out, not currently invested in the economy, because the market and everything else seems too risky. To turn the economy around, we need to get that money invested in job-creating enterprises again.

5. Free trade increases wealth. After NAFTA passed, the number of jobs increased in both Mexico and the US; economics is not a zero-sum game. Unfortunately, the lost jobs were localized in specific industries, which howled, especially if they were unionized. The larger job gain was spread across the economy; people in those new jobs had no clue they were working thanks to NAFTA. Some of them doubtless joined the chorus against NAFTA for "sending US jobs overseas."

Unfortunately, in a downturn, the political pressure is to put up trade barriers to "protect jobs!" Most economists believe the Smoot-Hawley Tariff Bill made the great depression longer and deeper. But even countries that promised at the economic summit to not do this are caving and putting up barriers. That will make things worse world wide.

To turn the economy around, the President and the leaders of both parties in Congress should pledge the following:

1. To reduce the Capital Gains Tax to 5%, and to keep it there for at least five years. Job-creating money would flood back into the stock market, as savvy investors scoop up the bargains. With the market rising, more money would flood in, as other investors fearful of missing the market recovery jumped on board. Recapitalized

companies could expand in good markets, creating jobs, which would increase economic demand. And those of us with 401Ks/IRAs would develop confidence in the future, thus be willing to spend more money now, driving demand—perhaps even in housing. (Bonus: government revenue from Capital Gains taxes goes up when the rate is reduced, due to increased economic activity—look it up.)

2. To tear down all tariff and trade barriers with all countries which are willing to establish free trade with the US. No exceptions. Call it the WWFTA. Investment would flow to where it was most efficiently used. And, BTW, the liberals have always been very concerned about the poor in the third world. Wouldn't giving them jobs be a lot better than taxing Americans to pay for foreign aid, most of which goes into the pockets of the corrupt oligarchs? When the world's economy booms, our economy booms.

3. Make America very business-friendly. That means killing card check, so the UAW, having built Ford, Chrysler and GM into the economic powers they are today, can't go into pro-business states and drive the Toyota and BMW plants out of the country. Make the entire country a right-to-work state. Reduce the paperwork and regulation businesses have to jump through. Maybe George McGovern, who discovered how hard it is to run a small business in a highly-regulated environment—in his case a country inn after he retired—could head a task force for meaningful regulatory reform. (yes, i know george has gone to that great paradice of free stuff in the sky.)

4. Stop welfare for corporations, from the Detroit bailout to farm subsidies. Let Detroit reorganize under bankruptcy protection to be able to compete—without bailouts, with Honda and Toyota. Let the market set the price for food, and more starving people could afford food around the world—or don't liberals want to feed the hungry? The government would have more money to spend on infrastructure needed for the economy, like roads and bridges. Obama's plan there was good, right up until he picked a Republican member of the Illinois' Political Combine to run it. Making it more the "The Chicago Way" than economic stimulus.

5. Limit lawsuits against business. Nothing would encourage small businesses like meaningful tort reform. Of course, with the League of Leftwing Lawyers in full charge of Congress this is unlikely to happen.

And the other parts of my economic stimulus plan fly in the face of everything the Democrats (and many Republicans) ran on. So we are as likely to see an economic recovery based on this as I am likely to see a personal economic recovery based on winning the Powerball

But that doesn't mean that isn't a great idea too.

Twenty Economic Facts of Life

The world economy is such a complex system that no single person—or group of people—can understand the hundreds of billions of variables and interactions that comprise the entire system. Thus it is understandable that economists—like experts in other disciplines—argue endlessly about what the results of various trends, policies and developments will be. These arguments are colored by each economist's worldview and life experience, as they are for the rest of us.

But there are some basic economic principles that have proven consistent, and that are fairly easy to understand. You may argue the physics of a complex system like the universe, but still have to agree that H20 turns from liquid to solid at 0°C at sea level on a fairly consistent basis, even if your worldview says it should freeze at 5°C. As Senator Patrick Moynihan reportedly quipped to a colleague, "You are entitled to your own opinion, but you are not entitled to your own facts."

But facts can be slippery things, starting with the old bromide, "Figures don't lie, but liars figure." In many of our current political debates, too many people seem to prefer their own facts, and to ignore the evidence of long experience, because the evidence doesn't fit their worldview.

Here, then, are what I consider to be Twenty Economic Facts of Life, which guide my thinking in policy matters.

1. People do more of what they are rewarded for doing, and avoid what they are punished for doing.

If that seems obvious, politicians and voters forget it all the time. Both JFK and Reagan lowered Capital Gains Taxes and discovered that government revenue went up, as more people invested money, rather than put it into other areas. Likewise, CGT increases have resulted in reduced government revenue. When I pointed this out to a liberal newspaper columnist in Madison, WI, his response was that it was a Republican, Pro-Business fact, and he wasn't interested in those kinds of facts. He felt entitled to his own facts. But promising to "soak the rich" in the name of fairness is often counter-productive for government revenue, however popular it is with economically-ignorant voters.

Maryland is a recent example. They decided to drastically increase taxes on people with million dollar incomes, only to find that the following year they had about half as many folks reporting million dollar incomes. Some of that decline was doubtless due to the recession, but a lot of it was due to millionaires relocating their legal domiciles, and often their businesses to states like Florida with no income taxes. Zero-income tax Texas is still doing fairly well in this poor economy while high tax California is crashing, and liberals can't figure out why.

When you punish people for investing in job-creating businesses, they will create fewer jobs, and you will collect fewer tax dollars, not more. It really is that simple.

Politicians also do what they are rewarded for, and their reward is votes. The next election is at most two or six years away. Voters love government spending and hate government taxes. So politicians get re-elected by voting for spending and against taxes. This results in an almost-permanent government fiscal crisis and ever-higher deficits. During my five terms in the Massachusetts senate, I observed one senator who *never* voted for a tax bill, but voted for every spending bill or spending increase to the state budget—with one exception. She always voted against legislators' and judges' pay raises, which, regardless of the merits, had minuscule fiscal impact on total spending. But it had a large PR impact, as with the help of a lazy press that never dug too deeply into the details of the budget, she trumpeted her fight for fiscal responsibility—these pay-raise votes—to her constituents. And she was re-elected year after year, becoming the dean of the senate. She wasn't the only one following this "spend, but don't tax" strategy.

2. There aren't enough "rich" to pay for everything we want.

The IRS reported that in 2006, only 5% of the taxpayers made $153,500 or above, but that 5% paid 60% of the total taxes. (This was under the Bush tax cuts, which Democrats say favored "the rich.") The 50% of the taxpayers with the lowest incomes paid a total of 3% of the taxes. "We'll spend and just raise taxes on the rich, they can afford it," is as fraudulent as a Ponzi scheme, because you soon run out of "the rich." There aren't enough of them, and the poor don't pay taxes, so when government spending goes up, most of it is going to come out of people in the middle, because that's where most of the money is.

The politicians will try to delay that reality through borrowing, hide it in fees, or disguise it in inflation. But when the government spends a lot more money, it's going to come out of the hides of middle income earners one way or another.

3. Politicians will sacrifice the country's long term economic interests for their short term political welfare.

President Hoover signed the Smoot-Hawley anti-trade tariff bill against the advice of a thousand economists. Many economists believe that was the key to a collapse of world trade, which turned what might have been a severe recession into the great depression. But, contrary to the myth that he did nothing, Hoover was under great pressure to do something, even if wrong, and he did what was politically popular, not what made economic sense. When it didn't work, he was defeated anyway.

Once Republicans got control of Congress in the 1990s, they started spending money in the kind of amounts they had criticized Democrats for, because spending gets you votes. Politicians using their own money to buy votes is illegal, but using our grandchildren's money to buy votes, by passing earmarks, pork barrel spending and entitlement programs, is not only legal, but practiced by both parties. Someone pockets every one of those dollars, and is thus inclined kindly toward the politician who provided it. The party out of power always criticizes this, as Obama did the Bush deficits (ignoring that they were approved in 07 and 08 by Democrat-controlled Congresses). But once in office, Obama's first-year deficit was greater than all eight years of the Bush deficits combined, as hungry supportive constituencies had to be rewarded in the name of economic stimulus, to keep them voting Democrat in the future.

Elections are short term, while deficits are a long term problem. Thus we usually have deficits.

4. Free trade increases economic prosperity

Free trade is popular with everyone, until it impacts their own income. Then workers and businessmen alike howl about "sending American jobs overseas." (Liberals always wanted to help the downtrodden in other countries—but that didn't mean the downtrodden should have jobs, only handouts. Like the poor in our cities.) The historic record is clear. Free trade increases prosperity among all the trading partners. After Bill Clinton and the Republican Congress passed NAFTA, the number of jobs in both countries went up—Ross Perot notwithstanding—just as the European Market has increased prosperity in Europe.

People circulating e-mails urging boycotts of "foreign" goods should recall how prosperous we were when international trade collapsed in the 1930s. But both businessmen and workers howl if they are the ones paying the price, so "saving American jobs" by barring trade will continue to be popular with politicians. Hillary Clinton, Bernie Sanders, and Donald Trump are only the latest politicians to pander to this ignorance.

5. Cause and effect in large economic systems are often impossible for most people to discern or understand.

When people who complain about high taxes and deficit spending still vote for their member of Congress because of the new bike path he brought to the district, making no connection at all, it's little wonder they can't understand economics. The jobs lost to NAFTA were concentrated in some industries and the workers and businessmen who lost out were very vocal. People demanded their public officials do something about the loss of jobs. Because the larger number of jobs gained were spread around the economy, people holding them usually had no idea they owed their jobs to free trade—and were doubtless clamoring against NAFTA in support of those who lost jobs!

Coupled with the voters' notorious short term memories, this gives politicians endless chances to manipulate the ignorant. As Lincoln might have said, "You can fool all of the people some of the time, and some of the people all of the time, and them's pretty good odds."

6. Waste is in the eye of the beholder.

Give me a couple of CPAs, a calculator and a laptop, and I believe that in a month or so I could balance the Federal Budget. After which, a howling, outraged mob would rip me into cat food. All our politicians say they want to bring down the cost of healthcare. One of the huge healthcare costs is malpractice insurance and the defensive medicine that results from the threats of lawsuits. So were these billions in savings on the table in "healthcare reform?" They were not. A majority of legislators, particularly among Democrats, are lawyers. Lawyers get the benefit of these lawsuits and don't see it as waste at all. It's not a topic for discussion.

This is why the rest of us may fume at the extravagance of the "Murtha Airport," but Congressman Murtha got re-elected by his constituents, who don't realize or care that to get their pork airport, Rep. Murtha has to go along with the other Congresscritters taking pork home to their districts, at the expense of his constituents.

7. Government never runs efficiently.

Business, which is organized with the sole goal of making a profit, has a hard time running efficiently. Non-profit organizations, where there are a lot of goals other than profit, have a bigger challenge. And in government, the bureaucrats are rewarded for following the rules, regardless of how much sense they make. Plus, they are subject to political influence in the decision making process, and the rules are set up to reward favored political constituencies, not efficiency. The results they strive to achieve are continued employment for both the bureaucrats and the politicians, not the efficient conduct of whatever the program's mission is.

Name a government agency or program that you'd hold up to the corporation where your IRA is invested as a model. The Post Office? The DMV? The Pentagon? Medicare, Medicaid, the VA, or the Indian Health Service? The Highway Department? Social Security? The Congress, state legislature, or city council? (Okay, I'm cheating a bit—we wouldn't really want them to be more efficient.)

A classic case was reported by John Steele Gordon in his essay, "Why government can't run a Business." According to Gordon, "In 1913, for instance, thinking it was being overcharged by the steel companies for armor plate for warships, the federal government decided to build its own plant. It estimated that a plant with a 10,000-ton annual capacity could produce armor plate for only 70% of what the steel companies charged. When the plant was finally finished, however -- three years after World War I had ended -- it was millions over budget and able to produce armor plate only at twice what the steel companies charged. It produced one batch and then shut down, never to reopen."

8. When government makes you poorer, it's a tax.

If the government spends money, but doesn't raise taxes, and instead prints more dollars, it causes inflation. (See Jimmy Carter.) If it gets really bad, it causes hyper-inflation, as in Zimbabwe, where (when this was written) it can cost billions of Zimbabwe dollars for a loaf of bread. Inflation makes your dollars worth less, so you are poorer. Government caused inflation is a hidden tax on your income and your retirement savings.

If the government passes legislation that makes things cost more, such as the proposed "cap and trade" energy bill to fight global warming, it makes you poorer. It might be necessary, or for a good cause. But if they make heating your home or buying gasoline 10% more expensive, there's no difference between that and putting a new 10% tax on energy. In either case you are worse off—they just don't call it a tax.

9. The free market makes better decisions than central planners.

One would think, logically, that one person in charge—a czar for the economy, to use the currently popular term—could look at the big picture and make better decisions. And that is what the statists always believe. But the opposite is true.

Every day in our economy, billions of economic decisions are made by millions of people. When you decide to buy whole wheat bread rather than white, the czar would have to be able to predict that, in advance, for you and 300 million other people, and order all the steps in production to increase whole wheat—for people like you, but not those who prefer white this week.

Each step of the way requires specialized knowledge and experience. The guy who knows how to make a tractor doesn't know how to grow wheat. The farmer doesn't know how to get it to the bakery; the baker doesn't know what sells in a particular neighborhood like the grocer does. There are hundreds of steps and decisions for every product. The czar would have to be God—which is why people always, *always* have higher standards of living in free economies than in planned economies. (Government bureaucrats and politicians only think they are God.)

10. Business people make economic decisions, politicians make political decisions.

Much was made of the "fact" that banks discriminated against blacks, "proved" by their giving home mortgages to whites at higher rates than to blacks. So the government stepped in, and created the Community Reinvestment Act to force banks to give loans to poor black people, thus earning votes for those politicians. This was followed by Fannie Mae and Freddie Mac, huge loan schemes guaranteed (though they claimed not) by the taxpayers to be sure poorer folks could own homes. Thus started the housing bubble which was the first domino in the great recession. Attempts by President Bush and some legislators to more tightly regulate Fannie and Freddie were beaten back by supporters, ever eager to cry "racism" to get more dollars for their voting constituencies.

But the brilliant economist Dr. Thomas Sowell points out the banks were in business to make a profit. If loans to poor blacks in the inner city were profitable, they—or someone else—would have been making them already. And Asians were getting mortgages at higher rates than whites—were Asians running the banks and discriminating against whites? No. Asians had better repayment rates than whites, and whites better than blacks, thus making loans to them safer and more profitable. Sowell, for those who don't know, grew up in a poor black family in NC.

11. There is no political freedom without economic freedom and property rights.

If you cannot own a home and a business and be free to run it as you wish, other freedoms are meaningless. If the government controls your shelter and your livelihood (from the root word "life"), it can tell you what to say, do, and think. You are a slave as surely as any slave on a plantation in the old south, because the Master controls where you can live, how you can live, and what you can eat and own. The right to own property is the most basis right, in terms of economic prosperity.

12. Government grows at the expense of individual economic and political freedom.

Most of us recognize that government is necessary to provide for the common defense, protect us from criminals, and provide infrastructure we cannot provide individually, like roads and harbors. We are neither anarchists on one end of the political spectrum, believing there should be no government, nor total statists on the other end (communists, Nazis, fascists, socialists) who believe the individual should always be subservient to the ruler's idea of the "common good"—that is, to the state. The statist tendency is always to build the power of government at the expense of the individual's freedom, as people keep telling politicians they should do something to solve perceived problems—and the politicians respond. But government owns most of the means of coercion—the military and police—and it has the power to take part or all of your income, to take your house, to tell you where to work. It was to thwart this tendency that the founders established the separation of powers—now much eroded— preserving to the states and the people any power not expressly granted to the federal government. And statists always believe that government should be bigger, that more programs are needed, without end.

13. Power equals money.

You have a full wallet, but the guy in the alley has a gun. Suddenly he has a full wallet. The more power government, large corporations, large unions, or criminal gangs have, the more money they will extract from the rest of us.

14. Corruption, crime, violence, and instability make people poor.

One has to look no further than our large cities to see this at work. Would you open a factory to employ people where you would be hit for bribes by the local government? If you had to hire people based on politics, rather than skills? If you couldn't get insurance because arson was rampant in the area? If crime made employees fearful of coming to work? Welcome to the American metropolis, run by Democrat bosses.

Many of the poorest third world countries are rich in resources, and have willing workers, but investors won't start businesses there for the same reasons. They prefer not to invest in corrupt, crime-ridden inner cities. Plus, there is always the fear that the third-world government thugs will seize your property. So the people languish in poverty, while the oligarchs get rich off them—and our foreign aid.

The classic example is Zimbabwe, which under the evil rule of a minority white government, led by Ian Smith, exported food to many other countries. But minority rule was "unjust," so the world, the US included, helped to bring down Smith's government and install black majority rule in the person of Robert Mugabe, a Marxist-Maoist. Mugabe appropriated white-owned farms and gave them to his black supporters, but was unable to appropriate the experience, knowledge, and work ethic of the white farmers. Famine ensued, tens of thousands died, black life expectance fell from 64 to about 36, hyperinflation and terror stalked the land. The people are desperately poor because of corruption, crime, violence, and instability, as investors do what is in their self-interest. And liberals called it "justice" because the statists had won.

15. The lower the cost of a "good," the more of it will be consumed.

When gasoline went to well over $4 a gallon, usage fell dramatically, burning the oil speculators and bringing down the cost. My step-daughter was driving home with the AC off to save pennies on a tank of gas, which she was paying for, then cranking up the AC in the house, which I was paying for—the AC at home was a free good to her.

No matter how many times this truth is proved, politicians still don't get it. Are expenditures for medical care too high with the average American paying 13 cents on the dollar out of pocket for care? Let's make it "free" and see if total costs go down.

People in supermarkets try free samples of foods they'd never give a second glance to, if they weren't free. "Cash for Clunkers" was predicted to cost $1B in three months, but it burned through $3B in one month. It was "free money." But even folks who hated the idea of the program figured if they were going to have to pay higher taxes to cover it, they might as well reap the benefits. (This is known as the "Tragedy of the Commons.")

16. Government does not create wealth.

Wealth is created when investors start businesses, hire labor, and produce goods or services. When government "stimulates" the economy by putting money in, it has to take money out of the economy elsewhere, through higher taxes (dollars spent on taxes don't get spent in other parts of the economy) or through borrowing (money lent to the government is not invested in the private sector).

And whenever government gives a dollar (or a dollar's worth of some good, like medical care) to someone who didn't earn that dollar, it must take that dollar from someone who did earn it through labor or investing (perhaps in a retirement fund.) The person who earned the dollar doesn't get the benefit of it—the other person does.

If I steal your wallet, and spend the money in it, is that better for the economy than if you had spent it yourself? Or is it just better for me and the favored people I spend it with?

17. Everyone tries to improve his or her own economic situation.

Whenever my wife and I are house hunting—all too often due to my career—we always think that there are houses just out of our price range that would be perfect. I'm sure if we could afford a million dollar house (we've never lived in a house that cost more than $250,000), we'd be dreaming of a $1.3M cottage. And so it goes. People work to improve the lives of their families and themselves—and appetites are unlimited. Economic systems that ignore people's commitment to self interest are doomed. The free market system harnesses people's efforts to improve their lives, to make everyone more prosperous. Other systems discourage economic activity and innovation.

18. Money isn't the only cost of something.

Time is a cost. My wife and I love yard sales and flea markets, and delight in finding bargains. But is the money we save worth the time investment? Probably not—especially when many of the treasures we find were unknown desires until we saw them. It's really a hobby, or entertainment rather than a sound economic strategy. If you did your grocery shopping at ten stores instead of one or two, you could take advantage of the sales and specials at each, and save money on your grocery bill. So why don't you? Because time is a cost as well, often a more painful one. Just learning where the sale items are takes a lot of time. (See Dr. Thomas Sowell's writings on the cost of knowledge.)

19. Bankruptcies and failure are vital to the economy.

It's not just success that makes our economy work. If a company can't fail, its owners and employees have no incentive to be efficient, to provide the most desirable goods and services at the best price. In short, it becomes like government, which can't fail because it can always get more money—from you. This is why the economic bailouts are so troubling to conservative, free-market economists.

20. There can never be equal outcomes and trying to achieve them is harmful.

It doesn't matter how many government programs you pass, or how much you talk about fairness or social justice, I'm never going to have the life style of Michael Jordan or Donovan McNabb. Oh, I can say it's racism that gives them a better, richer lifestyle than me, but the truth is they had slightly better athletic talents, a marketable skill I didn't have, and thus got ahead. No government program can give me justice and equality, by making my lifestyle—and everyone else's—equal to theirs. Nor is it desirable to bring everyone to the same level. If the outcome was the same for the kids who partied and did drugs as it was for Bill Gates, what is the incentive for hard work and creation?

In 1965, I was an 18-year-old private on mess duty in the Marines. I asked a fellow "messman" how come his coffee was so bad. "I make it double strength," he said. "If I make it regular strength, they drink three pots during chow. Double strength they only drink one, so I do less work and get paid the same." There, my friends, is socialism. When there are no incentives—except, perhaps, fear—for doing better, no one does better.

I have seen the future—and it doesn't work.

Fixing our electoral system

It's long been clear that our electoral system is broken. Unfortunately, there isn't a constituency for fixing it. Both Democrats and Republicans view any reform on the basis of how it effects their own short-term interests, rather than the good of the country.

I've been expecting a train wreck, and in 2000 we had it. The system threw up two focus-group candidates with a demonstrated contempt for campaign finance laws, who pandered to the fringe elements in their party to get nominated and to the center to get elected. That the Supreme Court should have had to decide between them, on a five-to-four vote, seemed only fitting.

Here's what must be done:

Primaries: The primary system should be scrapped. A national primary isn't the answer, because it aggravates the problem of campaign spending and favors well-heeled, well known candidates. We need a constitutional amendment mandating that all states participate in either a series of regional primaries, rotating the order of the regions from election to election, or a series of primaries starting with the small states. Minor parties could participate by petition, and if they received 5% of the vote would be declared established parties. Delegates should be bound to a candidate for at least two ballots.

Electoral College: Abolishing the College promotes regionalism and gives a corrupt city machine the chance to control the whole country, not just one state. And in a close election we'd have the Florida recount fiasco conducted nationwide. But we should eliminate electors, with each state's election officer casting the state's votes and bound by law to the results. And we should award electoral votes by Congressional district, as two states already do. This would keep every state in play and demand truly national campaigns, while the electoral vote would more closely follow the popular vote.

Campaign Finances: Most limitations founder on the First Amendment. Since you can't restrict a citizen's right to spend money on favored candidates, reforms often aid the candidates willing to subvert the spirit, and often the letter, of the law. And, yes, the names Clinton, Gore, and Bush come to mind.

Instead, we need to take the high cost out of campaigns by prohibiting television stations from selling political ads for issues or candidates. Since the airwaves belong to all of us, we can do it, taking 80% of the expense out of campaigns, and greatly reducing the power of rich special interests and wealthy donors. Other forms of advertising—direct mail, radio, newspapers, yard signs, bumper stickers—are much lower in cost and compete directly with each other. Involved volunteers would become more valuable than wealthy donors. (Since I wrote this, the development of cable and the internet has made it moot. I now think we should let anyone or any organization contribute as much as they want to a candidate, including businesses and labor unions, but that within 24 hours of receiving the contribution, the campaign would have to enter it into a national database on the Internet, so everyone could see who is supporting who.)

Voting: We need the system of numerical voting used in Australia, where you cast a "one" for your first choice, a "two" for your second choice and so on. If no candidate gets 50% of the "ones," the candidate with the fewest "ones" is eliminated, and that candidate's votes are apportioned to the other candidates according to each voter's second choice. Eventually a candidate receives a majority.

Currently, a candidate despised by 70% of the voters can win if the opposition votes are split by other candidates. Under a numerical system, citizens could vote their hearts for a Nader or Buchanan, and cast their second choice votes for a major party candidate. A McCain or Cruz might run as an independent and win, because voters would know that if he didn't, their second choice could still go to Bush or Gore and no harm done.

Exit polls: Okay, we probably can't constitutionally stop them, but we could revoke the broadcasting license of any station that calls an election on the basis of exit polling before the polls for that election close in every state. If the networks hadn't been so eager to call Florida that they forgot west Florida is in another time zone, Bush might have had enough votes to avoid the court fights. The alternative is staggered polling hours so the polls close everywhere in the country at the same time.

Voting: Sure, some folks were dumb. But when 19,000 ballots in one county are spoiled, possibly changing the outcome of a presidential election, something's wrong. If IQ is the test for voting, where do they draw the line? Punch card machines often make it impossible to determine what the voter intended. Can't afford new machines? Paper ballots are slow, but they don't have pregnant chads.

Absentee ballots should be in by Election Day, counted then, and included in each district's released totals. I heard there were enough uncounted absentee ballots from the 2000 election to have made Bush the popular vote winner as well. I doubt it, but it would be nice to know.

Internet voting: Forget it. Hackers regularly break into government systems, including the Pentagon. Some kid in Los Angeles could make Madonna president.

Press Two For Racism

If you treat one group of people better and another group of people worse purely because of their race or ethnic background would you agree that is racism? If so, then having Spanish on everything from phone voice-mail hells to government programs is clearly racist. After all, there are a lot of citizens, permanent residents and, yes, illegal immigrants whose native language is something other than English or Spanish. That immigrants from Mexico, legal or illegal, get to have everything presented in their native language while immigrants from Poland or Vietnam or Latvia or China do not clearly discriminates against those immigrants who come from a non-Hispanic culture. Oh, it's because there are more Hispanic immigrants than those from other language groups? So you can discriminate if a group is a minority, and it's okay? So if whites outnumber all other groups, it's okay to discriminate against the others? Given our litigation-happy culture, it won't be long before a smarmy lawyer figures that out and decides to cast aside political correctness in favor oo a payoff. Then we will see the courts tied in knots trying to promote "fairness"—the liberal chimera—for everyone.

The worse part is that the practice also discriminates against Hispanics as well. I have read that Hispanics who speak only Spanish earn significantly lower incomes than those who speak English, though because of the bi-lingual trend, those who speak both do best of all. But by making it easier for Hispanics to get by not learning English, you condemn them to poverty and welfare dependence. Which of course may be the point for political groups that depend on the government-dependent for their power base.

A last thought. By promoting a bi-lingual society, they promote conflict within the society. Yes, there are peaceful societies, like Switzerland, where there is more than one dominant language (though the Swiss have their stresses). But there are many examples, like Quebec, where it leads to political rancor, and sometimes violence, perhaps even disunion. America is a great country and a wonderful place to live, not because of the dominant race, but because of the dominant culture, which believes in hard work, self-sufficiency, integrity. (Don't laugh. If we have corruption here, at least we abhor and fight it. In all too many cultures, it is accepted and expected. And they are always backward in economics and human rights.) We also have long exposure to the benefits of free markets and property rights, the foundations of economic advancement. Note the difference in income in English speaking versus non-English speaking industrial democracies.

Immigrants who come here and join the dominant culture enrich it. But if they wish to bring a culture of corruption, anti-free markets, and disregard of property rights from their native lands to replace ours, we aide that to our destruction. We have enough challenges with the alternative culture that has grown up in our cities, which may destroy us, without importing the seeds of our destruction. If you don't believe me, look at Mexico, a country rich in natural resources and agricultural potential. Which way do the immigrants flow?

Poetry--The "Irish Pennants" from my poetry books

Casualty Call

The doorbell rang while she was baking bread.
She glimpsed them through the window by her door,
And slid down sobbing to the foyer floor;
Until she let them in he was not dead.
Her husband came to answer it instead.
"Are you okay?" He knew. He'd been to war.
"Mother, are you okay?" he asked once more.
"I'll never be okay again," she said.

Their son was buried two weeks to the day.
The rifles fired, a bugle sounded taps.
She was clear-eyed, her husband wept. Perhaps
He knew the price that they had yet to pay.
They grieved their son for years, then cancer came,
And as he died, he called the dead boy's name.

For Mother Corps

By Marines who often bled,
By the graves of all our dead,
We will take their place instead,
For Mother Corps.

With our DIs guiding hand,
By our country we will stand,
In the snow or in the sand,
For Mother Corps.

A Band of Brothers stands with thee,
Marines who served so faithfully
And went to war across the sea,
For Mother Corps.

Come and join the free men armed,
To keep our people safe from harm,
Hear the sounding war alarm,
From Mother Corps.

I loved Heroin Move Than I loved You

They told me I was "special,"
Could do what I could dream,
They gave me all the freedom
Of unearned "self-esteem."

Because I was so "special,"
Drugs could not hurt me,
Though scattered all around
The ruined lives I see.

First I snorted powder,
Then went to needles too,
And in the end I loved
Heroin more than you.

I'd steal and lie to get it,
I'd sell my body too,
Because when you are "special,"
Rules don't apply to you.

I threw away my future,
It all went up my nose,
My kids are sad and poor,
But that's the way it goes.

First I snorted powder,
Then went to needles too,
And in the end I loved
Heroin more than you.

You found me on the floor,
A needle by my side,
Did I look "special" then,
In vomit when I died?

First I snorted powder,
Then went to needles too,
And in the end I loved
Heroin more than you.

Lance Corporal John Payne

'Tis now the candle gutters low.
And now the night is almost fled.
And we must dwell on what's gone by,
And not what lies ahead.

We think of all the little things,
And deeds the world may soon forget,
And wonder why the good must go
Like candle flames, and yet...

He loved his family with his heart,
And cherished God, that much was plain,
Took pride in service to his Corps...
Remember now John Payne!

Marine Air

We say you're "swinging with the wing,"
You're skating, every man.
For only grunts are real Marines--
And then it hits the fan.

When we have wounded on the ground
Come choppers through the fire,
To pull our bleeding brothers out
When things are worse than dire.

While all around your close support
Breaks up their next attack,
You come in hot and fast and low
To knock the bastards back!

Then we are grateful on the ground,
The Wing came through again.
We thank our brothers in the air,
Our flying riflemen!

Molon Labe

We are a people free--
Our rights you'd disavow?
Defiantly we say,
Then come and *take* them now!

We won't give up our speech
Though you may call it hate!
That right is ours from God,
And not a whim of fate.

We won't give up our right
Our families to protect.
A people armed and free--
No yoke upon our neck.

We worship as we chose,
For all your laws and rules,
The State is not our God,
And we are not its tools.

We won't give up the wage
That buys our family's bread,
So they can buy the votes
Of parasites instead.

We won't give up our guns.
You'll have them anyhow?
Defiantly we say,
Then come and *take* them now!

Our rights are not from law,
Our rights are not from man,
They only come from God--
We'll *make* you understand!

Sonnet for AJ

Perhaps by chance, or that we tested high,
They ordered us to school. We grumbled some--
It seemed so safe--technicians seldom die.
We were Marines, and trained for what might come.
The seventeen who finished in our class
Were all close friends. (Except when we were not!)
Our comm was good, and as such comes to pass
We scattered through the Corps--the Jarhead's lot.

But Vietnam was waiting for us still.
They doled us out to outfits much the same.
'Twas all by chance we guarded base or hill--
And chance took AJ when the rocket came.
Why was he taken as a young Marine,
And we were left to keep his memory green?

There's Nothing Dignified in Death

There's nothing dignified in death,
When swords eviscerate a man,
Or shellfire rends the flesh apart,
Or bullets do the worst they can.

But there is love in standing firm,
In firing pit or wall of shields,
With cherished folk sheltered behind,
A man will die but cannot yield.

We will come for you

With wounded on the firing line
And half the outfit down,
The skipper calls for help and prays
He doesn't catch a round.

Battalion tells him to hold on,
"Here's what we plan to do,
Reaction force is on the way--
We will come for you."

Ambassador is on the horn,
The riots flare anew,
And then the Colonel tells him clear,
"We will come for you."

The word goes through the embassy,
Marines are on the way,
And mothers breathe a prayer of thanks--
Marines mean what they say.

The Recon Team is shot to hell,
And two are going fast,
They need a medevac at once,
Or neither man will last.

Then comes the word they're praying for,
The choppers will get through,
"Prepare to pop a smoke in ten--
We will come for you."

It is the code by which they live,
It's what Marines still do,
Their word's their bond each time they say,
"We will come for you."

Who is "Iron Mike"?

There's one down at PI,
And one at Quantico,
These statues standing guard
Over the truth we know.

There's one at Belleau Wood,
And others here and yon,
These statues standing for
The comrades who have gone.

But is the real Iron Mike
A statue cast in bronze?
We ask it over beers,
Debating pros and cons.

I think the real Iron Mike
Is in each brother's heart,
Marines who went and did,
Marines who played their part.

I think the real Iron Mike
Is in each sister's soul,
Marines who went and did,
Marines who met their goal.

Iron Mike's the young Marine,
Who saddles up once more,
To go out on patrol
In some forsaken war.

Iron Mike's the old Marine
Who goes to work each day,
To keep the family fed,
To hold the wolf at bay.

Iron Mike's the dead Marine
Who handed down our name,
Who kept it shining bright,
And we must do the same.

It's values that we hold,
A Corps that must not die—
If Mike's not in your heart
He not down at PI.

Robert A. Hall

You'll Never Be Alone

You'll never be alone,
For though my body die,
My heart will be with you,
And always at your side.

The breeze at setting sun,
The lights in midnight sky,
The kiss of rain at dawn,
With these I will touch you.

I'll taste your salty tears,
I'll share your happy laugh,
I'll walk each mile with you--
You'll never be alone.

Try not to grieve, my love,
For I'm not gone from you,
In truth we'll never part,
Rejoice our love is so.

You'll never be alone,
For God will not allow,
The parting of two souls
Who love like you and I.

I'll never be alone--
For I am joined to you.

Blank verse poem for my beloved wife, Bonnie